Networks and Marginality

LIFE IN A MEXICAN SHANTYTOWN

STUDIES IN ANTHROPOLOGY

Under the Consulting Editorship of E. A. Hammel,
UNIVERSITY OF CALIFORNIA, BERKELEY

Andrei Simić, THE PEASANT URBANITES: A Study of Rural-Urban Mobility in Serbia

John U. Ogbu, THE NEXT GENERATION: An Ethnography of Education in an Urban Neighborhood

Bennett Dyke and Jean Walters MacCluer (Eds.), COMPUTER SIMULATION IN HUMAN POPULATION STUDIES

Robbins Burling, THE PASSAGE OF POWER: Studies in Political Succession

Piotr Sztompka, SYSTEM AND FUNCTION: Toward a Theory of Society

William G. Lockwood, EUROPEAN MOSLEMS: Economy and Ethnicity in Western Bosnia

Günter Golde, CATHOLICS AND PROTESTANTS: Agricultural Modernization in Two German Villages

Peggy Reeves Sanday (Ed.), ANTHROPOLOGY AND THE PUBLIC INTEREST: Fieldwork and Theory

Carol A. Smith (Ed.), REGIONAL ANALYSIS, Volume I: Economic Systems, and Volume II: Social Systems

Raymond D. Fogelson and Richard N. Adams (Eds.), THE ANTHROPOLOGY OF POWER: Ethnographic Studies from Asia, Oceania, and the New World

Frank Henderson Stewart, FUNDAMENTALS OF AGE-GROUP SYSTEMS

Larissa Adler Lomnitz, NETWORKS AND MARGINALITY: Life in a Mexican Shantytown

Benjamin S. Orlove, ALPACAS, SHEEP, AND MEN: The Wool Export Economy and Regional Society in Southern Peru

Harriet Ngubane, BODY AND MIND IN ZULU MEDICINE: An Ethnography of Health and Disease in Nyuswa-Zulu Thought and Practice

Networks and Marginality
LIFE IN A MEXICAN SHANTYTOWN

LARISSA ADLER LOMNITZ
Instituto de Investigaciones en Matemáticas Aplicadas y en Sistemas
Universidad Nacional Autónoma de México
Mexico, D. F.

Translated by
CINNA LOMNITZ

Foreword by
ERIC R. WOLF

ACADEMIC PRESS   **New York   San Francisco   London**
A Subsidiary of Harcourt Brace Jovanovich, Publishers

ACADEMIC PRESS, INC.
111 Fifth Avenue, New York, New York 10003

United Kingdom Edition published by
ACADEMIC PRESS, INC. (LONDON) LTD.
24/28 Oval Road, London NW1

Library of Congress Cataloging in Publication Data

Lomnitz, Larissa Adler.
   Networks and marginality.

   (Academic Press studies in anthropology series)
   Translation of Cerrada del Cóndor.
   Bibliography: p.
     1.   Squatter settlements—Mexico—Mexico (City)
2.   Rural-urban migration—Mexico—Mexico (City)
3.   Mexico (City)—Social conditions.   I.   Title.
HN120.M45L6513   301.44'1   76-55974
ISBN 0–12–456450–X

An earlier version of this work was published in the Spanish language by Siglo XXI, Editores, S.A., in Mexico City in 1976, under the title *¿Cómo Sobreviven los Marginados?*

To Cinna,
Jorge, Claudio, Alberto,
and Tania

Contents

Foreword, by Eric R. Wolf   xi

Preface to the English Edition   xv

1 Introduction   1

    Some Preliminary Findings   2
    A Design for Survival   3
    City and Countryside in Latin America   4
    An Ecological View of Migration   5
    Urban Growth and Shantytowns   7
    A Theory of Marginalization   9

2 The Setting   15

    Mexico: Urbanization and Growth   15
    Underemployment in Mexico   16
    Mexico City: An Overview   17
    Low-Income Housing in Mexico City   18
    Cerrada del Cóndor   19
    Some Impressions of Shantytown Life   27

3 Migration   35

An Ecological Model of the Migration Process   38
Migration Processes in Latin America   41
A Historical Sketch of Migration in Mexico   43
Migration and Cerrada del Cóndor   44

4 Shantytown Economy   63

Cerrada del Cóndor: Occupational Structure   64
Unpaid Family Labor   67
Economic Levels   70
Occupation and Economic Level   76
Income and Economic Level   76
Housing and Property Ownership in Cerrada del Cóndor   78
Material Belongings   81
Economic Level and Life-Styles   84
Schooling and Economic Levels   88
An Informal Rotating Credit Institution: *Tanda*   88
Summary and Conclusions   89

5 Family and Kinship   93

Marital Roles   93
The Nuclear Family   97
The Household: Definition   99
Types of Households   100
Some Comparisons of Households   117
The Residential Pattern   118
Kinship   123
Relatives in the Country   129

6 Networks of Reciprocal Exchange   131

Classification of Reciprocity Networks   133
Networks in Cerrada del Cóndor   135
Analysis of a Residential Complex: Pericos Court   151
Networks and Kindreds: The Villela Macronetwork   155
Networks and Kinship   156

7   Compadrazgo   159

    Compadrazgo in Cerrada del Cóndor   162
    Some Conclusions on *Compadrazgo* in Cerrada del Cóndor   172

8   Formal and Informal Associations   175

    Cuatismo   175
    Local and National Associations   180

9   Reciprocity and *Confianza*   189

    What Is Reciprocity?   189
    Scales of Reciprocity in Cerrada del Cóndor   191
    Confianza: A Variable of Reciprocal Exchange   193
    Confianza and Exchange in Cerrada del Cóndor   199
    Patron–Client Relations: The *Cacique*   202
    A Final Note on Forms of Exchange   203

10   Conclusions   207

    Some Basic Concepts   207
    Networks   209
    Living in Cerrada del Cóndor   210
    The Future of Reciprocity   212

References   215

Index   223

Foreword

Rapid and intense urbanization is one of the salient features of this century. It goes on all over the world, but it is especially evident in Latin America. Age-old traditions are destroyed. Local ecosystems are uprooted. Millions abandon countrysides impoverished by decaying agriculture and seek new homes in the interstices of the expanding cities. As urbanization has gone on apace, so has the increase of the urban poor. Mexico City now has a population of about 10 million, of which 3–4 million are in the category of the economically marginal, the real poor. In this study, Dr. Larissa Lomnitz shows us how such poor people live and survive in one shantytown in the southern part of the city.

Dr. Lomnitz tells us how the inhabitants of this shantytown—still unrecognized by the authorities of government—were driven from their original homesteads either by their inability to make ends meet in the rural area or by the expansion of the city itself. To escape the upset of their means and places of livelihood they sought refuge in a deep ravine, the Cerrada del Cóndor, located in the midst of a middle-class neighborhood. There they proceeded to carve out a "niche" for themselves, to discover and define a set of resources that might underwrite their existence in the new habitat. But these resources barely suffice to this end. Cerrada del Cóndor is now home to a population of *marginados,* people pushed to the edge of the economic, social, and political order. They have become, in Dr. Lomnitz's evocative phrase, "the hunters and gatherers of the urban jungle."

Dr. Lomnitz uses the language of the ecologist to depict how this population migrated and relocated, but her account points well beyond mere ecological analysis. Occupation of new niches, in competition or commensality with other populations, conjures up a Darwinian process of biological selection. Dr. Lomnitz, however, shows us that such competition is in fact governed by larger forces, those of a capitalism controlled by corporations located elsewhere. These forces, responsive to capital movements and accumulation within the wider national and international economy, create the labor market within which the resources found in the Cerrada del Cóndor find their particular place. This is not the labor market of homogeneous quantities of labor power postulated in the models of many economists. It is, instead, a labor market which continuously differentiates the laboring population into segments and factions, in the very course of developing production. Marx foresaw something like this when he wrote in his *Grundrisse* that

> the laborers compete not only by selling themselves one cheaper than the other; but also by one doing the work of five, then ten, or twenty; and they are forced to compete in this manner by the division of labor, which is introduced and steadily improved by capital. . . . [Thus] the division of labor results in . . . the antagonism of private interests and class interests.

Dr. Lomnitz shows us how, in this process of differentiation, people like those of Cerrada del Cóndor are continuously pushed into occupations marked by low levels of skill, or by the use of residual resources and skills grown obsolete, or by the lack of stability in their employment. The processes of differentiation go on, indeed, within the Cerrada itself, yielding at least four differentiated categories of the poor. Not even poverty is homogeneous.

Yet Dr. Lomnitz shows us something else, and it is this demonstration which makes this book an outstanding contribution to our understanding of how the poor resist the burden of their poverty. In great detail and with anthropological sophistication, she illuminates the ingenuity and creativity by which these people mobilize effective ties of economic reciprocity through the mechanisms of kinship, ritual kinship, and friendship. These ties of reciprocity counteract the vicissitudes of poverty by evening out the risks of uncertainty and insecurity. They create a veritable economy of the poor, in which the guiding principles are not those of the market, but strategies which serve to bend off and blunt its negative effects.

At the same time Dr. Lomnitz shows us how market forces and the resistance to them co-exist dialectically in the lives of the urban poor. The people of the Cerrada offer their labor in the labor market, disadvantaged as they are by the terms of its operations. They fill occupations no one else wants to occupy. They are also consumers, even though they are frequently forced to scavenge off the leavings of others. They buy radios and television sets, furniture and furnishings; many pay rent for their houses. Toward the end of her concluding chapter, Dr. Lomnitz suggests who is the major beneficiary of this labor and consumption at the margins of the social and economic order. It is the urban middle class, which contracts most of the men of the Cerrada as day laborers and bearers of service and which hires their women folk as servants or maids. Thus the author poses a greater irony still. She calls attention to the degree to which Mexico City's ever expanding ''dependent'' middle class—dependent in large part on the huge governmental apparatus of the capital—depends in its turn on the growth of the urban poor, bereft of security and unprotected by the social services of the state.

Larissa Lomnitz has written a provocative book which adds greatly to our understanding of strategic processes at work in the modern world. By offering it in English translation, she has done even more. She has also shown the non-Spanish reading public something of the excellence of anthropology practiced beyond our borders. For both of these reasons, we are in her debt.

ERIC R. WOLF

Preface to the English Edition

The fieldwork for this book was carried out between 1969 and 1971 in Cerrada del Cóndor, a shantytown of about 200 houses in Mexico City. Because of the relatively small size of the settlement, repeated house-by-house survey was possible. Thus I was able to combine anthropological methods of participant observation with the quantitative methods used by sociologists and by economists.

Between October and December of 1969, after completing several economic and social surveys, I began to associate with three particular families in the shantytown. The male members of two of these extended families had rather unusual occupations: In one family all men were carpet layers; in the other, all were tombstone polishers. Eventually I discovered that all carpet layers in the shantytown belonged to the same kindred of 25 nuclear families who had migrated to Mexico City from a certain rural community in the State of San Luis Potosí. The striking correlation between kinship and occupation suggested the existence of some hidden mechanisms that might account simultaneously for the migration pattern and for the adaptation of the migrants to economic life in the city.

This idea proved fruitful and reinforced my conviction that participant observation is an indispensable requirement for the design and interpretation of quantitative surveys. This is particularly true if one believes, as I do, that research in the social sciences ought to strive for a global description of the culture. Kinship, housing, economy, ideology, and values are the integral parts of a culture: They can be analyzed separately only at the risk of distorting the whole.

As compared with the original Spanish edition, this translation contains a number of revisions and new interpretations. They are the result of a continuing process of rethinking the material; the data are identical in both editions.

I am indebted to my husband and translator, Dr. Cinna Lomnitz, for many valuable suggestions and for his faithful rendering of a work that grew in complexity as I strove toward its completion.

I am greatly indebted to Richard N. Adams for his detailed criticism and suggestions that went into the Spanish version of this work. The present version was prepared under the auspices of the Instituto de Investigaciones en Matemáticas Aplicadas y en Sistemas of the National University of Mexico, as part of my teaching and research duties at the Institute. I should like to thank Dr. Tomás Garza, director of the Institute, for his support of this work and for assigning the resources for its completion. I am indebted to María Elena Ducci de Colchero for her excellent maps and figures, and to Alicia Castillo for her cheerful and unfailing assistance and for her ability and patience in typing the manuscript.

On a more personal level I would like to thank my husband, Cinna, my sons, Jorge (who took the photographs), Claudio, and Alberto, and my daughter, Tania, without whose constant support I could never have undertaken this work.

I believe that much can be learned from the settlers of Cerrada del Cóndor. I have certainly learned a great deal from them. In addition, I have been fortunate in making valuable, lasting friendships in the shantytown. I would like to thank all my informants for their generous hospitality, and for the many hours that I spent talking with them and listening to the stories of their lives.

1

Introduction

This is the story of Cerrada del Cóndor, a shantytown in Mexico City. The suburban no-man's-land is made up of many steep ravines, reclaimed mudflats, and dusty slopes in the volcanic badlands, where 2 to 3 million people make their homes outside the pale of the economic and social amenities normally associated with a large modern metropolis. Beyond the poverty that meets the eye—the overcrowded housing conditions, the lack of urban utilities, and the cultural, political, and economic blight—I have attempted to describe the special circumstances of the daily lives of the shantytown settlers, and to understand the nature of the new (or perhaps ancient) adaptive strategies they have developed in order to survive.

This chapter is intended to familiarize the reader with the framework of theoretical concepts that are, I believe, essential for an adequate comprehension of what follows.

In the next chapter I shall summarize the development of Mexico and the evolution of Mexico City, as they relate to Cerrada del Cóndor, and I shall describe the shantytown itself. In successive chapters I shall analyze the migration process, the economy, the family and kinship patterns, and the reciprocity networks and associated mechanisms of survival value in the shantytown. Finally, I shall discuss some of the relevant theoretical points raised by the findings: reciprocity, the *confianza* concept, and the importance of informal economic exchange in complex urban societies.

SOME PRELIMINARY FINDINGS

My initial survey of the population of Cerrada del Cóndor (January 1969) showed that nearly 70% of the heads of families and their spouses were rural migrants. Most of the remaining 30%, although born in the Federal District, were sons or daughters of rural migrants. This initial finding—the predominantly rural origin of the shantytown settlers—turned my attention toward the problem of rural–urban migration patterns.

A migration survey brought to light the interesting fact that most of the present settlers had been assisted in their migration by some relative or relatives at the point of destination. This was true for rural–urban migration as well as for the frequent moves within the Federal District itself. The system of kinship ties between the city and the countryside immediately aroused my interest. Upon further exploration, it struck me that some groups of kinsmen in the shantytown tended to ply the same trades. For example, most adult males in a large kindred from the state of San Luis Potosí were carpet layers. Further inquiries uncovered the fact that assistance among kinsmen did not stop at migration but extended to mutual assistance in occupational training, housing, employment, and a host of other major and minor items of daily life.

It also struck me that the occupations held by shantytown settlers had one thing in common: They lacked any reasonable security features, such as job security, social security, or a reasonably safe monthly level of income. The settlers were either unskilled or semiskilled laborers working piecemeal or by the day, or they were self-employed craftsmen and traders without any working capital to speak of. Few if any of the settlers were able to find work every day; underemployment was the rule. Also, there was a remarkable lack of occupations bearing any direct relevance to industrial production. Rather, they were representative of what some economists called *tertiary activities* or *informal economy*. The term *marginality* has gained wide acceptance in Latin America, following studies done by the United Nations Economic Commission for Latin America (ECLA), especially the work of Quijano (1970:27–41) and Nun (1969); it designates social groups or strata having the characteristics I have just described.

At this point a new question arose: How do marginal people survive? Obviously, the low income level and the absence of job security that prevailed among the vast majority of the shantytown settlers represented no basis for survival. Moreover, shantytown families had no visible savings or skills that might have been useful in an emergency such as an illness or a lengthy spell of unemployment of the head of the family. Such emergencies were to be expected and in fact did occur quite frequently in Cerrada del Cóndor.

The question about the survival of marginal populations in modern cities thus became the central research problem of my book.

A DESIGN FOR SURVIVAL

What kind of systems or devices can be used to survive in a shantytown environment, considering the low level of skills and the extreme lack of security that prevails among Latin American marginals? The answer to this question will take several chapters to unfold. In a nutshell, what seems to be happening is this: Marginals occupy the bottom of the social scale in society. They have literally nothing. Their only resources are of a social nature: kinship and friendship ties that generate social solidarity. Accordingly, a type of social structure has evolved in the shantytown that mobilizes the social resources of the settlers on behalf of survival. This structure will be described at length here: It is called a *network of reciprocal exchange*.

The actual mechanisms of survival are a great deal more complex than might appear from the preceding outline. Reciprocity networks, for one thing, are not formal institutions. Their structure and functions must be brought out by anthropological research. Reciprocity is a form of exchange embedded in a long-term social relationship; it is not an impersonal, one-time transaction like market exchange. It is therefore important to understand the entire fabric of social relations, particularly kinship relations, in the shantytown in order to gain an insight into the economics of reciprocity networks. Last but not least, it is necessary to understand the general causes of marginality in the Latin American setting, since the problem of individual survival is closely related to the structural insecurity of the marginal strata resulting from their peculiar relationship to the urban industrial economy system.

Social life in the shantytown unfolds like a complex design for survival. Age-old institutions, like *compadrazgo* (fictive kinship or godparenthood) and *cuatismo* (a traditional form of male friendship), are mobilized to reinforce and strengthen the structure of local exchange networks. Characteristic residential patterns evolve, which optimize the resources of the group through various types of household arrangements. Even alcohol consumption, hitherto considered a symptom of social disorganization, can be harnessed to the objectives of group solidarity since it effectively prevents the accumulation of cash differentials among members of an exchange network.

A separate chapter is devoted to the subject of reciprocity. In the past, economists and economic anthropologists have tended to dismiss reciprocity as an archaic mode of exchange, which has largely disappeared from modern urban life and whose rudimentary remnants are preserved in economically unimportant institutions such as the annual exchange of gifts at Christmas time (Cook 1968:208–222). In this book, as in an earlier work (Lomnitz 1971:93–106), I attempt to make a case for reciprocity as a major form of exchange in complex modern societies. Social solidarity provides economic leverage to groups who use it either to survive or to consolidate their position in the social pecking order. The enduring importance of social connections and influence peddling in societies as different as Mexico, the United States, and the Soviet Union attests to the fact that reciprocity as an economic force is today very much alive. Moreover, the practice of reciprocity is found alongside market exchange in all strata of urban society, from the very poor to the very rich. The case of the marginal population, the fastest growing segment of Latin American society despite its glaringly inadequate support in the market economy, represents the most dramatic but by no means the only example.

The concept of *confianza,* which had been proposed as a tool in the analysis of reciprocal exchange (Lomnitz 1971:96, 103), is further developed in this book. *Confianza* is a Latin American native category that denotes mutual readiness to engage in reciprocal exchange. It represents a measure of the effective social distance that separates two potential or actual partners in exchange, and of the social relation in which it is embedded. In Cerrada del Cóndor *confianza* was conditioned chiefly by social proximity (kinship, *compadrazgo*), residential proximity, and socioeconomic equality (equality of wants).

CITY AND COUNTRYSIDE IN LATIN AMERICA

Major cities have dominated the Latin American political and economic scene, at least since the Spanish Conquest. Most Latin American cities were founded between 1520 and 1580. Spanish colonists have always been urban oriented; thus, in the Latin American colonies we find urban elites as far back as the early sixteenth century. In the words of Portes and Walton: "The city did not arise to serve, but to subdue [1976:9]." In other words, the conquerors settled in the main cities and initiated the military and economic subjugation of the countryside from these urban power bases.

The colonial pattern of urban dominance was maintained and reinforced after independence. The capitals of the emerging nations were as a rule located in the major cities. The urban elites had become accustomed to regarding the revenue from their rural properties as a permanent source of income to be spent on higher consumption. Little was reinvested in the development of the countryside. Eventually foreign capitalism took over the role of developing the basic resources (mining, commercial agriculture, manufacture, and commerce) of Latin America (Portes and Walton 1976:25–27).

Dependent capitalism became the principle around which the economic systems of all Latin American countries became organized. The centers of political and economical dominance eventually shifted from Spain to England to the United States (Castells 1974:70–73; Portes and Walton 1976: 24; Sunkel 1971). An incipient local entrepreneurial class arose toward the end of the nineteenth century, mainly in the manufacturing of consumer goods for the local markets. According to Quijano (1970:35), this trend became particularly dominant after the 1929 recession, when many local governments encouraged and subsidized an effort toward import substitution through the protection of local industries. Many of these industries were taken over by foreign investors after World War II; in general, recent trends in foreign investments have largely followed the existing patterns of industrialization.

Today Latin American economies are dominated by modern, urban industrial complexes, largely controlled by foreign-based corporations; this structure rests incongruously on a decaying traditional agro-extractive base. Such a basic disparity in the economic development of the city and the countryside has important economic consequences: (1) the deterioration of local or traditional industries that had formerly represented a major source of livelihood to the population; (2) the decline of popular trades and crafts; (3) a widening gulf between the productive capacities of the city and the countryside; and (4) deeper inequalities in the distribution of income.

Thus the modern trend of industrialization has actually reinforced the preexisting colonial pattern of predominance of urban elites over a backward countryside. Traditional labor-intensive industries have become displaced by foreign-based technology, which typically uses highly skilled labor in smaller numbers. The gradual shift from commerce and administration toward industry has made each of the countries increasingly dependent on external markets over which Latin America has little control. The deterioration of many primary products and the growing appetite of the urban population for imports and for consumption have also led to a chronic deficit in the balance of payments (Prebisch 1970:7). The resulting scarcity of capital and resources has further aggravated the tendency toward geographical concentration and the dependence on foreign initiative. Finally, the increasing concentration of wealth in the large cities has attracted huge crowds of unskilled labor from the countryside (Portes and Walton 1976:28; Safa 1976:3; Singer 1975:31–71).

AN ECOLOGICAL VIEW OF MIGRATION

The demographic imbalance between city and countryside is also due, in no small measure, to secondary effects of the concentration of industry in the major cities. These secondary effects are (1) advances in social legislation, leading to an improved protection of industrial workers in large cities; (2) the introduction of modern medical technology through the public health services, radiating outward from major urban centers; (3) improved communications (roads, telegraph, telephone, and television) linking the cities with the countryside; (4) an improved educational system; and (5) more effective contacts between city and countryside through compulsory military service, the expansion of tourism, and the growth of the provincial administrations.

Birth rates in Latin America continued at high levels, and death rates were dramatically reduced by medical and public health technology (Arriaga 1970:4). This represents a new demographic trend in Latin America. The annual population growth from 1935 to 1940 was still around 1.9%; the doubling period of the population was 37 years. By 1970 the rate of population growth increased to 2.9% and the doubling period had shrunk to 15 years (Prebisch 1970:25). One of the highest rates of population growth is found precisely in Mexico: 3.4% per year. These rates are up to three times higher than those prevailing in the industrializing countries of Europe and North America during the nineteenth century. As a result, the influx of labor to industrial centers has been much higher than at comparable stages of industrialization in the major industrial powers of the world (Balán, Browning, and Jelin 1973:16; Prebisch 1970:25). The impact of the population explosion might have been largely absorbed by a proportional increase of the productive capacity in the countryside. The opposite happened, unfortunately: The agricultural economy remained stagnant. In England, the industrial revolution had drawn its labor force initially from the surplus created by freeing the countryside from the chores of subsistence farming and small crafts. In Latin America, on the other hand, agricultural production had already been oriented to commercial markets long before industrialization (Balán, Browning, and Jelin 1973:17). Investments in agriculture were siphoned off into industry, and the countryside was left to decay.

This outline provides the theoretical basis of an ecological framework for the study of rural–urban migration, to be further developed in Chapter 3. Such a conceptual framework should be based on the recognition that the ecological niche of the peasant is fundamentally dependent on the availability and quality of agricultural land. Wherever land reform has been moderately successful in providing adequate land for the subsistence of the peasants, the rural population has become relatively stabilized. On the other hand, where land policies have been inadequate to ward off the combined impact of population growth, fragmentation of rural property, erosion, and impoverishment of soils, the balance of the ecosystem has been upset. The exodus of peasants may be attributed to a combination of positive and negative inducements: agricultural stagnation and pauperization of the peasantry, on one hand, and the monopoly on wealth and political power in the major cities on the other. The bulk of Latin American migrants were recruited from among the most impoverished sector of the peasantry: sharecroppers, wage-earning rural workers, and the landless peasantry in general. Thus, the Latin American migration process responds to an ecological catastrophe rather than to the economic inducements of industrialization. ''The shift out of the agricultural sector in Latin American countries is taking place as a reaction to population growth and agricultural stagnation, rather than as a response to mechanization and greater productivity [Balán, Browning, and Jelin 1973:17].''[1]

URBAN GROWTH AND SHANTYTOWNS

According to Cardona and Simmons (1976:19), in 1940 there were 4 Latin American cities with a population in excess of 1 million; 4 between 500,000 and 950,000; and 8 between 125,000 and 500,000. By 1960, 10 cities had exceeded the 1 million mark. The proportion of city dwellers in the total population increased from 39.3% in 1950 to 46.9% in 1960. The rate of population growth in localities of more than 20,000 inhabitants has been about 5.2% and is still increasing (Urquidi 1969:141). At the same time, the rural-based agricultural labor force decreased from 63% to 41% in the period 1930–1970 (Prebisch 1970:31).

Urban growth has always been a characteristic effect of industrialization. However, comparisons with the industrializing nations during the nineteenth century are not entirely relevant because the industrial technology then required large amounts of unskilled labor. Today large masses of cheap labor are no longer a condition for industrial growth. Latin American industry tends to operate with the capital-intensive technologies developed by advanced industrial nations under conditions of labor scarcity (Balán, Browning, and Jelin 1973:16–17). As a result, the social context of urbanization has been radically different in Latin America. Employment opportunities in industry are proportionally shrinking. Although 13.7% of the economically active population were gainfully employed in industry in 1925, the proportion had decreased to 13.4% in 1960 (Castells 1974:66–68).

In the absence of a direct relation between urban growth and employment in industry, an increasing redundancy of urban population in terms of industrial productivity develops. There may be a spurious absorption of rural–urban migration into the unskilled service occupations; nevertheless, the introduction of scientific and technological advances appears to increase rather than diminish the lag between population growth and capital accumulation (Prebisch 1970:7). As a matter of fact, for the period 1950–1965, the overall rate of growth of the labor force has been 2.5%, but the increase in service occupations has been as high as 3.8% (Prebisch 1970:31). In terms of social consequences of the rural–urban migration process in Latin America, one might say that the chronic saturation of

[1]This and subsequent quotes cited to Balán, Browning, and Jelin 1973 are from Jorge Balán, Harley L. Browning, and Elizabeth Jelin, *Man in a Developing Society* (Austin: Univ. of Texas Press). © 1973 by University of Texas Press.

the absorption capacity of migrants in the urban economy has tended to accen-
tuate the ecological segregation of migrant strata in the urban environment. In
effect, the proliferation of squatter settlements in the large cities has resulted in a
dual structure of urban land allocation: "one formal and governed by capitalist
market forces, and the other informal and ruled by popular demand [Portes and
Walton 1976:29]."

Large-scale rural–urban migration in Latin America began after World War II.
At first the old residences in the downtown areas were subdivided into one-room
units and transformed into slums. The residents of these central slums enjoyed
and still enjoy certain urban facilities, including water, drainage, public transportation, electric power, garbage collection, schools, markets, and sometimes rent
control. As a result, the downtown slums were soon filled to capacity. About that
time, certain contingents of urbanized migrants began to move out of the slums
into squatter settlements on the outskirts of the towns. Turner and Mangin (1968)
have called this new trend "the *barriada* movement." Once the major squatter
settlements had been established, they were able to operate as reception centers
for rural migrants coming in directly from the countryside.

In the case of Cerrada del Cóndor, as we shall see, groups of relatives provide
the necessary linkage of information and assistance for the eventual absorption of
the new arrivals from the countryside.

In this book the terms *shantytown* and *squatter settlement* will be used more or
less interchangeably. According to Leeds (1969:44), a squatter settlement is a
residential zone of illegal or unregulated origin, where the rights of land tenure
are uncertain or ambiguous. Thus, most shantytowns develop under an implied
or actual threat of forcible eviction, although the landholdings may eventually
become legalized through government action.

Anthropologists have adhered to one of two major points of view concerning
shantytowns: (1) Shantytowns are hotbeds of contagion, crime, and social disorganization; and (2) shantytowns are rural islands of social reconstruction and
community life in an aggressive urban milieu (Morse 1965:51). Frank Bonilla
(1970:73) has described the *favelas* of Rio de Janeiro as a cancer that spreads
throughout the city. Shantytowns are dehumanized places, built out of waste
materials, contrasting with the shiny glass-and-concrete skyscrapers of the
modern city. Bonilla estimates that the *favelados* of Rio de Janeiro represent 33%
of the total city population. The daily life of the *favelados* is plagued with
apparently unsolvable problems, such as social disorganization, illiteracy, mal-
nutrition, illness, occupational instability, alcoholism, irregular sexual unions,
and crime. Yet the shantytown provides a certain type of social cohesion and may
even be described as an integrating influence: a place where migrants can learn
new ways of solidarity and certain forms of social and political action. Not the
shantytown but the nation is in need of reform, says Bonilla. The nation has
compromised its own future by abandoning half its population to senseless pov-

erty. *Favelas* are not so much hotbeds of social disorganization as of social revolution.

Turner (1970:1–4), Matos Mar (1962:177), and Mangin (1967:65–68) describe shantytowns as places where families work hard to make the best of their limited possibilities. Family ties remain strong and social problems such as alcoholism, theft, or mistreatment of women are not necessarily worse than in other urban areas. According to Mangin, shantytowns actually contribute to the national economy insofar as they provide a solution of sorts to a housing problem that government and private enterprise have been unable or unwilling to face.

Mangin's work has become popular among planners, particularly outside Latin America, who interpret it as saying that the problem of shantytowns somehow represents its own solution. According to this school of thought, shantytowns should realistically be accepted as a normal part of urban growth.

Both Turner and Matos Mar have stressed the housing aspects of shantytown development. Turner sees official policies as largely counterproductive, because the imposition of "modern" housing standards actually bans all low-cost construction and represents an incentive to real-estate speculation and the exploitation of the marginals. Those unable to invest in legally approved housing are forced to become squatters or victims of rent sharks.

Portes and Walton (1976:38–43) have attempted to estimate the proportion of shantytown population in the major cities of Latin America during the 1960s. Some typical figures are as follows: Cali, Colombia, 30%; Caracas, Venezuela, 35%; Santiago, Chile, 25%; Guatemala City, Guatemala, 10%; Iquitos, Peru, 64.7%; Lima, Peru, 24.4%; Rio de Janeiro, Brazil, 30%; Mexico City, Mexico, 40%.

Portes and Walton point out that the proportion is increasing, since "greater numbers of the urban poor, and higher land values, lead to an increasing shift toward illegal means of securing shelter and hence an increasing frequency of land invasions [1976:44]."

A THEORY OF MARGINALIZATION

The social structure of Latin America is in a state of flux. We are witnessing the emergence of a strong middle class, which has begun to differentiate according to occupational sectors (bureaucracy, politics, commerce, the liberal professions, the technocracy, the small entrepreneurs, and the military), and according to economic strata (lower, middle, and upper-middle class). Likewise, the urban working class tends to split into an industrial proletariat and a so-called informal or marginal sector (Nelson 1969:3–5), which contains social groups variously described as "the poor," "the traditional sector," "the culture of poverty," "the marginals," or "the reserve labor force." These social groups are not really new to Latin America. It can be argued that rural–urban migration has merely transferred the poor and the unemployed from the countryside to the city (Safa 1976:10–11). Moreover, there have always been poor people in the cities themselves. However, the increasing differentiation within the Latin American working class and the emergence of a new industrial proletariat in the cities suggest the need for the adoption of a more precise terminology. Peattie (1974: 101–112) has objected to the usage of the term *marginality*. She argues that both the industrial workers and those excluded from industrial jobs "are components of . . . urban society [1974:107]." Other social scientists tend to shrink from the term *marginality* because they believe it to be derogatory. In this book I shall use *marginality,* because (1) it is descriptive of the cleavage in the working class between those who participate in industrial production and its associated benefits, and those who do not; and (2) it is widely accepted and understood in Latin America, where its usage has become firmly established.

The early literature on marginality in Latin America dealt indistinctly with several closely interrelated phenomena, such as urban poverty, rural–urban migration, and shantytowns.[2] The squatter settlements that had appeared around the edges of Latin American cities during the late 1940s were marginal in a geographical and ecological sense, since they were located outside the urban limits and beyond the reaches of normal urban facilities. Gradually the term *marginality* came to be applied to many social, economic, and psychological aspects of shantytown life. Parra (1972:221–225) and Sotelo (1972:129–139) have traced the history of the concept of marginality from early psychocultural notions through the present, relatively well-defined economic and sociocultural school of thought. Inevitably each social discipline has come to associate the concept of marginality with its own approach and lines of research; thus, psychologists tend to view marginality in terms of personality changes and adaptation to urban life, whereas economists are more interested in aspects of employment and economic development. The group of sociologists associated with DESAL[3] views marginality in Latin America as a society-wide phenomenon going back to the early colonial period, and stresses those aspects that refer to the lack of involvement in the political decision-making process.

Richard Adams has provided a broad conceptual framework for the study of marginality (1974:37–68). According to Adams, marginalization is a form of

---

[2]There is a great deal in the anthropological and sociological literature related to poverty, shantytowns, and migration (e.g., Bataillon and Rivière d'Arc 1973; Bonilla 1970; Roberts 1973; Cornelius 1971:95–105; Leeds 1969:44–86; Lewis 1959a:387–402, 1959b, 1964, 1966:19–25, 1969a; Mangin 1967, 1970; Matos Mar 1962; Morse 1965:35–74; Safa 1974; Sotelo 1972:129–139; Turner 1970). See annotated bibliographies in the works of Butterworth (1971), Cornelius (1971), Kemper (1970), Mangalam and Schwarzweller (1968), and Muñoz, Oliveira, Singer, and Stern (1972).

[3]DESAL (Centro para el Desarrollo Economico y Social de America Latina) is a Catholic scientific institution which started in Santiago, Chile and later moved to Bogotá, Colombia. It specializes in studies on social development in Latin America.

social entropy. All technology aims at the transformation of natural resources into manufactured products plus waste. No industrial process is 100% efficient. There is always a residue of energy or inert matter that admits no further processing, which can only be recycled at great expense. Similarly, the organization of society into increasingly complex social structures is achieved at the considerable cost of marginalization of certain sectors or strata of society. "Structuring" is the process by which mankind, in its attempt to control its environment, paradoxically places ever greater sectors and elements of this environment beyond its control. An increment in order at the center of the society necessarily entails an increment in disorder at its periphery.

Thus marginalization may be seen as the result of the concentration of wealth, industrial organization, and political power within a society. Industrial powers "set up the hinterland basis for secondary development; and marginal development occurs as a concomitant of both. Both primary and secondary developments generate marginal sectors [Adams 1974:53]." In the advanced capitalist economies, marginalization is largely contained or counteracted through welfare, as it is in the socialist economies through full-employment policies that imply the existence of a large underemployed sector. In so-called Third World countries like Mexico, no nationwide strategy concerning the control of marginality has yet emerged.

Adams holds that, independently of the political system, all industrialization processes are accompanied by an accelerated differentiation that tends to create power differentials within the society. The exercise of power is always directed from the top to the bottom: It implies either exploitation or marginalization. Whenever the logic of the structuring process renders any given sector of society unfit for further use within the system, this sector is gradually divested of real power or participation in the economy. It becomes *marginalized* in the sense that it exists increasingly at the margin of the dominant economic and social system. Nominally it remains a part of the system, but to the extent that it is divested of any real decision-making power, the system also loses any real control over it.

Many social scientists agree today that "underdevelopment" is not just a stage in the process of becoming another Western industrial power. (See, for example, Adams 1974:38; Quijano 1970; Sunkel 1971.) For example, the modern Mexican economy is both qualitatively and quantitatively different from the British or American economy of the late nineteenth or the early twentieth century. Many more differences than similarities may be noted; for instance, the income per capita is considerably lower than it was in the industrialized countries at comparable stages of development. Characteristically, the Third World nations develop through a combination of borrowing and readaptation. Massive underemployment is generated among the traditional population, which remains unskilled from a modern industrial point of view. This type of marginalization is rendered more acute through the introduction of capital-intensive technologies in the presence of a glutted labor market resulting from the population explosion.

Technological expansion in the great industrial power centers of the world creates an increasing marginalization along the periphery of these power centers, e.g., Latin America (Adams 1974: passim; Quijano 1970:53–65; Sotelo 1972:138–139; Sunkel 1971). Underdevelopment in some countries is thus seen as a direct consequence of industrialization in others. The introduction of new technology creates an excess labor force, which is irreversibly excluded from insertion in the productive process. Marginalization in effect creates an "excess population" from the urban industrial point of view. Some economists have objected to this interpretation on the grounds that marginality represents actually the "labor reserve force" postulated by Marx. The main question seems to be whether marginality is functional or dysfunctional from the point of view of capitalism. The classical Marxian analysis holds that any excess of labor supply tends to depress wages and to increase profits. This was particularly true during Marx's lifetime, when industrial technology was labor-intensive and required a large unskilled labor force. A Marxist argument in support of the "surplus population" point of view has been provided by Nun (1969:11–27; see also Sotelo 1972:31–136).

Members of the urban industrial proletariat (i.e., industrial workers protected by union membership and social security) are usually well aware of their privileged position as compared to the marginal sector. They tend to support closed-shop practices that preserve access to jobs for themselves or for their close relatives (Balán, Browning, and Jelin 1973:306). Although initially many rural migrants were able to gain access to industrial jobs in cities, this is no longer the case. The economic and social barriers preventing marginal populations from becoming assimilated into the urban industrial economy have become increasingly rigid. Predictions made by social scientists in the late 1940s and 1950s concerning the transient nature of marginality and the eventual assimilation of marginal populations into the industrial proletariat have not come true. Second- and third-generation marginals are growing up in Latin American shantytowns, and their prospects of gaining access to industrial jobs are slimmer than were those of their parents.

In conclusion, marginality is the result of a stratification process taking place within the Latin American working class as a consequence of industrialization. There is a growing distinction between the industrial proletariat and the marginal strata, according to whether they enjoy job security and other benefits of social legislation. The marginals are largely occupied in unaffiliated manual labor, unpaid family labor, and small-scale family enterprise. A typical cross-section of marginality would comprise trades and occupations such as these: construction workers, housemaids, house repairmen, waiters, barbers, gardeners, janitors, street vendors, and practitioners of traditional trades and crafts that have been devalued by industrialization. Quijano (1970:80) distinguishes between a marginal petty bourgeoisie (including traders, artisans, and small-scale manufacturers) and a marginal proletariat (mostly unskilled laborers). However, there is also some stratification in degrees of poverty and insecurity within each of these marginal sectors. The borderlines between the marginal proletariat and the industrial proletariat are blurry because of intrafamily capillarity: There are sometimes industrial workers as well as marginals within the same family. Such cases tend to become less frequent, however, since the relatively more affluent industrial workers tend to move out of shantytowns and away from their poorer relatives.

Another reason for the blurriness of the borderlines of marginality is the presence of brokers, who specialize in mediating between the marginals and the urban industrial economy. For example, the foreman of a construction gang performs an essential function in marketing the unskilled labor of his relatives and neighbors; he earns much more than any of the members of his crew. Yet he remains a member of the marginal strata since he depends on social resources, such as kinship and neighborly relations, for his livelihood.

The articulation between the marginal strata and the modern sector of the urban economy is also provided by brokerage of another sort. There are local leaders who speak for the shantytown settlers and who act as political go-betweens in all dealings with the authorities or with the bureaucratic apparatus in general. Finally, there is a group of small entrepreneurs (owners of repair shops and the like), whose social and economic positions fluctuate between marginality and the lower middle class.

The core group of marginality may be defined on the basis of two characteristic features: (1) It lacks a formal articulation or insertion in the urban industrial process of production, and (2) it suffers from chronic insecurity of employment. This core group has also been called by Latin American economists the *informal sector,* i.e., that part of the economy not directly regulated by the law of the market (ILO, PREALC 1974a:9). In general, marginal entrepreneurs are self-employed and marginal laborers are free-lancers. Neither group is normally covered by social security; marginal traders are not licensed and do not pay taxes.

Economists of the International Labor Organization (ILO, PREALC 1974b: 1–2) propose a distinction between visible and invisible unemployment in Latin America. In the industrialized countries the labor force is either employed or unemployed; in underdeveloped economies such as those of Latin America, on the other hand, there is a large gray zone of underemployment caused by the underutilization of human potential even among a part of the fully employed working force. The introduction of modern technology in successive waves of modernization has caused a stratification according to productivity within the industrial economy itself. The major results of the ILO study were as follows: (1) An extremely high proportion of the working force is actually both self-employed and underemployed (typically small traders, barbers, artisans, and so on); (2) the population that appears as "unemployed" in the statistics is largely composed of young people and unmarried women; and (3) those officially classified as part of the working force fall into three different groups: (a) those who hold stable jobs with fixed incomes; (b) those who hold stable jobs with fluctuating incomes; and

(c) those who hold irregular jobs with fluctuating and sporadic incomes. The last two categories may be described as hidden and overt underemployment, respectively. Overall results in three Latin American cities (Asunción, Paraguay; Santo Domingo, Dominican Republic; and Managua, Nicaragua) showed that 31% of the labor force was idle at the time of the survey. Of the remaining working force, 30% lacked any job or income stability. In the marginal areas it was found that 30.5% of the labor force was idle at the time of the survey. Almost 80% of these jobless were either women or young people between the ages of 15 and 24. Nearly half of the idle population had been jobless for at least 12 months.

Another study (Souza and Tockman 1975:8) defines the "informal sector" as the set of persons and enterprises engaged in nonorganized activities (lacking any distinction between capital and labor), where wages are not exclusively monetary, and where the requirements of social legislation, such as minimum salaries and so on, are not met. The technologies used are largely traditional and obsolete. The sector includes the lowest strata of urban society, beyond the reach of organized labor and social security. The occupational composition of the sector includes domestic service, occasional workers, self-employed workers, and workers in small enterprises (up to four people). The survey also includes in the informal sector those workers who earn less than the minimum legal wage. The results were as follows: 46% in San Salvador, 57% in Asunción, 48% in Guayaquil, Ecuador, and Iquitos, and 50% in Santo Domingo. The preceding figures may not be typical of all major Latin American cities. However, chronic underemployment is but one aspect of the marginal problem: It is a result of the general exclusion of marginals from the process of decision making in their national societies. On the whole, members of the marginal sector in Latin America are left to their own devices as far as the business of survival is concerned. How do they survive?

The Setting

MEXICO: URBANIZATION AND GROWTH

Toward the beginning of the twentieth century, Mexico was a rural nation. About 10% of the population lived in cities of 15,000 inhabitants or more.

After 1940 the country experienced a period of accelerated growth, which has now leveled off to a constant rate. The number of intermediate cities has increased, the proportion of young people in the population has become appreciably higher, and the rate of net demographic growth has risen to one of the highest in the world: 3.4% per year in 1970. Economic growth has been even faster (6.4% in 1970), but the regional distribution of growth has been spotty. Most of the economic development has benefited the larger cities.

In 1970 the urban population in Mexico reached 44.6% of the total population. During the initial period of industrialization (1940–1955), the highest rates of economic growth were found in construction (8.8% per year) and manufacturing (6.9% per year). After 1955 these figures continued to increase but the number of new jobs began to decline. This new trend was due to a shift away from the production of consumer goods and toward the production of capital goods, as well as to the introduction of modern capital-intensive technology. The small and medium-sized concerns, which had provided a large share of the labor market, were no longer able to compete with the modern corporations and were eliminated. The impact of new technologies was beginning to be felt in a slowdown in the service industries.

Agriculture began to slacken noticeably after 1955. The farming economy had been growing at the rate of 5% per year, but this rate proved impossible to sustain. By 1960 agriculture had become stagnant and mass migration to the cities had begun. The continuing investment and increased output in the agricultural sector corresponded almost entirely to commercial farming, which employed but a small minority of the peasant population (Secretaría 1976:66–71).

Thus the social and economic growth of the country evolved toward the present situation of "two Mexicos: a modern sector which includes industry, high output services and cash crops . . . and a traditional sector which may be associated with unirrigated farming and an urban population lacking steady jobs or occupations [Bazdresh 1973:18]." By 1963 the top 10% of the population was benefiting from 50% of the national income, whereas 40% of the population at the bottom had to share 11% of the national income.

UNDEREMPLOYMENT IN MEXICO

In 1960 an estimated 40% of the Mexican labor force was employed in so-called low productivity activities (Alejo 1973:7–9, 11–12). This proportion has remained stationary ever since and is not expected to change. Underemployment was estimated at 35–45% of the labor force in 1970, distributed as follows: agriculture, 60%; services, 31%; commerce, 22%; manufacturing, 18%; building, 14%; mining, 13%; transportation, 8%; public administration, 6%; power industry, 4%; petroleum industry, 3%. These high rates of underemployment were attributed to "an inability of the modern high productivity sector to generate enough jobs, and an inability of the educational system to generate enough qualified personnel [Alejo 1973:1–2]."

Only one out of four adult Mexicans has a steady economic activity. The proportion is decreasing, since the rate of growth of the labor force is now less than 2% per year, well below the population growth. Jobs generated by industry lag at least 1.5% per year behind the increase in the agricultural population.

According to the Department of Labor (Secretaría 1975:31–32), the underemployment situation is more critical than is the unemployment problem. Only 6% of the labor force was unemployed in 1970. At the same time, 61% of the labor force declared average yearly earnings below the equivalent of the minimum legal wage. About 70% of the unemployed and of the underemployed labor force is located in rural areas. The Secretary of Labor has stated that 48.5% of all Mexican families live on less than 1000 pesos a month, about the minimum legal wage (P. Muñoz Ledo, *Excélsior*, February 7, 1973).

According to official statistics, the future outlook is grim. The occupational structure is expected to remain stationary at best:

> There is transgenerational accumulation of poverty and underemployment, because jobholders in low-productivity occupations cannot afford to feed their families properly or to provide an education which might enable their offspring to attain higher-productivity jobs. In this group the transgenerational capillarity is minimal and improves only slightly by migration to the major cities. According to recent projections, assuming that the economy grows at an average annual rate of 8% and provided that important adjustments can be made in the regional–sectorial partition of resources under conditions of stability of internal prices as well as external payments, we might look forward to maintaining by 1980 the same absolute levels of unemployment and underemployment which prevailed in 1970 [Alejo 1973:13].

MEXICO CITY: AN OVERVIEW

The present population of the Mexico City metropolitan area is around 10 million. It is the largest of 17 Mexican cities in the range above 100,000 population. Originally an agricultural nation, Mexico now has one of the highest urbanization levels in the world. Annual population growth in Mexico City was around 6% in 1970.

Up to 1930 the urban area of Mexico City included the 12 city delegations, plus the suburban areas of Coyoacan and Atzcapotzalco, which then contained only 2% of the urban population. From 1939 to 1950 there was an explosive growth of the city within the limits of the Federal District. Finally, after 1950 the city expanded across Federal District boundaries into the adjoining areas of the State of México (Unikel 1971:250, 255, 269).

This expansion was fed principally by the impoverished countryside population. In 1965 the difference in wealth between the rural and urban sectors could be deduced from the available figures for per capita net product of the labor force in each sector of the economy:

primary (mainly agriculture):	2, 421 pesos
secondary (mainly industry):	12,905 pesos
tertiary (mainly services):	12,685 pesos

The preceding figures are in pesos at the 1950 currency value. Since the secondary and tertiary sectors are largely urban based, the figures reflect an important differential in per capita income between the city and the countryside (Palerm 1969:11–12).

By 1960 only 55% of the residents of Mexico City had been born within the city; 44% were first-generation migrants. In a single 3-year period (1962–1965) the urban industrial labor force increased by 15% (from 2,416,000 to 2,779,000), whereas the agricultural labor force increased by 8% (from

6,505,000 to 7,092,000). Notice that, although the urban rate of increase was almost twice the rural, the numerical growth of the peasantry still exceeded the urban growth in absolute figures. In view of the high underemployment rates and the low per capita income levels in the countryside, this means a continuing high rate of emigration to the city.

In 1974 an estimated 5.7% of the economically active population of Mexico City was unemployed and 35.3% was underemployed (Cornelius 1975:231). This was significantly better than the estimated 70% underemployment in the countryside. A high proportion of the rural migrant labor force was absorbed by the building industry, because construction provides a large number of unskilled jobs under conditions of cyclic or intermittent employment, without social security benefits and at low pay levels. Yet these jobs are reckoned as "high productivity employment" in the available statistics.

According to Unikel (1976:44, 46) the urban growth trends were as follows:

	Migrants	Total population increase
1940–1950	847,197	1,228,610
1950–1960	739,053	1,930,933
1960–1970	1,488,529	3,445,123

During 1950–1960 there was a decline, in both absolute and relative terms, of the rural migration into Mexico City. However, after the agricultural development became stagnant the figures doubled and have since remained at a high level.

Other studies provide roughly comparable figures within the uncertainties of the estimates. Thus, Bataillon and Rivière d'Arc (1973:62) put the figure of the marginally employed in 1960 at 605,000 for Mexico City. Ifigenia Navarrete (*Excélsior,* November 4, 1976) quotes a total of 2,464,000 unemployed for all of Mexico in 1971, thus marking a net increase of 1,958,000 over the figure corresponding to 1960. If the latter figures were to be accepted as reliable, the increase in unemployment during 1960–1970 would be roughly the same as the rural migration into Mexico City for the same period.

LOW-INCOME HOUSING IN MEXICO CITY

There has been relatively little specific research on shantytowns in Mexico. A general classification of low-income housing has been provided in a government-sponsored report by Turner (1971). According to this report, we may distinguish four main types of lower-class housing in Mexico: government low-cost housing projects, squatter settlements (*colonias populares*), slums (*vecindades*), and shantytowns (*ciudades perdidas*).

Government-sponsored housing usually consists of apartment blocks with relatively high housing standards, with a total population in 1970 estimated at 500,000 persons. This type of housing is not generally accessible to marginals, since it is preferentially awarded to industrial workers and government clerks. The so-called *colonias populares* (also called *asentamientos informales*) comprise a wide variety of settlements on undervalued real estate (sloping ground, mudflats, and so on). Their property status is irregular, either because of squatting (*colonias de paracaidistas*), or because the settlers acquired their lots from illegal developers (*fraccionamientos ilegales*) (Cornelius and Lomnitz 1975:5–6; Ward 1975:5–7). These squatter settlements occupy about 41.5% of the built-up area in Mexico City (according to Ward), and their total population was estimated at about 3.3 million in 1970. They are mostly located in the peripheral zones of the metropolitan area, and represent relatively stable evolving standards of housing. The population in these settlements is growing at an average rate of 5% a year in Mexico City.

Vecindades are central-city slums, typically in the form of alleys containing 20 to 50 rented rooms each. In some cases, *vecindades* are old town-houses of the prerevolutionary upper classes that have been subdivided into individual rooms. Many of these slums are rent-controlled and have very little population turnover. The residents tend to form stable family networks. Their total population in 1970 was estimated at 2 million for the Federal District (Turner 1971:1–4).

Finally, *ciudades perdidas* are small shantytowns of high population density and extremely low living standards, which may be found typically in the interstitial areas of decaying urban zones. The settlers normally pay rent for their huts. The total population of these settlements was estimated at 200,000 to 300,000 people in the Federal District. Turner finds that the two last-named systems or types of irregular settlements (slums and interstitial shantytowns) tend to have a stable or slightly decreasing population, with deteriorating housing standards.

At present most of the growing settlements, including Cerrada del Cóndor, belong to the second type, i.e., shantytowns with medium population density that spring up in the peripheral zones of the city, either through direct squatting or through the agency of free-lance developers, whose title to the land is often dubious or irregular. Some of these settlements are inhabited by urban industrial workers, and others are settled predominantly by marginals. Altogether their population includes roughly 40% of the total population of the Federal District.

CERRADA DEL CÓNDOR

Cerrada del Cóndor is a relatively small settlement: It contains around 200 dwellings. Its inhabitants are not squatters. The shantytown occupies the south-

Partial view of Cerrada del Cóndor, with the opposite slope of the ravine in the background. Notice black patches indicating the entrances of abandoned "sand mines."

The shantytown dwellings follow the relief of the erosional slopes of the ravine. The topography is characteristic of dissected volcanic ash flows along the western edge of the Valley of Mexico.

ern slope of a deep ravine for a length of about 10 blocks; its maximum width is about 2 blocks. There is a cemetery on the opposite slope of the ravine. The ravine is an affluent of the old Mixcoac river and it runs dry most of the year. The general location of the shantytown and its adjoining middle-class and lower-class neighborhoods may be seen in Figure 2.1.

The western hills, or *lomas*, of Mexico City are volcanic ashflows, which have been deeply dissected by ravines. The general aspect of these erosional features is quite characteristic. The flanks of every ravine are pockmarked with caves dug into the hillside for the purpose of extracting sand for use as building material. These sandpits may tunnel into the hills for several hundred yards. They once provided a means of livelihood for the original settlers of Cerrada del Cóndor, but in recent years they have been banned by city ordinance, because the tunneling represents a hazard to construction.

From an administrative point of view the shantytown of Cerrada del Cóndor would be reckoned as part of the upper-middle-class neighborhood of Las Aguilas, within the delegation of Alvaro Obregon (Federal District). Las Aguilas is a relatively recent neighborhood (developed during the 1940s); it has a church, a public school, and two religious schools. There are urban utilities, transportation, and facilities of every kind. Most of the development is of one-family homes, and the land is very expensive. The northern ravine, which forms a boundary to the neighborhood, has been neglected by the developers. There are few middle-class homes fronting directly on the ravine; in general one finds a transitional lower-class buffer zone between the elegant residences of Las Aguilas and the ravine proper. Here we also find a few small neighborhood shops that cater to Cerrada del Cóndor settlers; a small textile factory, a private kindergarten, a police patrol booth, and a number of vacant lots.

Looking northward across the ravine and above the cemetery on the other side, we see the old lower-middle-class neighborhood of Merced Gómez. Just west of the low houses of Merced Gómez rise the new apartment blocks of Lomas de Plateros, designed for middle-class occupancy. Still further upstream we find a number of shantytowns and squatter settlements, such as Tarango (a 10-minute walk from Cerrada del Cóndor) and Puente Colorado, where it was still possible in 1973 to purchase small plots of land. Several families of Puente Colorado and Cerrada del Cóndor are interrelated through kinship.

The houses are apparently scattered at random over the hillside though their distribution actually obeys underlying social structures, particularly kinship. (See Figure 2.2.) A few of the dwellings are clustered together as *vecindades* (rows of rooms facing on a central alley) or *solares* (rooms sharing the same plot of land and facing on a common yard). The hillside between the houses has remained more or less in its original state; it is generally dirty and unkempt. The bottom of the ravine serves as a public latrine for over 50% of the population of the

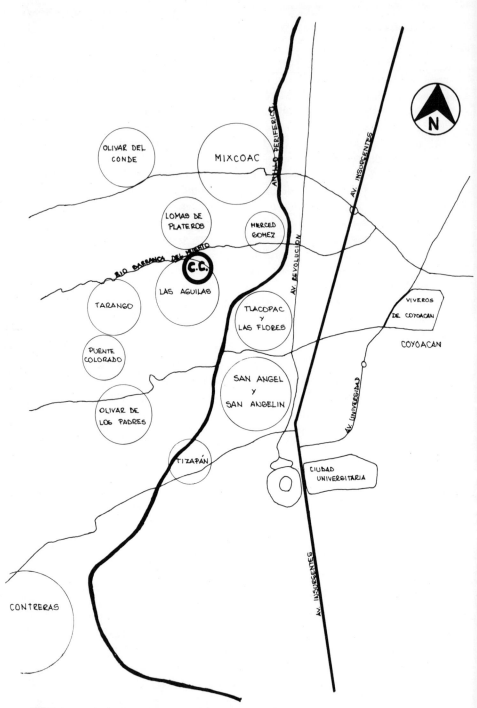

Figure 2.1. Map showing the location of Cerrada del Cóndor (C.C.) within the southern sector of Mexico City.

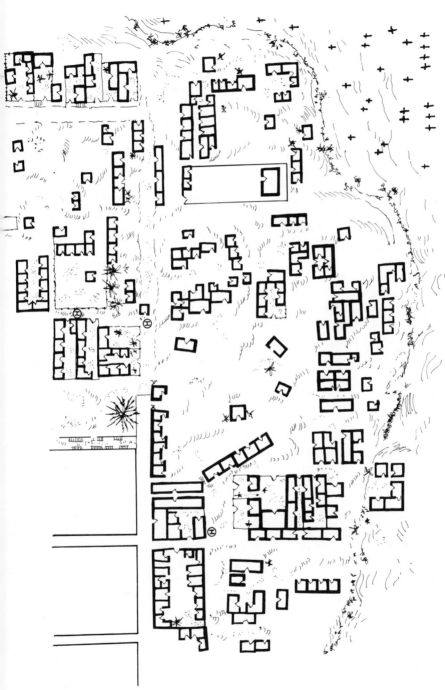

Figure 2.2. A map of the shantytown, showing the nearest urbanized street of Las Aguilas (upper left), and part of the cemetery on the opposite slope of the ravine (lower right). Public water faucets are represented by H.

shantytown. A public garbage dump at the eastern boundary of the shantytown represents a further health hazard.

The shantytown has no paved streets, no drainage, no gutters, no power or electric street lighting, no telephones, no garbage collection, and no water except for three public faucets and seven outlets in private homes. The public water faucets were installed as a result of pressure by groups of settlers. People standing in line and gossiping in front of a public water faucet represent a common sight in the shantytown. Any waste liquids are thrown outside the houses and trickle downhill. Small children are allowed to relieve themselves in public in front of their homes.

There is a special relationship of symbiosis between informal settlements and middle-class neighborhoods in Mexico City (Antochiew 1974; Cornelius and Lomnitz 1975:7). For example, in some of the northern districts of the metropolitan area, such as Naucalpan, Atzcapotzalco and Zaragoza, about 45% of the built-up area is occupied by "informal" settlements, whereas the remaining 55% is occupied by industrial areas and middle-class neighborhoods. The latter provide jobs (as gardeners, maids, and servants) for an important sector of the marginal population. On the other hand, the settlers in the shantytowns use the public transportation, the utilities (water, illegal hookups to power lines, and so on), the public schools, the public markets, the health centers, and other services found in the adjoining middle-class neighborhoods. In the case of Cerrada del Cóndor, there are two bus lines through Las Aguilas a few blocks away from the shantytown, as well as in Merced Gómez and Lomas de Plateros on the opposite side of the ravine. A police booth two blocks from the shantytown is staffed by a captain, a sergeant, and two policemen who "come down on Sundays to pick up the drunks." Most of the settlers also use nearby shops and markets in Las Aguilas, Merced Gómez, and other middle-class areas, particularly for tortillas, tortilla dough, drugs, and foodstuffs. Most shantytown children between the ages of 7 and 13 go to the public school of Las Aguilas, about 15 blocks away, or Merced Gómez across the ravine. Some mothers take their children every day to the Mexican Institute for Childhood Protection (IMPI), where they can get a school breakfast against payment of 20 centavos and a show of clean hands. Some of the women also participate in the classes for mothers and young girls that are taught there.

Within the shantytown proper are three small shops, which sell bread, crackers, candy, soft drinks, tinned sardines, condensed milk, fruit, chili, and (in two of the shops) beer. In addition, there are several small stands within or outside homes. There is a *tianguis* (free market) in the shantytown on Sundays. The mailman goes into the shantytown for mail delivery.

Cerrada del Cóndor does not exist on official city maps. Yet it has been there since the early 1930s and the settlers are not squatters in the strict sense of the term. Few of the settlers are homeowners; most of them pay rent for the *piso* or plot on which their homes are built (see Table 4.10, in Chapter 4). The homes themselves are either owned or rented by the settlers. Most of the land in the shantytown is owned by two heirs of the original owner. None of the construction in the shantytown has been carried out according to city ordinances, and therefore the shantytown is threatened by the same administrative measures, including possible eviction, as a squatter settlement. A more real threat of eviction arises because of the high value of real estate and the increasing demand for middle-class housing. When I visited Cerrada del Cóndor in late 1973 I found that 20 homes I had previously surveyed were gone. These homes were the ones closest to Las Aguilas and they had been "cleaned out" to make way for middle-class residential construction. The evicted families had scattered; some had been able to find a place to live elsewhere in Cerrada del Cóndor or in neighboring shantytowns such as Puente Colorado.

Origin of the Shantytown

The site now occupied by Cerrada del Cóndor used to be uninhabited land until 1929. It was purchased in 1913 by a man who used it mainly for growing seedlings of fruit trees. Sixteen years later he leased the area of the ravine to a man who installed a small brickmaking plant. This man eventually purchased the land and built his home there. During the 1930s he allowed some of the workers at the brick kilns to build their homes there. He also sold small plots to 15 families, most of whom came from the State of México. A family of caretakers from the sandpits east of the present shantytown later decided to settle there.

During the early 1940s urban development of the neighborhoods of Las Aguilas and Merced Gómez began. Some of the construction workers rented plots of land from the owner of the brick factory. Others came to the general area as caretakers of plots or constructions, and eventually moved into the shantytown. Soon they were joined by many relatives from the countryside.

In the 1950s the owner died and the brick factory was closed down. The descendants of the owner began leasing the plots or houses to settlers. The population of the shantytown increased rapidly because of rural–urban migration and because of the southward expansion of the city, which dislodged many of the original inhabitants of the districts of Mixcoac, Las Flores, Tlacopac, and Merced Gómez. During the 1960s the population of the shantytown increased by 119 families; 87 had relatives or friends living there. Operation of the sandpits was discontinued around that time. The ravine became a purely residential area. There was a great deal of construction of new dwellings by owners, for their own relatives as well as for renting out to settlers. Clusters of extended or jointed family households sprang up throughout the shantytown. The first families of settlers born in the shantytown appeared at that time, mostly in dwellings adjoining those of their parents. Clusters of kinship-related settlers from various parts

TABLE 2.1

Reasons for Moving to Cerrada Del Cóndor[a]

Number of previous moves in Mexico City	1930-1940				1940-1950				1950-1960				1960-1970			
	A	B	C	D	A	B	C	D	A	B	C	D	A	B	C	D
0					4	2					10	1	1	1	60	1
1	1		2				1				3	2	8	4	10	9
2							1		6	1	3	1	1	1	2	2
3									2				1		7	
4															3	1
5							1		1				1			
6+													1			1
Unknown												1			2	

[a]A = displaced by urban growth; B = seeking privacy from relatives;
C = moving in with relatives or friends in Cerra da del Cóndor;
D = more conveniences in Cerrada del Cóndor.

of the country constituted centers of attraction for new migrants from the same geographical areas.

According to Table 2.1, based on my survey of 162 households in 1971, only 3 families had settled in Cerrada del Cóndor by 1940. Nine additional families had settled there by 1950, 30 between 1950 and 1960, and 119 between 1960 and 1970. It is significant that, during this last decade, as many as 63 families established their initial urban residence in Cerrada del Cóndor. These families included direct migrants from the countryside to the homes of relatives in Cerrada del Cóndor, as well as young couples constituted in the shantytown. During the same period, 31 families arrived in the shantytown after only one previous residence elsewhere in the Federal District, and 6 families after two changes of residence. Most residents chose the shantytown because they had relatives or friends living there.

The number of settlers who had left the shantytown prior to the 1971 survey could not be determined with any degree of reliability. Hence the figures of Table 2.1 include only those settlers who were still living in the shantytown by 1971. The number of families who moved away from the shantytown between 1969 and 1971 is estimated at between 25 and 30 families. Some of them (not more than 5 families) returned to their villages; the others moved to other areas in the Federal District, often to Puente Colorado where small plots for sale were still available. In general, outward migration from Cerrada del Cóndor was motivated either by family reasons or by the availability of more favorable residential conditions elsewhere.

SOME IMPRESSIONS OF SHANTYTOWN LIFE

Mexico City shantytowns located in ravines are effectively hidden from observation. Cerrada del Cóndor becomes visible only when you are inside it. The initial impression is of an assemblage of low, single-story shacks or brick cabins made of inexpensive materials and scattered at random. It has a transient look, more like a camp than a permanent settlement. Roofs are weighed down with stones, wires hang from power lines, tins and metal scraps are found in heaps around the dwellings, bricks and old plumbing fixtures are apparently strewn about in disorder. There is a characteristic shantytown smell, compounded of used clothes, stale mattresses, and fecal matter.

The place looks extremely dry and dusty most of the year. During the rainy season, however, the alleys become rivers of mud. Some bushes and small trees grow on the slopes, between the houses, but they do not seem to yield any noticeable shade. The general impression is neither urban nor rural; the shacks are too small and too close together for a typically rural environment. In another shantytown in Mexico City, children of school age, when asked whether they lived in the city or in the countryside, were unable to give consistent answers.

The dwellings are unpainted structures made mostly of bricks or adobe. They have little mortar and no outside finish, so that the owner may easily take them apart and reuse the bricks elsewhere. Most homes are one-room dwellings with a wooden door and no windows. The door is normally left open during the day, and there is a plastic or fabric curtain hanging across the opening for privacy. Most settlers grow flowers or ornamental plants in tin cans placed around the house or hung on the walls. Outside each door there is usually a metal washbasin where water is stored for personal washing, bathing children, washing dishes, and doing the laundry. Often there are two or more such tubs to a family, and it is possible to see the settlers washing their faces, cleaning objects, or scrubbing their children in the tubs. These washbasins may also be a source of additional income for housewives who take in washing. A washboard made of fiber or some similar material completes the installation. Clotheslines with dripping laundry are seen everywhere in the shantytown.

During the daytime, radios are blaring from nearly every door. Women and young girls are busy washing, cooking, and minding the small children playing in the gutter in front of the homes. The style of dress is largely urban. Though many construction workers still wear straw hats and *huarache* sandals, otherwise the men dress like the Mexico City working class: dungarees, shirt, and shoes. Elderly migrant women tend to wear dark-colored dresses with skirts below the

Carrying water from the public faucet into the shantytown. Notice the typical arrangement of clotheslines.

A view of Cerrada del Cóndor, showing why shantytown children are at a loss to decide whether they live "in the country" or "in the city." (Cruz Azul is the name of a national soccer team.)

The shantytown in the early afternoon. Notice the variety of housing quality. Electricity is pirated by hooking onto the power lines. Children at play are supervised by an older sister.

Rainfall has dissected minor creeks in the "streets," which provide drainage. Pails, tubs, and pots are emptied into the street. Many homes have TV antennas.

Roofs on Class D dwellings are weighted down with stones. The entire dwelling is easily taken apart and moved to another site, with a minimum loss of building materials.

knees and a shawl (*rebozo*) for covering the head, as is customary in the country-side. Younger women mostly wear secondhand urban dress such as blouses with skirts or cheap print dresses. Young girls wear blouses with short skirts or pants, as well as inexpensive dresses, all of which may be found in the stores or at the nearby market. Young boys are dressed in hand-me-downs from their brothers, mostly ill-fitting clothes, with their shirttails hanging out. Synthetic fabrics and plastics are dominant; women as well as children characteristically wear shoes made entirely of molded plastic.

I realize now that an objective description of shantytown life is a difficult accomplishment. Fortunately, there exist numerous descriptions of shantytowns by anthropologists and other writers. If the Latin American reader should not wish to rely on these, there is all too often a shantytown within walking distance, which he or she may explore at leisure. In this book one will find no stress on the more sensational aspects of poverty: the filth, the promiscuity, the arguments and fights between people who must live together in a tiny space with the barest minimum of material comforts. It is not a place to look for beauty or harmonious interpersonal relationships. Yet, I believe, the fact that a strong social fabric persists, that norms and values are upheld, and that persons of admirable strength of character are so frequently encountered in these shantytowns should give pause to those who are inclined to be pessimistic about the future of mankind. One might even go so far as to say that the contemporary challenge of minimum consumption and maximum recycling of resources has been successfully (though unwittingly) met by the marginals. It is not a pleasant solution, perhaps; but one that can no longer be ignored, given the ceaseless growth of marginal strata all over the world. I am convinced that the settlers of Cerrada del Cóndor have a message for all of us, if we could but interpret it correctly.

A typical day in Cerrada del Cóndor starts before sunrise, when most men and women get up. Around 6 A.M., most men as well as some women go to work. Many walk to work, others take the bus. As the sun rises over the mountains the bustle in the shantytown begins. Lining up in front of the public water faucet are long queues of women, children, and old men, waiting to fill their buckets. Most of these buckets are made of empty used cans (for the most part, square cans that originally contained animal fat). Some of the old men balance two of these cans at the ends of a wooden yoke, which they use to carry water to the homes of settlers for a few centavos. The public water faucet is the informal meeting place of the shantytown, much like the village well was in the countryside. There is a great deal of exchange of news and gossip while waiting in line with the empty buckets.

Most of the women start working on their laundry early in the morning. While they soak and scrub in front of their homes, the transistor radios are blasting soap operas or popular music. Most shantytown women are soap opera fans and rarely miss an episode. Meanwhile, the young girls help their mothers in sweeping, running errands, and watching over their small brothers. Little boys, as a rule, are more pampered than little girls, though they too have to help with errands, particularly carrying water. There are two school shifts; some children go to school in the mornings, whereas others go in the afternoons. Those children who are not away at school or running errands for their mothers are usually seen playing around the dwellings in groups according to age. Every family owns some toys, and there are many broken toys strewn about the shantytown. The games differ according to sex and age. For example, boys of school age tend to play ball or marbles. There are also a few gangs of adolescent boys who are no longer going to school and who do not yet have jobs. They may be seen sitting around near the entrance to the shantytown or leaning against a wall, talking.

During the morning hours there are small groups of jobless men talking outside the small shops where beer is sold. By midmorning the shantytown is bustling with activity. Street vendors walk by offering their wares to the women who work or sit out of doors. Elderly men and women set out stands in front of their homes with small amounts of merchandise. The items for sale on the street include bread, clothing, chairs, ice cream, fruit, and so on. The women buy whatever they need, or they send their children to the store. The water carriers carry water back and forth; women and children wait for their turn at the faucet; children are playing, and some men tell jokes or compliment the women, if they have had a few beers. About noon, the children who go to school on the afternoon shift start washing up or taking a bath in the tanks in front of their homes. They eat their lunch of tortillas, beans, or noodle soup. After they go and the children from the morning shift return, the women can relax for an hour or so. In the afternoon they may finish their housework, listen to the radio, or watch a soap opera on television. There is also a lot of gossiping and visiting among relatives and neighbors on afternoons.

Television is an important cultural influence in the shantytown. Children watch television after school; if they do not have a set at home they visit with neighbors who do. More important, ownership of a television set tends to ensure the presence of the men after work.

Between 7 and 8 P.M. there is a light evening snack, mostly coffee and tortillas, and then to bed. The lucky owners of a television set may sit up or watch the screen from their beds until late at night.

Sundays and holidays differ from weekdays mainly because of the number of men to be seen in the shantytown. Many men stay home and drink, or go for a drink to the store or the *pulquería* (an unlicensed place serving *pulque,* a traditional fermented beverage made of agave juice). Groups of men go out for more serious drinking, for visiting with friends, or for a soccer game. The soccer aficionados (either players or watchers) often take their boys along; but outings of the whole family are rare, especially for large families. Such an outing may cost at least the equivalent of one or two working days' wages.

Young couples with fewer children do occasionally go out to picnic in some of the city parks, or visit relatives in the country. But once the family starts growing, women and children have to stay home except for shopping, going to church, or visiting a relative within the metropolitan area. Television and radio then become the major surrogates for contact with the world outside the shantytown, as well as the main form of entertainment and diversion. It takes the women's minds off the gray realities of their daily lives.

Migration

The study of internal migrations as an ongoing demographical and sociological process represents one of the major problems in contemporary social science. The lack of a unifying point of view among the wealth of contributions by sociologists, demographers, anthropologists, and economists on this subject has already been pointed out. A number of reviews help bring out the range and the diversity of viewpoints which prevailed in the field of migration studies (Balán, Browning, and Jelin 1973; Butterworth 1971; Cardona and Simmons 1976; Cornelius 1971; Kemper 1971a; Mangalam and Schwarzweller 1968:6–7; Muñoz, Oliveira, Singer, and Stern 1972; Sayers and Weaver 1976:10–29; Stepick and Stepick 1975).

Demographic studies of migration tend to favor (implicitly or explicitly) the so-called push–pull hypothesis. According to this hypothesis the causes of a specific migration process may be analyzed in terms of two components: (1) the "push" or repelling force from the place of origin, and (2) the "pull" or attraction to the place of destination, i.e., the city. The variables most commonly used by demographers in illustrating this process are age, sex, ethnic origins, education, occupation, income, distance to urban centers, and other factors that admit quantitative treatment and statistical processing. There has also been some effort to incorporate sociopsychological factors such as attitudes, aspirations, motivations, values, community identity, institutional influences, and other less easily quantifiable variables. However, the more notable advances in the demographic treatment of migrations have probably taken place in the field of mathematical modeling and in the development of statistical techniques (Mangalam and Schwarzweller 1968:7; Sayers and Weaver 1976:20–29).

Two major approaches to the migration problem have been dominant in the field of sociology: (1) *historical structuralism,* favored by many Latin American scholars, and (2) the *modernization* approach, represented mainly by North American sociologists. The approach of historical structuralism (Muñoz and Oliveira 1972:32–34) emphasizes aspects of social change within a framework of Latin American economic dependence on foreign power centers. Underdevelopment in Third World nations is not merely seen in relation to the development of the major industrial powers but as actually caused by the rise of these powers to economical and political prominence. Specifically, Latin America is seen as the traditional economic hinterland of the United States and of a few other Western powers. The patterns of dependence between nations tend to be duplicated within each Latin American country; thus, large cities represent secondary centers of domination with respect to the countryside. The hegemony of major cities is viewed as a direct cause of the marginalization of the traditional peasantry in its own hinterland. In the historical structuralist view, the migration process in Latin America is seen as a symptom of the imbalance that has been introduced into the traditional economic structure of the region by a process of industrialization based on foreign power centers.

Against this large-scale backdrop of historical development of the socioeconomic structures one can find a number of studies concerned with the motivations of the migrants, construction of typologies and models, social mobility, social problem analysis, acculturation, and the problems of decision making and adaptation to the urban environment. These studies have become collectively known in Latin America as the modernization school. Most research is centered on the individual as the unit of analysis: This approach is reflected in the use of variables such as attitudes, motivations, aspirations, and similar psychological concepts (Mangalam and Schwarzweller 1968:6–7; Muñoz, Oliveira, Singer, and Stern 1972:32–34; Parra 1972:221–225; Sayers and Weaver 1976:28). According to the critics there has been a tendency to stress aspects of personal decision and adjustment at the expense of the elements of social interaction in migration phenomena. On the whole, however, it seems that the two views address themselves to different levels of analysis: Whereas the historical structuralists discuss the macro social factors involved in the origins of large-scale migration processes, the modernizationists study the migration problem at the scale of the individual migrant.

Until recently the dominant model among anthropologists (again, explicitly or implicitly, as the case may be) has been the so-called folk–urban model attributed to Redfield (Balán, Browning, and Jelin 1973:149; Kemper 1971:610; Uzzell,

1976). Basically this model postulates two ideal poles at the extremes of a continuum: (1) *folk society,* which is characteristically small, homogeneous, traditional, and formal; and (2) *urban society,* which is described as the exact opposite of folk society.

> The lineage of this model is long and impressive, dating at least as far back as the mid-nineteenth century with Maine's "status and contract," recurring in Tonnie's "Gemeinschaft und Gesellschaft," Spencer's "military and industrial," Durkheim's "mechanic and organic," and finally descending to contemporary variations on "traditional and modern." . . .
> The community of origin, the village in the rural–urban migration sequence, was said to be characterized by close, intense, and emotionally gratifying familiar and communal interpersonal relationships. By definition . . . the other end of the dichotomy, the city as the community of destination must display opposite characteristics of distant, cold, and impersonal social relationships. In such perspective the migrant is seen as being wrenched from the community of origin of which he was an organic part, and embarking alone upon the journey to the great city . . . [where] unshielded by any sort of social protection provided by the family of other "primary" groups, he is confronted by the full force of an impersonal, even hostile, urban environment [Balán, Browning, and Jelin 1973:149].

Although Redfield himself never used this model in relation to migration (his folk–urban continuum was set up as a scale of reference in comparing traditional communities within a given culture), some of his followers as well as his opponents began to attribute the difficulties of the acculturation process suffered by peasant migrants in cities to a supposed loss of folk-type cultural traits that they had brought with them from their communities of origin. This extrapolation of Redfield's model has been very widely used.

At present a majority of anthropological studies on migration discusses the degree of adaptation of the migrants to urban culture.[1] Such observations often appear to contradict the predictions of the model proposed by Redfield's followers.

Now, a peasant arriving in a large city does not actually undergo anything like the supposed transition from folk society to urban society. Prior to migrating, peasants have been in contact with cities through many aspects of their culture. On the other hand, every large city contains "rural" islands and these are precisely the spots where rural migrants tend to congregate. The discrepancies of the folk–urban migration theory can hardly be blamed on Redfield, who never intended his model to apply to individuals. The process of disorganization, secularization, and individuation described by Redfield clearly refers to changes in the culture of the community as a whole. The individual acculturation of

---

[1]For example, Lewis (1952:230–246); Butterworth (1971:257–274); Munizaga (1961); Kemper (1974:1095–1118); Lomnitz (1969:43–71); Cardona and Simmons (1976:30–31); Du Toit (1976:61–64); Halpern (1976:94); such authors have studied groups of migrants who tended to cluster together according to their places of origin and who managed to maintain most of their family structures and cultural traits without any noticeable symptoms of social disorganization.

migrants is a complicated process that necessarily depends on many other factors beside the relative position of their community of origin on the folk–urban scale.

Another anthropological approach to migration studies, which is achieving some recent prominence, consists in analyzing certain intermediate social structures such as groups, quasi-groups, and social networks (Lomnitz 1976b:133–150; Wolfe 1970:224–226). This approach aims at two kinds of results: (1) providing a better understanding of the social mechanisms that promote and facilitate the migration process; and (2) bridging the present gulf between historical structuralistists and modernizationists, by providing an intermediate level of analysis. "Individuals do not make decisions in a vacuum or as abstract members of a socio-economic category, but as a result of their interaction with others. . . . The concept of social network . . . represents a microstructure, a middle-range level of abstraction situated between the large-scale social structure and the individual [Wolfe 1970:227]."

The presence of relatives and friends in the city has emerged as a major factor of selectivity in the rural–urban migration process of Latin America. (See examples in Browning and Feindt 1971; Bryce-Laporte 1970; Butterworth 1971; Du Toit and Safa 1976; Kemper 1974; Lewis 1952; Mangin 1970; Roberts 1973.) During the early years, a large part of the contingent of migrants was made up of young, unmarried, male migrants. At that time the migrants gravitated toward the central slums of large cities, where they underwent a period of adaptation (Turner and Mangin 1968). However, as the process matured the flow of migrants became greater, and spanned the full range of the rural population. Entire families, including the young and the very old, migrated together. The process became increasingly unselective as to age, sex, or skills. Where the central slums of Latin American cities have become filled to capacity, the new migrants now go directly from the countryside to the peripheral shantytowns where they are expected by relatives or friends (Brown 1972).

The dominant mechanism, as we see it, involves an exchange of information and assistance by and through social networks that span the gap between the city and the countryside. These networks encourage, regulate, or otherwise influence the migration process, beginning at the stage of decision making back in the village and continuing through the complex problems of adaptation and survival in the city. Today the study of these networks represents a major frontier in urban anthropology in Latin America.

AN ECOLOGICAL MODEL OF THE MIGRATION PROCESS

A consensus exists among migration experts on the following points: (1) The study of internal migration processes requires a unifying viewpoint and a model sufficiently general and broad to encompass all aspects of migration; (2) such a model should be interdisciplinary; (3) the folk–urban model used by anthropologists has become obsolete; (4) the migration process is caused by the interaction of economic, social, psychological, and environmental factors at various levels: the macrohistory of economic relations between nations and classes, the microprocesses on the individual scale, and the intermediate level of social groups and networks; (5) an ecological approach may be successfully used as a conceptual framework in processes of interaction between society and the environment; and (6) a close affinity appears to exist between the holistic approach of anthropology and the concept of an ecological system.

I do not intend to propose a theory of migration, but rather a conceptual framework that may be useful in describing the migration process through the inclusion of data from different disciplines and analysis at different levels of generality. Human ecology is a branch of anthropology that deals with the adaptation of human societies to their natural environment. Every population adapts to its physical environment, in terms of food, shelter, and clothing, and in its attempt to fit biological needs to specific requirements of the ecological niche it happens to occupy. In addition, every social group is also a culture bearer. As such it must develop adaptive mechanisms that become incorporated in its set of social relations, to ensure the survival of the group by means of orderly, regular, and predictable patterns of competition and cooperation. The economy, the culture, and the social structure are important parts of the ecological system in a human population (Cohen 1968:1–2).

The ecological approach treats human society as one link in a complex chain that includes the fauna, the flora, and a wide range of geographic and climatic factors. This chain is known as the *ecosystem*. "Anthropologists have found that factors such as geography, the distribution of natural resources, climate, crops, cattle, and relationships with neighboring populations may influence the evolution of society to a considerable degree. These factors are major components of the ecosystem and societies must adapt to them [Hole 1968:357]."

I propose to describe migration as a process of geographical displacement of human populations from one ecological niche to another. Three stages may be distinguished in such a process: (1) imbalance, (2) transfer, and (3) stabilization, discussed in the following sections.

Imbalance. During the imbalance stage, the temporary or permanent saturation of an ecological niche takes place, imperiling the survival or the physical safety of some human group. The imbalance may be due to cumulative factors such as population increase, differential economic opportunity, or the deterioration of agricultural soils; or it may be caused by relatively sudden events such as an accelerated population explosion, a foreign invasion, or a natural disaster. There are also cases of intermittent or periodic imbalance that are due to economic or environmental cycles; these may cause seasonal migrations.

Transfer. The stage of transfer includes all those factors related to the migration proper that determine the rate, human composition, and other features of the migration. Some of these factors are means of transportation, time–space coordinates of the migration, and the description of the migrant group as to age, family status, ethnic composition, schooling, and so on. The time–space patterns of the migration process obviously depend on the severity of the imbalance in the original niche as well as on the expectations of the migrants to find a better ecological niche at their selected locality of destination.

Stabilization. The stage of stabilization involves a return to the state of ecological balance, i.e., an adaptation of the migrant group to its new ecological niche. It includes the process of social acculturation: institutional change within the group, changes in family structure, and changes in cultural traits such as language, religion, leisure activities, and political organization. The period of stabilization may range from months to decades; it may involve a variety of reactions originating from within the host ecosystem, from violent rejection through tolerance to total absorption. Some migrations are so massive as to cause fundamental changes in the ecosystem of destination; or the technology of the new group may be so advanced as to displace the indigenous culture, as in the case of the Spanish conquest of America. Other migration processes produce a sequence of cultural mergers and fusions, e.g., in the Valley of Mexico during the Chichimec invasions, or in the Latin American cities of today.

Stabilization takes place in three phases, as follows:

1. *Settlement.* As migrants are incorporated into a new ecological niche of an ecosystem, a sequence of adaptive processes is triggered. These processes depend largely on the mode of integration (from assimilation to rejection) achieved by the migrants in their new milieu.
2. *Interaction.* The migration process brings changes in the new ecological niche—social and ethnic conflict, marginalization, introduction of new technologies, and so on. These changes are not limited to the human component of the ecosystem but may refer to alterations of the environment: new patterns of land use, changes in residential patterns, or the saturation of services and facilities that may occur in large cities.
3. *Feedback.* The migration process affects the original ecological niche of the migrants, not merely by depleting it but also by modifying the imbalance that originated the process. If the new ecological niche is satisfactory from the standpoint of survival and development of the migrant group, this information may reinforce the incentive for new groups to migrate. On the other hand, the economic contributions from successful migrants may channel new resources into the original ecological niche and thus help stabilize the stiuation at least temporarily. Both phenomena are observed in rural–urban migration.

MIGRATION PROCESSES IN LATIN AMERICA

The processes of rural–urban migration represent but one type of migratory phenomena found in history and in prehistory. Migrations have been extremely common and widespread, and may be cited among the fundamental processes of social change.

In Latin America there has been a recent saturation of the ecological niche that for thousands of years provided a livelihood for the peasantry. This saturation was caused by the explosive growth of the rural population, the fragmentation of rural landholdings, and the erosion and impoverishment of soils. The resulting imbalance was further augmented by the development of large cities, which are increasingly monopolizing all national resources (Browning 1965:4; Unikel 1976:56; Urquidi 1969:141). Thus the Latin American countryside has fallen behind the large cities in vital aspects of modernization (including health and sanitation, welfare, education, and cultural facilities) and has remained relatively unprotected against the impact of natural disasters (droughts, floods, earthquakes) as well as against episodes of political violence.

A classification of these factors in terms of push or pull, as in the earlier anthropological literature on migrations, describes two sides of the same coin. In the context of an ecological framework, what matters is that the imbalance affects particularly the economically and socially depressed areas in the countryside, because of improved conditions elsewhere in the prices of basic foods and commodities; better educational, social, and housing facilities; better protection against violence, illness, and natural disasters; better economic opportunities, as well as the opportunity to participate more actively in the sociocultural movement of modernization propagated via the mass media (M. Whiteford 1976:96–99).

In Latin America, "although rural poverty is the factor which pushes the migrants off the land, the exodus is selective and poverty in itself is not a sufficient cause of migration [Butterworth 1971:87]." Selectivity factors are those factors that may facilitate or inhibit migration. They include age, sex, and educational level of migrants; distance to the nearest large town; the availability of communications (roads, bus service, mass media) linking the city with the countryside; and, very important, the presence in the city of networks of relatives who are willing to extend assistance to the potential migrants.

The factors controlling the transfer stage of the migration process may be of three kinds: space factors, time factors, and selectivity factors. Space factors involve such geographical variables as may pertain to the routing of the transfer; some migration processes occur in stages whereas others are direct from the village to the city. Similarly, the time factors govern the duration and temporal pattern of the migration; some migrations occur in waves or currents, some are transgenerational, and so on. Finally, selective factors control the type of individual who is more likely to migrate. Migrant groups often represent a highly nonrandom sample of the population of the locality of origin.

Kemper points out that there are two conflicting views on selectivity factors in Latin American migrations: "Some hold that the migrants are poorly prepared for urban life . . . while others state that the better prepared elements in each rural community are more likely to abandon it in search of better opportunities [1971:617]." These two views are not altogether incompatible. A report of the United Nations (quoted by Butterworth) points out that

> the migration process is not a simple movement of peasants towards large cities, nor are the migrants generally among the poorest or least adapted members of their communities of origin. They include representatives of different social strata . . . many of which acquire some prior experience of urban life . . . as a result of compulsory military service. Many migrants are craftsmen or semi-skilled workers; some young men have secondary schooling . . . village craftsmen or non-farmers find it easier to migrate than the *peon* who may lack any useable urban skill. Again, the semi-literate are more likely to migrate than the illiterate and those having relatives in the city more than those who lack such relatives [Butterworth 1971:87].

In fact, however, several studies have shown that the migrants are not among the most able or the more highly skilled. According to Butterworth (1971:92), age is the only universal factor of selectivity; yet, Cornelius (1975:22) and Cardona and Simmons (1976:28) found that this may be true only of the initial or pioneering group of migrants. Once the young migrants have established a foothold in the city they promote the migration of their remaining relatives without age selectivity. My data confirm their findings. The most "able" may frequently be an individual who is fortunate in having social or kinship ties within the city. Likewise, selectivity on the basis of sex may vary from place to place. In some countries or regions a majority of migrants are women, because of the availability of job openings as housemaids. Often there are compensating factors that tend to even out the distribution of migrants by sex. Selectivity factors may vary, then, depending on a wide range of conditions such as technology, the political and kinship systems, systems of values, and other social variables in the community of origin, as well as on the psychological characteristics of the migrant (Cardona and Simmons 1976:19–48; Du Toit 1976b:49–76).

The stabilization stage has been more widely studied in Latin America, as it includes the process of adaptation or acculturation of the migrant in the city. Available research has been directed toward one or more of the following aspects: changes in family structure; the concept of "culture of poverty"; studies of shantytowns; changes of personality or world image; the cognitive orientation of the migrant; and studies of marginality. Most of these studies have referred in one way or another to the bipolar model attributed to Redfield.

A HISTORICAL SKETCH OF MIGRATION IN MEXICO

The history of Mexico prior to the Spanish conquest has been a history of invasions and migrations.[2] After the sixteenth century, however, the Spanish colonial regime imposed strict rules against the migratory mobility of the population. The hacienda system of land tenure required a resident labor force, tied to the property and to the owner of the hacienda in various permanent ways, usually through debt bondage.

The hacienda system remained through the end of the nineteenth century. However, during the revolutionary period of 1910–1940 major changes were introduced in the system of land tenure, and therefore in Mexican society. During the period of revolutionary violence, from 1910 to about 1921, the population decreased from about 15 million to 14.3 million. By 1924, more than 1.3 million hectares of hacienda lands had been distributed to the peasants. As the hacienda lands were carved up into *ejidos* (corporate farms), an unattached *campesino* (peasant) labor force was created. Also, thousands of peasants formerly tied to the haciendas were mobilized into the various revolutionary armies. At the time more than three-quarters of the country population were rural.

By 1940 the population of the country had increased to 19.6 million, of which 83% belonged to the lower class, most of them (60.7%) to the peasantry. Petroleum and the railroads were nationalized and industry increased. In 1940 about 10% of all Mexicans were living in states other than the one in which they were born. The large cities, such as Mexico City, Guadalajara, and Monterrey, were growing at about four times the average national rate. By far the greatest contingent of migrants settled in Mexico City. The year 1940 also marks the beginning of a period of rapid economic growth in Mexico.

Rural states such as Chiapas, Oaxaca, and Guerrero, as well as traditional mining states such as Zacatecas, Guanajuato, and San Luis Potosí, lost a large proportion of their inhabitants through migration. Thus, the State of Michoacán had lost nearly 15% of its native-born population by 1950. Government economic policy stimulated the growth of cash-crop agriculture in irrigated lands as against the traditional farming sector, which still includes roughly 85% of all landholdings in Mexico. There has been a slowly rising standard of living in the major cities and in the industrial, commercial, and mechanized agricultural sectors, as against stagnation in the traditional agricultural and mining sectors.

Between 1950 and 1970, approximately 4.5 million Mexicans migrated from rural to urban localities. Most of the migrants were landless peasants and small subsistence farmers, the poorest sector of the rural population. During the 1960s migration contributed more than 43% to the growth of the Mexico City met-

[2]This section has been largely based on data from Wright (1976:30–49).

ropolitan area—roughly, 1.8 million migrants per decade. By 1970 the population of the capital exceeded 8.4 million (as compared with about 1.5 million in 1940). At this rate the population of Mexico City is expected to reach 14.4 million by 1980. The city population in 1975 was increasing at a rate of about 2600 inhabitants per day. The economic pressure on the countryside during the same period may be estimated from the fact that there has been a 17.4% increase in the number of landless agricultural peasants in Mexico between 1940 and 1960. In conclusion, the pattern of internal migration in Mexico has been similar to that of other underdeveloped countries in the stage of industrialization, where a few major urban areas have begun to expand rapidly, attracting thousands of migrants from the overpopulated and depressed traditional countryside.

MIGRATION AND CERRADA DEL CÓNDOR

General Characteristics of the Settlers

In 1969 I made a survey of 389 heads of nuclear families and their spouses in the shantytown of Cerrada del Cóndor. The sample included 264 persons (67.6%) born outside the Federal District and 125 (32.4%) born in the Federal District. All informants born outside the Federal District were considered migrants, independently of age at time of migration. These included settlers who reached the Federal District as small children. So-called village-centered migrants, i.e., seasonal visitors to the shantytown, were not included in the sample even though it was recognized that many such temporary migrants would eventually settle in the shantytown.

As one examines the origins of the 125 individuals in the sample who were born in the Federal District, one finds that most of them are also of rural origin. Table 3.1 shows that a majority of the parents of these settlers were migrants. As

TABLE 3.1

Migrant Origin of the Parents of Settlers Born in Cerrada del Cóndor[a]

	Number	Percentage
Both parents migrants	49	39.2
One parent migrant	22	17.6
Both parents born in the Federal District	50	40.0
Unknown	4	3.2
Total	125	100.0

[a]From a sample of 125 heads of nuclear families or their wives.

TABLE 3.2

Age of 389 Heads of Families and Wives

Age	Number	Percentage
15-19	19	4.9
20-24	75	19.3
25-29	59	15.2
30-39	117	30.0
40-49	58	14.9
50-59	28	7.2
60+	22	5.6
Unknown	11	2.8
Total	389	99.9

to the 50 individuals born of Federal District parents, most of them turned out to come from small rural towns within the Federal District that have since been absorbed into the metropolitan area. I propose to call these people *passive migrants,* because they have made the transition from rural to urban settlers without actually moving away from their places of origin. In conclusion, it may be said that the vast majority of settlers in Cerrada del Cóndor are at most one generation removed from their rural origins.

Age.   Table 3.2 shows that most of the population of the shantytown is under 40.

Geographical Origin.   The sample of heads of family and their spouses included representatives of 18 different states of Mexico, plus the Federal District. The states of México and Guanajuato are overrepresented; this is true for Cerrada del Cóndor and the Federal District as a whole. More than 60% of our sample originated either from these two states or from the Federal District.

The migrants may be divided by states of origin into five distinct groups: (1) migrants from the states of Guanajuato and México, including depressed agricultural areas adjoining the Federal District (45.2%); (2) migrants from San Luis Potosí (11.4%), all of whom were members of the same kindred in Cerrada del Cóndor; (3) migrants from Veracruz, Zacatecas, and Hidalgo (about 6% each); (4) migrants from Querétaro, Guerrero, Michoacán, Puebla, Jalisco, and Oaxaca (2–4% each); and (5) migrants from Coahuila, Morelos, Tamaulipas, Tlaxcala, Aguascalientes, and Chihuahua (1–2 migrants in each group).

Population of the Locality of Origin.   Table 3.3 shows the distribution by size of localities of birth for the heads of families and spouses of migrant origin in Cerrada del Cóndor. The population figures for the localities declared as their birthplaces by the informants were obtained from the National Census of 1960; they are thought to be roughly representative of the population at the time of

TABLE 3.3

The Population of the Locality of Origin of Migrant Heads of Households
and Spouses According to 1960 Census

Population	Number	Percentage
Under 2,500	180	68.2
2,500-10,000	32	12.1
10,000-25,000	25	9.7
25,000-100,000	2	.7
Unknown	25	9.7
Total	264	100.4

migration. In the case of small localities the informants tended to give the name
of the nearest village as their birthplace; this leads to a bias toward overestimat-
ing the population of the locality of origin. It is concluded that the vast majority
of the migrants in the shantytown are rural in origin.

The Ecological Model of Migration Applied to Cerrada del Cóndor

The Stage of Imbalance.   In this section I shall attempt to describe the migration pattern as observed in Cerrada del Cóndor, using as example a group of 25
adult migrants from the *ejido*–hacienda Villela, in the township of Santa María
del Río (State of San Luis Potosí). These results will be presented jointly with a
tabulated survey for the population of Cerrada del Cóndor as a whole, in order to
allow an interpretation to emerge concerning the migration pattern of the shantytown.

   In Cerrada del Cóndor I found 30 heads of families or spouses who came
originally from the State of San Luis Potosí: 25 among them came directly from
the *ejido*–hacienda Villela. In 1971 this group formed 22 nuclear families, all of
them interrelated through a maze of kinship and *compadrazgo* ties. The central
core of this kindred was the Fernández family, including a total of 16 nuclear
families.[3] Originally all of these *Villelinos* had been landless fieldhands who
hired themselves out for a small daily wage. Jobs were few and far between. The
informants were unanimous in stating that their reasons for migrating were
"poverty," "no jobs," "hunger." Those informants who had been either too
young or too old to migrate on their own accord agreed that "life is easier here in
the shantytown." Let us compare this situation with the results of the survey
carried out on a shantytown-wide basis, as shown in Table 3.4.

[3]As elsewhere in this book, the actual names of the informants have been changed.

TABLE 3.4

Causes of Migration

Cause	Number	Percentage
Work	128	48.4
Need to stay with husband or parents	88	33.4
Family reasons (other than economical)	26	9.8
Unknown	22	8.3
Total	264	99.9

Roughly one half of all informants gave economic reasons for migration. Some of the typical responses were as follows: "There were no jobs," "I had no land," "There was not enough land to feed my family," "Everything is dead down there, so I came up here to see if I could find some work," "I had no food for my children." Only 9.8% of the sample stated family reasons other than purely economic as a main motive for migration. The remainder were members of households who had migrated jointly with their husbands or their parents.

A major reason for the disastrous economic situation of most migrants in their places of origin may be inferred from their occupations. Most of them were either landless peasants or attached to a family of landless peasants. The sample included 13.7% "members of other occupations," such as cobbler's apprentice, lumberjack, pig killer, bricklayer, charcoal maker, food trucker, truck driver, laundrywoman, janitor, farm maid, watchman. Only four informants had had any land of their own. Two of these had shared their parents' property, a third said his property had been "small and poor," and the fourth had decided to migrate because his land was flooded by a reservoir.

The data in Table 3.5 bring into focus the imbalance stage of the migration process. The migrants in Cerrada del Cóndor abandoned their ecological niche because it had ceased to provide a reasonable guarantee of their physical survival. They were peasants without land and without work.

Let us look more closely at the locality of Villela. One part of it is still a hacienda. The process of land expropriation and distribution has been a slow one; it began under the Cárdenas regime (1936–1942), but the size of the lots assigned to the peasants did not take the population increase into account. The present average size of family lots has shrunk to 4.7 hectares, most of it nonirrigated land. The arable surface is but a fraction of the total, because of the poor soil and the lack of economic means. Farmers in the *ejido* grow corn and beans for home consumption only; even so, the yearly crop lasts merely 2 or 3 months. Therefore the peasants "must necessarily go out and look for work elsewhere in order to complement their incomes [Alemán 1966:135]."

TABLE 3.5

Occupation Prior to Migration of Heads of Families and Wives

Occupation	Number	Percentage
Landless peasant (hired field-worker)	77	29.2
Artisan	1	.4
Worker at occasional jobs and service occupations	15	5.7
Peasant (propertied)	4	1.5
Too young to work	54	20.5
Worker	16	6.1
Miner	3	1.1
Skilled worker	1	.4
Housewife or unmarried peasant woman	93	35.2
Total	264	100.1

In 1960 the township of Santa María del Río had a population of 4841 "urban" inhabitants plus 33 ranchos, *ejidos*, or localities, with a grand total of 27,042 inhabitants. Like most *ejidos*, Villela had less than 1000 inhabitants; most localities of origin of settlers in Cerrada del Cóndor were in this size range.

The Stage of Transfer. The migration process from Villela to the Federal District began during the decade of the 1950s: Young Juan Pérez Fernández decided to migrate to the city jointly with his brother and a few friends. They were eager to try their luck and get away from the miserable conditions in the *ejido*. No one in the group had friends or relatives in the Federal District. After various adventures, three members of the original group (the brothers plus one friend) found work in the sandpits that then adjoined Cerrada del Cóndor. They settled in Cerrada del Cóndor and were joined, a few years later, by the mother of Juan Pérez Fernández, his nieces Juana and Elvira Fernández, and their respective children.

Since then, by successive stages of migration, the remaining Fernández kin have all migrated to Cerrada del Cóndor. This includes Señora Lupe, mother of the Fernández girls, and her remaining descendants. Her last daughter arrived in 1964 with her seven children, after her eldest boy (then 14 years old) had been sent ahead to work and stay with Señora Lupe. The remaining Villela families in the shantytown are relatives or descendants of the friend who had migrated with the Pérez Fernández brothers; in the meantime they all have become related through alliances or *compadrazgo* with the Pérez Fernández kindred.

The Villela story may be regarded as characteristic of the migration pattern in Cerrada del Cóndor. The three initial migrants were young innovators, unmarried at the time of migration, and willing to try their luck in the large city. Once they had found a place to settle, they became as it were the bridgehead for the staggered transfer of their kin from the village to the shantytown. Except for the

TABLE 3.6

Age at Migration of Heads of Families and Wives Born Outside Mexico City

Age	Number	Percentage
Under 13	56	21.2
13-18	78	29.5
18-25	54	20.5
25-40	54	20.5
Over 40	8	3.0
Unknown	14	5.3
Total	264	100.0

initial three migrants, all other Villelinos moved directly from the *ejido* to the shantytown, without any intermediate stages or stops. Several of them were unmarried at time of migration; some unmarried girls had found live-in jobs as housemaids prior to their arrival in Mexico City. Elderly people were brought directly to the shantytown by their descendants.

It is important to test whether this pattern of migration applies to most migrants in Cerrada del Cóndor. Let us analyze the results of our 1969–1970 survey of all heads of nuclear families and their spouses in the shantytown.

Tables 3.6–3.9 show the age of migration, routing of migration, birthplace, and current residence of parents. The data show that 88.3% of the migrants in the

TABLE 3.7

Routing of Migration for Heads of Families and Wives

	Number	Percentage
A. Village to Mexico City		
Directly	228	86.4
Not directly	22	8.4
Unknown	14	5.2
Total	264	100.0
B. After arrival in Mexico City		
Directly to Cerrada del Cóndor	58	22.0
Not directly[a]		
0-2 years	10	3.8
2-5 years	34	12.8
5-10 years	39	14.7
More than 10 years	84	32.0
Unknown	39	14.7
Total	264	100.0

[a]Amount of time spent in Mexico City before arriving in shantytown.

TABLE 3.8

Most Recent Residence of Parents of Heads of Families or Their Wives

	Number	Percentage
Their birthplace		
Both parents	153	50.67
One parent	35	11.59
Federal District		
Both parents	49	16.22
One parent	30	9.93
Elsewhere		
Both parents	7	2.32
One parent	3	.99
Unknown	25	8.28
Total	302	100.00

shantytown came straight from the village to Cerrada del Cóndor. Only 1.9% of the informants returned to the village before deciding to settle down permanently in the city. Only 17 informants in a total sample of 264 stopped over in a provincial town before migrating to the Federal District.

There are two distinct groups among the migrants. One group of migrants arrived directly in Cerrada del Cóndor from the village; this includes practically all migrants from Villela. It is extremely unlikely for a migrant fresh from the countryside to find a place of residence by himself in a shantytown such as Cerrada del Cóndor without the benefit of assistance and shelter provided by a relative. A second and more numerous group of migrants lived in the Federal District for periods on the order of 10 years before they settled in Cerrada del Cóndor. Many of them had been originally displaced by the southward growth of the city into formerly rural or semirural districts.

TABLE 3.9

Birthplace of Parents of Migrant Heads of Families and Wives

	Number	Percentage
Both parents from migrant's birthplace	228	86.5
Both parents from elsewhere	8	3.0
One parent from migrant's birthplace	8	3.0
Unknown	20	7.5
Total	264	100.0

The large number of cases of direct migration to the Federal District seems highly significant. In order to eliminate the possibility of a transgenerational migration process I have also collected information on the place of origin of the parents of the informants, showing conclusively that only 3% of such parents were born elsewhere than at the birthplace of the informant. This eliminates the possibility of a migration process extending over two generations; this conclusion is also corroborated by the fact that most migrants come from very small localities.

Juan Pérez Fernández and his young companions from Villela reached the city and looked for whatever jobs they could find. At first they worked in the sandpits, then as brickmakers and bricklayers. Finally Pérez Fernández found a job as a carpet layer; at present 13 of 19 jobholders of the Villela group work as carpet layers. Thus the assistance offered to new arrivals from Villela by the established residents was not limited to food and lodging. It extended also to job guidance for the heads of families. Male adult relatives in general were introduced to a relatively lucrative trade in spite of the possible competition this might entail to the older residents. The results show that this operation was highly successful, since it permitted the wholesale migration of the Villela group: The population of Villela, 564 in 1950, had decreased to 489 in 1960. This net population decrease may have something to do with the successful migration of Juan Pérez Fernández and his encounter with Cerrada del Cóndor.

In 1965 the group of 25 heads of households and their spouses from Villela included 14 illiterates and 6 self-taught literates, i.e., adults who have learned the rudiments of reading and writing after migration. Only 2 members of the group had any schooling beyond the fourth grade; one of them had lived in the Federal District since childhood. These literacy figures are roughly representative of the population of Cerrada del Cóndor, as Table 3.10 shows.

Migrants who have never been to school comprise 43.2% of the population. This figure is to be compared to 16.8% for the Federal District. Those who had between 1 and 3 years of schooling (and who therefore may have learned reading and writing though little else) include 33.4% of migrants as against 42.4% of those born in the Federal District. Only 1.9% of the migrants had any schooling beyond the sixth grade.

Let us now look at the time pattern of migration in Cerrada del Cóndor. Migrants from Villela arrived in a continuous stream since the process began around 1950. Hardly a year has gone by without some new arrival from Villela. The corresponding figures for the shantytown as a whole, shown in Table 3.11, indicate that there has been a continuous current of migration since the late 1930s. After 1950 there was an upward trend in the rate of migration though it appears to have stabilized gradually.

The actual details of the migration process are fairly uniform. The preferred mode of transportation is by *camión* or interstate bus. Migrant families carry their

TABLE 3.10

Schooling of Migrant and Nonmigrant Heads of Families and Wives

Schooling	Migrants		Born in Mexico City		Total	
	Number	Percentage	Number	Percentage	Number	Percentage
None (illiterate)	91	34.5	12	9.6	103	27.4
Self-taught	23	8.7	9	7.2	32	8.2
First to third grade	88	33.4	53	42.4	141	36.0
Fourth to sixth grade	36	13.6	38	30.4	74	18.6
Beyond sixth grade	5	1.9	4	3.2	9	2.3
Unknown	21	7.9	9	7.2	30	7.5
Total	264	100.0	125	100.0	389	100.0

TABLE 3.11

Time of Residence in Mexico City of Migrant Heads of Family and Wives

Year of arrival	Number	Percentage
1960-1969	74	28.0
1950-1959	72	27.3
1940-1949	51	19.3
1930-1939	34	12.9
Before 1930	12	4.55
Unknown	21	7.95
Total	264	100.00

modest personal belongings on the bus; these include chiefly clothing and pots and pans. Unmarried migrants carry a package with clothing and little else. Beyond getting settled in the city few migrants have any but the haziest plans; they have no clear conception of city life. Most of them expect to remain in Mexico City, though a few hope to return to the village eventually. Initial plans seem to have little influence on the eventual decisions of the migrants, and the number of returnees seems to be very low.

The Stage of Stabilization.   Let us now evaluate the adaptation of the Villela migrants to their new ecological niche in Cerrada del Cóndor. The three pioneers from Villela were young men under 20 without any acquaintances in the city. All others headed directly for the shantytown where they took up with relatives who were in residence there.

One informant described the situation as follows: "My sister sent word for us to come. Once we got to Cerrada del Cóndor we were lodged at the home of a cousin; we all slept in the same bed. There was no room to turn around in the bed." Once she had settled in Cerrada del Cóndor, the same informant gave shelter to her last remaining sisters who had remained behind in Villela, following the same pattern. This sister had seven children at the time of migration.

The occupational integration of the Villelinos was described by an informant as follows: "The first one to get here was my cousin Pérez and he got my brother in [as carpet layer]. Then came another cousin so he got him in too, then he got me in and so we all got to learn the trade and to bring the others in."

Members of the Villela kindred maintain a very active family life. There is a great deal of visiting and economic solidarity; they live in extended households or in groups of interrelated households. The men have their own soccer club. Their adaptation to city life appears to be satisfactory to them; no one thinks of going back to the village. There is no visible family disorganization. Not even the oldest grandmothers show sentimental yearnings for the native soil; their dominant memory seems to be "we were ever starving." Kinship solidarity has

TABLE 3.12

City Contacts of Migrants at Migration Time

Contact	Number	Percentage
Relatives	109	41.3
Friends or countrymen	4	1.5
Job givers	16	6.1
None	28	10.6
Migrating with husband or parents	74	28.0
Unknown	33	12.5
Total	264	100.0

extended to all aspects of life. A Villela man who died not long ago was buried by the kindred; all relatives contributed to the expenses of the funeral.

Perhaps the outstanding factors of success in the Villela migration process have been their propensity of migrating in family groups, and their utilization of established relatives in the Federal District. These features are typical of the shantytown as a whole, as shown in Tables 3.12 and 3.13.

TABLE 3.13

Marriage Status of Heads of Family and Wives at Time of Migration

Status	Number		Percentage	
	Subgroup	Total	Subgroup	Total
Too young to marry	60		22.6	
Unmarried (independent)	88		33.4	
Total		148		56.0
Married				
Childless	22		8.3	
With children	72		27.2	
Migrated alone, family followed				
later	5		1.9	
Total		99		37.4
Unmarried or widowed with children		4		1.6
Unknown		13		4.9
Total all subgroups		264		100.0

In conclusion, the typical migrant to Cerrada del Cóndor may be portrayed as follows: A landless peasant, he originates from an economically depressed agricultural region. His educational level is extremely low. He migrates within a family group, usually at an early age. He migrates directly from the village to the city and finds a place to stay at some relative's home in the Federal District. His relatives provide food, shelter, and job orientation during the initial period of residence. Once he has settled down, the new migrant eventually brings his own relatives to the city, including especially his parents or grandparents and his unmarried close of kin.

It is of some interest to compare these conclusions with similar data obtained from migrants in Monterrey. According to a recent survey, "the great majority of migrants leave their communities of origin at a relatively early age [Balán, Browning, and Jelin 1973:150]." About one-third of the sample left their villages before the age of 16, and roughly two-thirds left before the age of 21. Fully 63% of the informants migrated directly from their villages to the city of Monterrey. The reasons given for migration were predominantly economic: Sixty percent migrated directly in search of work. Fewer than one-fifth of the sample migrated singly, all others migrated in family groups. There were relatives expecting them in the city in 84% of all cases. The most common form of assistance consisted of food and shelter: "Our data suggest that the kinship network is rather effective in taking care of the basic needs of the migrants when they arrive [Balán, Browning, and Jelin 1973:160]." And 58% of the migrants actually lived in the homes of relatives or friends during the initial period of their stay in the city. Balán, Browning, and Jelin also found that 92% of the informants expressed satisfaction over the results of their migration (1973:155). Cornelius (1975:22) has confirmed these findings in his study of six *colonias proletarias* of Mexico City. He found that 37% of all migrants had reached the city alone; the remainder had come as members of a family group. Nearly two-thirds of the sample of migrants had been preceded by members of their extended families. Upon arrival, more than three-quarters of all migrants received some form of assistance from relatives already established in the city.

In this section I have attempted to show how the ecological model of migration might be applied to Cerrada del Cóndor. In order to complete the analysis of the third stage of the process (stabilization) we need the data on economy and social organization of the shantytown, which will be discussed in the following chapters.

Intraurban Migration and Cerrada del Cóndor

As we have seen, most of the settlers in Cerrada del Cóndor (78%; Table 3.7) came to the shantytown after prior residence elsewhere in the metropolitan area.

A survey of all households in the shantytown has yielded some detailed data on the migration history of these settlers prior to their arrival in Cerrada del Cóndor.

The pattern that emerges from these data is different from that reported as typical in a classic study on shantytowns in Lima (Turner and Mangin 1968:154–162). Among 164 informants only 23 gave the central slums of the city as their initial place of urban residence (usually because they were born there). The remaining informants had either been born in the southern sector of the metropolitan area or had migrated there directly from the countryside.

Mexico City is so large that no single individual can know the whole city. Even in the neighboring residential district of Las Aguilas there were quite a few residents who seemed totally unaware of the existence of Cerrada del Cóndor. It would be highly unusual for an inhabitant of the central slums to hear about some remote zone of refuge tucked away among the hills of the southern reaches of the city. On the other hand, marginal people in nearby areas would be more likely to know about such places, and to look for them when they became displaced by the southward growth of the city. The few settlers who were born in the central city had been invariably led to Cerrada del Cóndor by the presence of relatives, or by job offers in the area.

Some families had moved as many as eight times within the Federal District, but always within the southern area. The initial place of residence of the migrant appears to determine the eventual zone for subsequent moves. For example, a family might start out in Olivar de los Padres and move from there to Tizapán, and from Tizapán to Cerrada del Cóndor; or, to take another example, from Mixcoac to Tlacopac, to Las Aguilas, and from there to Cerrada del Cóndor (see Figure 3.1).

The ecological model of migration applies to intraurban changes of residence within the Federal District, as it does to rural–urban migration. In this case, the stage of imbalance usually involves a displacement caused by the rapid growth of the city. The inhabitants of the semirural communities at the outer edge of the city are dislodged as a consequence of rising property values. Owners of small properties are subjected to considerable political and economic pressures and are forced to sell out to the developers. Another common type of pressure is the lack of space encountered by a growing family living in a single room, usually with the parents of either husband or wife.

The transfer stage involves the problem of selectivity. A major reason for moving to Cerrada del Cóndor, in preference to some other place, is the presence of relatives living in the shantytown. A further reason is the presence of certain economic advantages: the possibility of buying a plot, for example, or the existence of relatively low rentals, or the possibility of finding a job nearby. Table 3.14 summarizes the main reasons given by informants for moving to Cerrada del Cóndor.

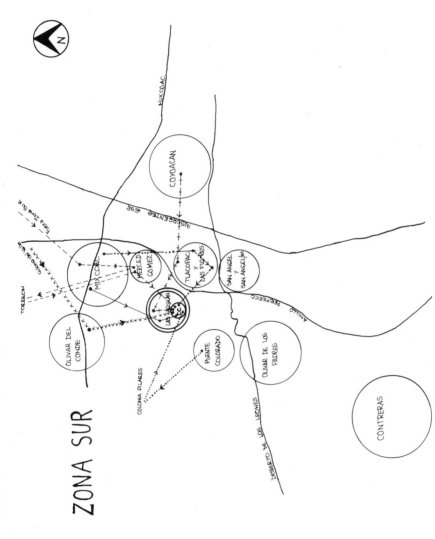

Figure 3.1. A map of residential movements of six Cerrada del Cóndor families within the urban area. Each line pattern represents a different family. The pattern is typical in that most residential moves occur within the southern sector of the city.

TABLE 3.14

Reasons Given for Moving to Cerrada Del Cóndor[a]

	Number	Percentage
Jobs in the brick plant, building and construction, sandpits, or as caretakers of plots	22	13.01
Cheaper rentals or a chance to buy a plot	31	18.3
Desire to live near relatives or friends	64	37.8
Displaced by urban growth (reason explicitly given)	28	16.5
More privacy (trouble with in-laws and the like)	24	14.2
Total	169	99.81

[a] Census by residential unit.

Case Histories

1. A young couple (husband aged 23, wife aged 21, both born in the Federal District).   The husband was born in Merced Gómez (southern zone), where his parents were taking care of a plot. When the owner of the plot died, they were evicted. The family then moved to Olivar del Conde (southern zone). They lived there for 10 years. They moved to Cerrada del Cóndor because his father wished to live near some relatives who were working in the sandpits and living in the shantytown. The wife was born in La Villa (northern zone). When she was 4 her parents moved to Cerrada del Cóndor where her maternal grandmother lived. Some years later they moved to Pericos Court, still within Cerrada del Cóndor; but later they moved back in with her grandmother. There she met her present husband; they married and moved into an independent room in Cerrada del Cóndor.

2. Couple (husband aged 62, wife aged 54) with four children.   This couple migrated 24 years ago from a ranch near Celaya, State of Guanajuato. They initially moved in with an aunt in Tlacopac (southern zone). When the aunt "threw them out," they moved in with a brother of the husband who worked in Las Aguilas (southern zone), a suburban farming area at the time. But they began hearing "the rattling of chains" at night and so had to look for an unhaunted place; they moved back to Pilares street in Tlacopac. Some years later, the husband found work in some brick kilns in the neighborhood of Portales (southern zone). There they lived for some time until they had an opportunity to buy their present plot in Cerrada del Cóndor. They built a home consisting in a series of rooms where their two married sons are now living with their families. Their married daughter moved to another shantytown where she was able to buy a plot. Another married daughter lives in Cerrada del Cóndor; her husband was originally from San Luis Potosí and met his present wife in the shantytown. This young couple has already moved several times, always within the shantytown.

The preceding case histories are fairly typical. Most migrants look for a place to live where they have relatives, and their subsequent moves are made within the same general area of the city unless they have relatives elsewhere. People who were born in the Federal District also tend to move within the general area of their birth, unless they have relatives in another part of town (see Figure 3.1).

The number of residential moves depends on various circumstances, chiefly of economic nature: "We have to pay rent so we move about from place to place." Table 3.15 shows the statistics of the number of residential changes per family, starting with marriage or with arrival in the Federal District. Residential moves prior to marriage are not counted. The category "0 moves" includes the cases of residents of Cerrada del Cóndor who were married in the shantytown but had not

TABLE 3.15

Residential Mobility of Nuclear Families within the Mexico City Metropolitan Area[a, b]

| Number of moves since marriage or migration | Years since marriage or since moving to Mexico City (if already married) | | | | | |
	0-5	6-10	11-15	16-20	21+	Total[c]
0	34	13	4	1	5	34.8
1	17	18	7	6	7	33.5
2	2	4	6	3	10	15.3
3	0	5	0	1	4	6.1
4	3	3	2	0	1	5.5
5	0	0	1	0	2	1.8
6+	0	0	1	0	1	1.2
Unknown	0	0	1	1	1	1.8
Total[c]	34.1	26.2	13.4	7.4	18.9	100.0
Average	.6	1.2	1.9	1.4	2.0	
Median	0	1	1	1	2	
Ratio between more than 2 and less than 2 moves	.1	.39	.91	.57	1.5	

[a]Including moves within Cerrada del Cóndor.

[b]Total sample = 164 households.

[c]Expressed in percentages.

TABLE 3.16

Age of Heads of Family and Wives at Time of Survey

	Born in					
	Mexico City		Countryside		Total	
Age	Number	Percentage	Number	Percentage	Number	Percentage
15-20	11	8.8	8	3.0	19	4.9
20-25	37	29.6	38	14.4	75	19.3
25-30	17	13.6	42	15.9	59	15.2
30-40	29	23.2	88	33.3	117	30.0
40-50	16	12.8	42	15.9	58	14.9
50-60	6	4.8	22	8.3	28	7.2
Over 60	6	4.8	16	6.0	22	5.65
Unknown	3	2.4	8	3.0	11	2.8
Total	125	100.0	264	100.0	389	100.0

yet set up independent housekeeping. They usually lived in extended-family arrangements with parents or relatives.

Either migration into Cerrada del Cóndor directly from the village or moving into a separate home after marriage is counted as one move. Moves within the shantytown are also counted. The correlation between years of marriage and number of moves is fairly significant. The high number of cases of fewer than three moves reflects the fact that Cerrada del Cóndor is a relatively young community. (See Table 3.16.)

Incidentally, it has been observed that unmarried people move frequently for job reasons. This is particularly true for young women working as maids. There are also 15 cases of families who went back to the village for a time and finally returned to the city.

After marriage there are changes in residence every 5 to 10 years on the average. One might conclude that the residential mobility of the population of Cerrada del Cóndor has been high, but it is perhaps not very different from working-class or middle-class mobility in Mexico City or other industrial cities. Kemper (1976:121–122) has found a somewhat higher mobility among Tzintzuntzan migrants in Mexico City; they moved on the average of every 2 years, as long as they did not have a home of their own. Ward (1975:19) has studied three squatter settlements in Mexico City at different stages of development and found that the settlers had moved, on the average, five times prior to the period of his survey.

The influence of dislodgement through urban growth may be studied in Cerrada del Cóndor. Many settlers give as their previous address one of the new middle-class developments (such as Mixcoac, San Angel Inn, Tlacopac, Coyoacan, or Las Aguilas) that have sprung up near the shantytown. The tendency toward a preferential transition from central slums to peripheral shanty-towns is not observed. According to research by Brown (1972), Ward (1975), and Kemper (1976), it appears that such a tendency may indeed have existed in Mexico City until about 1950, when the capacity of the slums was exceeded and rent control was imposed in the central city.

In conclusion, the study of intraurban migration may be used to confirm the general migration pattern brought out by applying the ecological model. The major features of this pattern are as follows:

1. *Imbalance stage.* Imbalance is caused by displacement through economic processes (economic deterioration in the countryside, or progressive dislodgement through urban growth, in the case of rural communities located in suburban areas) in the economic niche of the Mexican traditional rural population.

2. *Transfer stage.* The peasant becomes a migrant. Except for a relatively small percentage of young unmarried pioneers who spearhead the migration process in each rural community, the succeeding waves of migrants travel in family groups. Kin-mediated migration is the rule, both for rural–urban and for intraurban migration.

3. *Stabilization stage.* The successful resettlement of the migrants in the urban environment depends on adaptive socioeconomic mechanisms, which will be discussed in the remaining chapters of this book.

Shantytown Economy

The occupational structure of marginality in Latin America may be described as follows: (1) low-productivity occupations that utilize obsolete skills and residual production resources; (2) nonproductive occupations that require little or no specialized skills; and (3) occupations in low demand and with unstable labor markets (Balán, Browning, and Jelin 1973:19; Quijano 1970:80).

Muñoz, Oliveira, and Stern (1972:325–358) have shown that occupational groups defined by a marginal structure and earning less than the equivalent of a minimum wage include roughly one-quarter of the economically active adult population of Mexico City. The dominant occupations in this marginal sector are as follows: construction workers or bricklayers, street vendors, waiters, shoeshine boys, watchmen, janitors, domestic maids, and others.

This estimate is in essential agreement with a government report (Secretaría 1975:31–33), which displays the marginal sector in Mexico City as follows: (1) According to occupational structure, 576,358 persons were employed as domestic servants, unaffiliated laborers, or workers in small family-type enterprises; and (2) according to income, 780,176 persons earned less than the minimum legal wage. These figures were based on the 1970 census statistics. If one assumes that a breadwinner maintains an average five-person family, an estimate of between 3 million and 4 million people for the marginal sector in Mexico City is reached.

CERRADA DEL CÓNDOR: OCCUPATIONAL STRUCTURE

According to my survey of households in Cerrada del Cóndor (completed in 1971), the gross occupational structure of the shantytown is roughly as follows: over 60% of heads of households are unskilled laborers; 30% are in commercial and service occupations, and 10% work in industry. However, the type of work entrusted to the industrial workers is also of the service variety; they are janitors, gardeners, night watchmen, and so on.

The individuals included in Table 4.1 represent exclusively heads of households. There are many more settlers, men as well as women, working in the shantytown. The category "unskilled laborers" includes house painters, bricklayers, workers in the sandpits, brickmakers, gardeners, trucker's helpers, bakers, carpet layers, and others generally described as "apprentices." They usually make less than the minimum legal wage and have no job security. This type of labor might be locally described as "peon work"; a peon is an unskilled laborer who works at a wide variety of occupations, according to unforeseeable demand. Peons are subject to random periods of unemployment.

TABLE 4.1

Occupation of Heads of Residential Units at Time of Survey

	Number	Percentage
A. Men		
Unskilled worker or apprentice	51	32.9
Skilled free-lance worker	48	31.0
Industrial worker	16	10.3
Service worker	5	3.2
Commerce (vendors or shopkeepers)	7	4.5
Employee	8	5.1
Property owner receiving rental income	5	3.3
Unemployed	15	9.7
Total	155	100.0
B. Women		
Unskilled worker	1	4.5
Servant	12	54.6
Employee	1	4.5
Commerce (vendors and shopkeepers)	4	18.2
Property owner receiving rental income	1	4.5
Housewife (no independent income)	3	13.6
Total	22	100.0

A "skilled free-lance worker" is a peon who has become specialized in a certain line of work. He is called a *maestro* and his specialization may refer to any of a number of trades: He may be a baker, construction worker, carpet layer, electrician, driver, carpenter, glazier, tombstone polisher, shoemaker, smith, potter, furniture maker, or repairman who specializes in household appliances. Such workers are called *eventuales,* because they work either on a daily basis or on a job-rate basis, according to demand and without job security. Their income is rated higher than that of a peon; typically it was around 60 to 80 pesos a day in 1971. Since demand is variable, they tend to lack a stable income. A few *maestros* enjoy a stable clientele, but even so the number of clients is usually too small to ensure work the year around.

"Industrial workers" are peons who enjoy a certain amount of job security because of their employment in industry. A handful of them were slightly more specialized (one tractor driver for a construction company, and a few mechanics). The job security of such "industrial" workers is lower than that of the industrial proletariat; typically, they would lose their jobs in the event of sickness. "Employees" are also unskilled workers, but they draw a salary because of employment in a department store or in some agency such as the Department of the Federal District. Their tasks are essentially the same; they are janitors, gardeners, sanitation workers, and the like. Industrial workers and employees are the only workers in the shantytown who enjoy a conventional salary as well as social security benefits.

"Service workers" include icemen, soft drink vendors, water carriers, watchmen, waiters, housemaids or domestic servants, and others. "Commerce" includes street vendors of flavored ice, flavored jelly, newspapers, chickens, eggs; and three local shopkeepers. Their sales are normally restricted to the shantytown. Altogether some 10% of the heads of households (both men and women) extract their means of livelihood from the shantytown itself, as salesmen, makers of tortillas, water carriers, shoemakers, barbers, shopkeepers, and property owners who receive rental income. There are five families in the latter category who live in the shantytown and obtain a small income from the lease of their properties.

Most households headed by women derive their income from domestic service. Such women either work as maids or as laundrywomen. Other typically female economic activities include tortilla making and street selling (flavored shaved ice, *nopales,* or lunches for construction workers on building sites). The income level of households headed by women tends to be significantly lower.

An analysis of the occupational histories of the settlers affords some interesting generalizations. A migrant who reaches the city without prior work experience (except as a peasant) finds himself at an initial disadvantage with respect to marginals who have begun their occupational careers in the city; eventually,

TABLE 4.2

Occupational History of Male Heads of Nuclear Families

Type of Occupation	Initial job					
	Peasant		Unskilled worker		Other	
	Number	Percentage	Number	Percentage	Number	Percentage
A. Second job						
Unskilled worker	65	82.1	26	40.6	0	0
Skilled worker	3	3.8	17	26.5	12	54.5
Industrial Worker	6	7.6	13	20.5	4	18.1
Service worker	3	3.8	3	4.6	2	9.0
Commerce	1	1.3	1	1.5	1	4.5
Employee	1	1.3	1	1.5	1	4.5
Landlord	0	0	0	0	0	0
Unemployed	0	0	3	4.5	2	9.0
Total	79	99.9	64	99.7	22	99.6
B. Job at time of survey						
Unskilled worker	27	34.2	22	34.4	0	0
Skilled worker	24	30.4	19	29.7	9	40.9
Industrial worker	5	6.3	6	9.3	5	22.6
Service worker	4	5.0	4	6.2	1	4.5
Commerce	6	7.6	0	0	1	4.5
Employee	4	5.0	3	4.6	1	4.5
Landlord	0	0	3	4.6	2	9.0
Unemployed	9	11.4	7	10.9	3	13.5
Total	79	99.9	64	99.7	22	99.5

however, his occupational pattern tends to even out with that of the other marginals. Table 4.2 shows that the eventual occupational structure is the same for migrants as for nonmigrants. The sample used in this table included a total of 163 male heads of nuclear families (*not* heads of households).

The initial urban occupation of peasant migrants is almost universally unskilled labor. This is practically the only type of work available to a migrant. As acculturation proceeds, the migrants begin to gain access to other forms of employment, though the total proportion of such jobs remains severely limited. One may speak of an *occupational structure of marginality* as such, which depends but little on the initial conditions or the occupational history of the individual. The mean occupational status of a given marginal tends to improve slightly in time, only because the category of "free-lance skilled worker" represents a natural second level of the peon category. Unfortunately it is all too frequently the terminal level. Fully one-third of all unskilled laborers remain unskilled all their lives, irrespective of whether or not they were migrants. On the other hand, those who begin their occupational careers as skilled workers or as servants tend to continue in these trades; they never drop back into the peon category. This proves that the unskilled laborers represent in fact the lowest occupational level in the shantytown.

UNPAID FAMILY LABOR

The intensive use of unpaid family labor in the shantytown may be seen as an integral part of the informal economic system based on reciprocal exchange networks, which will be described more fully later in this book. The free economic cooperation of wives, children, and the elderly is but one aspect of a more generalized interfamily cooperation system.

A large family has a positive economic connotation in marginal society. This is due to the widespread use of unpaid child labor, as well as the utilization of relatives for emergency assistance during periods of loss of work. Children represent a ready source of income to a nuclear family, because their cooperation is permanently available and their maintenance cost is insignificant. They squeeze into whatever space is left over in the room, eat whatever food is available, and wear any used clothing. They will skip school whenever the economy of the household needs them. Peasant children in Mexico begin their economic careers before they are 10 years old. Their labor is water carrying, fruit picking, corn shelling, cattle raising, and so on. Girls help around the house and in child care, as well as in the preparation of foodstuffs and in the raising of domestic animals.

In the urban environment, children likewise begin their work careers at an early age. They shine shoes, sell chewing gum on the street, clean windshields and watch over parked cars for a tip; they carry packages for customers at supermarkets; they deliver tortillas for their mothers, gather metal scraps and other waste products, beg for stale bread and tortillas from door to door for use in feeding their pigs or chickens, and take care of the home while mother is out working. Few children complete the legally required 6 years of primary school. Male children frequently start working with their fathers around the age of 10. They may share their father's income as "apprentices" until they are ready to go out and work by themselves.

According to the results of my survey, as many as 27% of the present heads of families were working before they were 10 years old. About 68% were working before the age of 15. (See Table 4.3.)

Many informants were uncertain as to whether unpaid family labor should be regarded as work; this fact must be taken into account when interpreting the table. Similar observations have been made in Monterrey: "The blurriness of the transition in Mexico undoubtedly has some effect on the reliability of information collected in the Monterrey survey, for different men use different sets of implicit criteria in their responses [Balán, Browning, and Jelin 1973:118]." About 70% of my sample are migrants of peasant origin, though 21.2% of these migrated before the age of 13; their first formal jobs were probably held in the city. The rest of the migrants presumably started their work careers in the village. The difference between migrants and nonmigrants as to the age of first remunerative employment is not significant. In any case, children work as unpaid laborers in various occupations much before they earn their first salary.

The following passage illustrates the prevalence of this situation in Mexico:

> In a rapidly changing and developing society like Mexico's for those men participating in the technologically more advanced sectors of the economy where roles are more clearly defined, the transition from education to work is clear. But this is not the case in other sectors of the

TABLE 4.3

Initial Working Age of Wage Earners Who Are Heads of Families

Age	Born in the country		Born in Mexico City		Total	
	Number	Percentage	Number	Percentage	Number	Percentage
Under 10	30	20.6	18	27.7	48	22.6
10–15	72	49.5	26	40.0	98	46.2
15–20	24	16.5	15	23.0	39	18.4
Over 20	3	2.06	1	1.54	4	1.88
Unknown	18	12.4	5	7.7	23	10.8
Total	147	100.0	65	100.0	212	100.0

TABLE 4.4

Number of Wage Earners per Residential Unit

	Number	Percentage
None	5	2.8
Father only	83	46.1
Mother only	12	6.7
Son only	9	5.0
Mother and father	29	16.1
Father and sons	17	9.4
Mother and sons	9	5.0
Mother, father, and sons	14	7.8
Unknown	2	1.1
Total	180	100.0

economy where it is often difficult to establish a clear cut moment when the men may be said to enter the labor force. There are mainly two situations where the boundary between work and non work status is difficult to draw. One is involvement in any type of family enterprise, whether rural or urban, where members of the family group contribute their labor without receiving any income.... The other situation is paid work but of unstable and occasional nature. Both are particularly important for the Monterrey study ... as a large proportion of the men began their occupational lives in these positions [Balán, Browning, and Jelin 1973:114–115].

Difficulties with the interpretation of census figures are encountered when dealing with the unpaid labor of children, women, old people, and other relatives within the household. (See Table 4.4.) In Cerrada del Cóndor, the wife has some income of her own in about 35% of all households. Many women work part time, in addition to their economic obligations in and around the home. Practically all women get some small income from baking and selling tortillas, raising pigs or chickens for home consumption or for profit, gathering *nopales* for sale, collecting tin cans and other salable items in garbage dumps, and so on. Old people mind the home while the mother is out working, or earn small sums of money as water carriers, or vendors of small quantities of foods and other items at sidewalk stands. An economic valuation of activities such as raising pigs, chickens or other fowl, or cattle in shantytowns has never been officially attempted, probably because the status of such enterprises is illegal. In my experience, at least half the households in shantytowns complement their diets and their incomes through raising farm animals. Pigs, chickens, turkeys, and rabbits are common; sheep, goats, and cows are by no means unusual. They represent an important source of cash reserve, as well as practically the only source of meat in the shantytown diet.

ECONOMIC LEVELS

A shantytown settler who earns the minimum legal wage (32.50 pesos or $2.60 a day in 1970) should theoretically be making 975 pesos ($28) a month if he works every day. Only two settlers in Cerrada del Cóndor, both of whom employees, were earning 1300 to 1500 pesos a month. Not counting the heirs of the main real estate owner in the shantytown (who were earning up to 5000 pesos a month in rentals), all other settlers were earning the equivalent of a minimum legal wage or less, depending on their job stability. Actually, *all* unskilled laborers were consistently earning less than the monthly equivalent of the minimum legal wage, even though the minimum wage requirements are normally met in the case of contract labor, typically in construction work. The trouble is that most unskilled laborers cannot find work every day.

Shantytown incomes are invested in food, rent, alcohol, and a few consumer items. For the purpose of gaining a quantitative insight into socioeconomic conditions, I carried out a project aimed at defining differential levels in standards of living within the shantytown. This project included a survey of material belongings in all shantytown households. The following variables were selected: (a) housing; (b) furniture; (c) electrical appliances; (d) stoves; and (e) population density per room. Each variable was graded on a scale of three, as follows: 1, good; 2, fair; 3, poor. Table 4.5 describes the meanings assigned to each of these ratings.

Each domestic unit was inspected separately and graded according to the scale in Table 4.5. The appliances were rated on a yes or no basis, as shown on the list. Finally, correlations between pairs of variables were computed, and a contingency table was obtained as shown (Table 4.6).

An interpretation of this contingency table is obtained as follows. As might be expected, all correlation coefficients were positive, thus proving that all five variables are in some way indicators of the standard of living of a household or family. The highest correlations were found between the following three variables: housing, furniture, and electrical appliances. The variable of population density per room was found to have a significantly lower correlation coefficient than the other four variables, presumably because the number of people in a household depends largely on factors other than the economic level.

The correlation between "electrical appliances" and "stove" was very high; on the other hand, the correlation between "stove" and "housing" or "furniture" was less significant. This indicated a possible split in the middle range, in the sense that some households rated as fair in terms of housing and furniture owned high-grade appliances whereas others did not. This hypothesis was subsequently tested in the field and was found to be highly significant and important. It was discovered that there is a boundary that runs across the middle-income range between families of predominantly rural living style and families that had

TABLE 4.5

Ratings of Variables Used in Determining Economic Level

Variable	Rating	Description
Housing	Good (1)	Brick or cement-block construction with concrete or corrugated metal roofing. Three or more rooms. Running water, light, bathroom, or latrine. Cement or tile floor.
	Fair (2)	Two rooms with or without kitchen. Brick construction. Corrugated metal roofing. Cement floor. No bathroom, or bathroom shared with others. Light. No running water.
	Poor (3)	One room with or without lean-to for cooking. Construction of brick or other used materials. Dirt or cement floor. No utilities. Poor state of repair.
Furniture	Good (1)	Living room furniture, dining-room furniture of metal and plastic. Chairs, closets, night tables, dish racks, adequate beds.
	Fair (2)	Tables (one for eating and one in the kitchen, usually), chairs, closet, dish rack, beds. The furniture may be either urban (metal and plastic) or rustic (unpainted wood).
	Poor (3)	Beds. Bench or small table. Clothing is kept under the bed or hanging from a nail. No dining table. No chairs.
Electrical appliances	Yes (1)	One or more of the following: record player, food blender, or sewing machine.
	No (2)	None of the preceding, except radios, electric irons, and television sets, which may be found at any economic level.
Stove	Gas (1)	Gas stove used for cooking.
	Oil (2)	Oil stove used for cooking.

TABLE 4.6

Correlation Coefficient between Variables Used to Define
the Economic Level

	Housing	Furniture	Appliances	Kitchen	Population density per room
Housing	1.00	.95	.78	.70	.56
Furniture		1.00	.86	.59	.39
Appliances			1.00	.73	.24
Stove				1.00	.19
Population density per room					1.00

become visibly urbanized. The latter were invariably found to have been residents of the Federal District for at least 10 years. In the end we were left with a four-level classification of economic status in the shantytown, as shown in Table 4.7.

The following case histories were selected as typical for each of the levels.

Case Histories

Level A. Rufino Saldivar, aged 62, five children. The family migrated to the Federal District as a unit, 40 years ago. Señor Saldivar has worked as a gardener, a brickmaker, a construction worker, and so on. At present, with the assistance of his wife, he mans a small foodstand in the shantytown. They bought a plot 24 years ago. Two married sons live on the same plot, in rooms of their own. One daughter lives elsewhere in Cerrada del Cóndor, and a second daughter lives with her husband in another shantytown in the Federal District. The Saldivars own their home. It is made out of brick and mud, with tin roofing and cement floor. There are two bedrooms, an oratory (tiny room for lighting candles to saints' images), and a kitchen. There is an ample yard with dogs, chickens, turkeys, pigeons, and a pig. There are two double beds accommodating five people (the couple, two unmarried sons, and a 1-year-old grandson). There are pillows, bedclothes, and blankets; a gas stove, various pots and pans, earthenware dishes, cups, spoons, and a dish rack. There is a dining-room table with six chairs, and there are two wooden closets. The outhouse has a standard ceramic-type sanitary bowl. There are electric outlets, and there is a water faucet in the middle of the yard. The appliances include a food blender, a radio, an electric iron, and a television set. The Saldivars

TABLE 4.7

Stratification of Economic Levels in Cerrada del Cóndor[a]

Level	Residential units			Variables			
	Number	Percentage	Housing	Furniture	Appliances	Stove
A	14	7.8	Good	Good	Yes	Gas
B	17	8.9	Average	Average (urban)	Yes	Gas
C	43	23.8	Average	Average (rustic)	No	Oil
D	106	59.5	Poor	Poor	No	Oil
Total	180	100.0				

[a]Based on a survey of 180 residential units.

all live together as one extended family; one of the married sons owns the only automobile in the shantytown. They spend 20 pesos a day in food and up to 100 pesos a month in clothing. There are many images of saints: Señor Saldivar does not drink and is very religious. He organizes periodic pilgrimages.

Level B. Pedro Alfonso, a carpet layer, feeds a family of nine. He rents the piece of property on which his home is built for 80 pesos a month. Señor Alfonso owns the brick and the cardboard roofing of which his home is made; the floor is of cement. There are two rooms, and a gas stove. There are three beds for the whole family. There is a dining-room table and another small table; there are dishes, glasses, pots and pans, spoons, but no forks. They have four chairs, two armchairs, a record player, a food blender, an electric iron, a television set, a radio, and a sewing machine. There is a crucifix and an image of Saint Martin. There are many toys, balls, and a tricycle. There are plants, dogs, and two pigs. They use the bathroom of their father-in-law (Señor Saldivar of the previous example). They hook up to the power line and use the public water faucet. They have tin water containers for bathing the children before they go to school. There is some good clothing.

Señor Alfonso earns about 1000 pesos a month when he has a job. There are no other wage earners. The family is among the better-off people in the shantytown. They spend 6 pesos a month on school, 3 pesos a day on transportation. Food expenditures are unknown. Señor Alfonso drinks beer, tequila, and *pulque* on Saturdays and Sundays.

Level C. Family of Salvador Soto, unskilled carpet layer. This is a young couple (23 and 24) with four children. The wife does not earn. They pay 175 pesos a month in rent. They own the building materials for their home, which consists of a single room plus lean-to kitchen, made of bricks with corrugated fiber roofing and dirt floor. There are two beds, two tables (one for eating), five chairs, and two or three small benches; a dish rack, a wooden closet, pot and pans, glasses, and spoons. There is a radio, a television set, an electric iron, a tortilla pan, and a washbasin. They share an outhouse with other people and they use the public water faucet. They cook on an oil stove. There are pictures, toys, and plants.

Señor Soto gives his wife 150 pesos a week for household expenses. She spends 20 pesos a day on food, 1 peso a day on schooling, and 2 pesos a day for transportation to take lunch to her husband. "He does not drink much."

Level D. Family of Martin Moreno, who works as machetero (loading and unloading freight trucks). The family of eight people lives in a brick room with cardboard roofing and cement floor. They cook inside the room,

TABLE 4.8

Occupation and Economic Level[a]

	Level A		Level B		Level C		Level D	
	Number	Percentage	Number	Percentage	Number	Percentage	Number	Percentage
Unskilled worker	0	0	1	.6	4	2.2	40	22.3
Skilled worker	2	1.1	9	5.0	14	7.8	25	14.0
Commerce	2	1.1	1	.6	4	2.2	3	1.7
Employee	3	1.7	1	.6	3	1.7	1	.6
Landlord	3	1.7	0	0	3	1.7	0	0
Unemployed	0	0	0	0	6	3.3	16	9.0
Industrial worker	3	1.7	2	1.1	6	3.4	7	3.9
Service worker	0	0	2	1.1	3	1.7	15	8.4

[a]Based on a survey of 179 heads of residential units.

on an oil stove. They have two beds, bedclothes, and blankets. There is a
rustic table for the oil stove and a few pots; there are dishes, cups, and
spoons. They sit on the beds for eating, as there are no dinner tables and
no chairs. There is a metal shelf for clothing. They use the bottom of the
gully for a latrine. They hook up to the power line and use the public water
faucet. There is a radio, a picture, a washbasin, some toys, and two dogs.
That is all.

Husband and wife are both earning (she does washing three times a
week in nearby residences and earns 25 pesos a day). Señor Moreno
earns the minimum wage and gives his wife 125 pesos a week for household expenses; they spend around 25 pesos a day. Señor Moreno pays 60
pesos a month on the rent of the room and the plot it is built on. He spends
the rest of his wages on drink.

OCCUPATION AND ECONOMIC LEVEL

As an example of the application of economic level indicators I shall now
present some additional survey data, which bear on various aspects of the standards of living in the shantytown. Table 4.8 shows how the type of occupation is
correlated with the economic level.

The table shows (rather dramatically, I believe) that the occupational structure
in level A is the exact inverse of that in level D. Level A includes the industrial
workers, the employees, and the small landlords, all of whom enjoy a certain
stability of income. Level D, on the other hand, includes a majority of unskilled
laborers and unemployed, none of which are found in level A. Levels B and C
are intermediate and typically include a majority of skilled laborers or *maestros*.

INCOME AND ECONOMIC LEVEL

There is no direct correlation between type of occupation, wages, and income in
the shantytown. Monthly income depends largely on the number of actual work-
days in an average month rather than on the daily wage. However, there is a good
correlation between economic level and income, as shown in Table 4.9.

Nearly half the families in level D had a monthly income below 600 pesos. At
the intermediate levels (B and C) more than half the families were in the 600–
1200-peso bracket. As to level A, nearly 80% of the families in this level had an
income above 1200 pesos a month.

The skew in the distribution of incomes is at least as significant as the mean
income. In levels C and D incomes are skewed toward the lower end of the

TABLE 4.9

Income and Economic Level[a]

Monthly income per family	Level A		Level B		Level C		Level D	
	Number	Percentage	Number	Percentage	Number	Percentage	Number	Percentage
Less than 600 pesos	0		0		8	18.60	49	46.67
600-900	1	7.4	4	25.53	14	32.56	31	29.52
900-1200	2	14.29	5	29.41	9	20.93	7	6.67
More than 1200	11	78.57	6	35.30	2	4.65	6	5.71
Unknown	0		2	11.76	10	23.26	12	11.43
Total	14	100.0	17	100.0	43	100.0	105	100.0
Mean monthly income	$1150		$1030		$820		$720	

[a] Based on a survey of 178 residential units.

income scale; thus, the modal income, which is the one occurring most frequently in the sample, is lower than the average. On the contrary, in levels A and B the incomes are skewed toward the upper end of the scale. In other words, although families in levels B and C have incomes between 600 and 1200 pesos, low incomes are relatively more frequent in level C than in level B. One out of five families earns less than 600 pesos in level C; none earns less than 600 pesos a month in level B.

The minimum legal wage applies actually to male occupations only. Service jobs normally filled by women or children are subject to conventional wages, which rarely reach the legal daily amount. Yet the individual earning power depends on the amount of available work as much as on the actual wage.

HOUSING AND PROPERTY OWNERSHIP IN
CERRADA DEL CÓNDOR

Housing and property ownership are important elements in the shantytown economy. Most of the property in Cerrada del Cóndor originally belonged to just one owner. There has been neither squatting nor collective occupation of land as in other shantytowns. Only 7.4% of the heads of households own their properties; all others pay rent, with the exception of 6.3% who enjoy free rent as caretakers and 4.7% who are exempted from the payment of rent for various reasons. (See Table 4.10.)

Many settlers rent the plots on which their homes are built; this occurs in a 17.2% of cases. When such a settler decides to move he takes his dwelling apart, and keeps the bricks and other materials for reuse in his next dwelling. Only nails, mortar, cement floor, and other expendable materials are wasted. He may also decide to sell his dwelling to the next occupant for a conventional sum, e.g., 1000 pesos (in one documented case).

Table 4.10 shows the property situation in Cerrada del Cóndor in 1971. There is a clear correlation with economic level; about 90% of the heads of households in level D pay rent, as against less than 30% in level A. The situation may be further clarified by analyzing the structure of real estate property in the shantytown. The major owners of Cerrada del Cóndor live at the edge of the shantytown. They own about 90 individual plots, with or without their residential units. In addition, there are 17 small property owners, 11 of which are shantytown residents. Most of these own just the plot of land they live on, but a few have a small income from additional plots that they rent to settlers. There are 17 families who pay no rent, either because they are relatives of a property owner, or because they are caretakers of the plot on which they live. Some of them are

TABLE 4.10

Property Status and Economic Level[a]

	Level A		Level B		Level C		Level D		Total	
	Number	Percentage	Number	Percentage	Number	Percentage	Number	Percentage	Number	Percentage
Owns both house and plot	10	5.7	0	0	3	1.7	0	0	13	7.4
Renting plot	0	0	4	2.3	5	2.8	21	12.1	30	17.2
Caretaker of plot	0	0	2	1.1	2	1.1	7	4.0	11	6.3
Renting both house and plot	4	2.3	8	4.6	25	14.2	67	38.2	104	59.4
Renting for free	0	0	3	1.7	6	3.4	8	4.5	17	9.7
Total	14	8.0	17	9.7	41	23.2	103	58.8	175	100.0

[a]Based on a survey of 175 residential units.

former workers in the brick kilns, who have been exempted from paying rent in recognition of past services.

Thirty heads of residential units "pay rent for the floor," i.e., they pay between 30 and 120 pesos a month for the use of a plot. All others pay rent for both plot and dwelling, in amounts varying from 110 to 280 pesos a month in most cases. The range of rentals is large. One family is paying 400 pesos a month for a relatively large and well-built house. Another family is paying 300 pesos per month. Rentals fluctuate in accordance with the quality of the terrain and the type of the dwelling. Another factor is the personal relationship between the renter and the landlord. The principal landowner of the shantytown frequently grants special rent privileges to relatives, *compadres,* former workers in the brick kilns, or to some settler who needs a break.

The major types of construction in the shantytown are shown in Table 4.11.

By "brick" (*tabique*) I mean the ordinary construction brick. Most of the housing in the shantytown is made of brick with corrugated metal roofing. Many bricks are rejects from construction sites; settlers who make a living as construction workers have access to such materials. There are cement floors in 53.3% of all houses, and dirt floors in 25.9% of them.

A residential unit may have one or more rooms, according to the breakdown in Table 4.12. The term *lean-to-kitchen* refers to a small enclosure made of cheap or temporary materials, with a cardboard or metal roof. This enclosure is built against an exterior wall of the dwelling and is used for cooking, much as in the traditional Mexican peasant house. Meals are served individually, not in family gatherings; mealtimes are very irregular. The term *kitchen inside* means that the cooking is done in a bedroom. Sometimes the cooking is also done in the open, in front of the entrance to the room. Most rooms in Cerrada del Cóndor measure 3.0 by 3.5 meters on the average. There is a slight difference in the density of

TABLE 4.11

Shantytown Construction Types

	Number	Percentage
Brick with zinc or asbestos roofing	97	60.4
Cement block with zinc or asbestos roofing	23	14.2
Adobe with zinc or cardboard roofing	20	12.1
Wood, zinc, or brick mixed construction	9	5.4
Random waste materials	4	2.4
Unknown	9	5.4
Total number of dwellings surveyed	162	99.9

TABLE 4.12

Number of Rooms in a Residential Unit

	Number	Percentage
One room (kitchen outside)	55	30.6
One room (kitchen inside)	48	26.6
Two rooms (kitchen outside)	17	9.4
Two rooms (kitchen inside)	17	9.4
Three or more rooms (kitchen inside)	25	13.8
Unknown	18	10.0
Total number of residential units surveyed	180	99.8

occupancy, depending on whether cooking is done inside or outside the room. In the first case the average density is 5.4 people, as against 6.2 if the cooking is done outside. As an interesting sidelight, the census figures indicate that 28% of the population of the Federal District (i.e., a total of 1,793,596 persons) were living in single-room dwellings in 1970. Any residential unit having more than one room is usually the home of an extended family, a group of several nuclear families (see Chapter 6). The density of occupancy may be slightly lower in this case. For two-room dwellings with lean-to kitchens the average density is 4.0 persons per room; the density is higher (5.0) when the cooking is done inside. Dwellings of three or more rooms belong usually to homeowners who have built a more comfortable home for themselves and their descendants.

Another relevant factor concerning the quality of a dwelling is the presence or absence of utilities. No standard utilities are provided in the shantytown; therefore their presence in a specific residential unit is significant in terms of economic level. There are seven cases of private water outlets within residential units; however, only one of those homes has internal plumbing for kitchen and bathroom. The general sanitary situation in the shantytown may be gathered from Table 4.13.

MATERIAL BELONGINGS

Oscar Lewis (1969b:4) once published an inventory of material belongings for 14 families (83 persons) in a Mexico City slum. All 14 families lived in one-room dwellings made of adobe with cement and cardboard roofing and lean-to kitchen. Their economic situation closely matched our levels C and D as described in Cerrada del Cóndor. In the case studied by Lewis the total number of beds in the slum was 23, which comes to 1.6 beds per family. In Cerrada del Cóndor the situation was as shown in Table 4.14.

TABLE 4.13

Sanitary Facilities per Residential Unit

Type of facility	Number	Percentage
Own latrine (ceramic unit or rustic outhouse)	18	11
Shared ceramic unit	28	17
Shared outhouse	6	4
None (bottom of ravine used)	84	52
Unknown	26	16
Total number of residential units surveyed	162	100

My findings indicate an average of 2.1 beds per residential unit. The higher number, as compared to Lewis's findings, is due to the dwellings of levels A and B in Cerrada del Cóndor. Most couples share a bed with one or two children. Whenever there is a second bed it is used by other adults in the household with another child or two; the remaining children sleep on straw mats or mattresses on the floor. There are only 23 cases of "adequate" number of beds, meaning one bed per couple or per single adult or child. Such cases are either level A residential units, or households of couples without children.

The pattern of bed occupancy may be deduced from Table 4.15. The *mode* is the value that occurs more frequently in the sample; for example, for one-bed families the average number of users is 4.0, yet the case that occurs more frequently is two people to a bed. The fewer beds, the higher is the number of people per bed. These results indicate that the number of people per bed is not a

TABLE 4.14

Number of Beds per Residential Unit

Number of beds	Number of residential units	Percentage
0	1	.6
1	50	30.8
2	59	36.4
3	33	20.4
4	10	6.1
5	1	.6
6	3	1.8
Unknown	5	3.0
Total number of residential units surveyed	162	99.7

TABLE 4.15

Bed Occupancy

Number of beds in residential unit	Number of people per bed	
	Mean	Mode
1	4.0	2
2	3.1	3
3	2.5	2 or 3
4	2.6	2 or 3
5	2.4	2
6	1.4	1

reliable indicator of economic level, since the modal value fluctuates rather slowly about two persons per bed.

In the slum studied by Lewis all families had at least the following pieces of furniture: a bed, a mattress or bedspring, a table, and a shelf for an altar or for dishes. Other articles, such as a chair, a closet, and a radio, were frequently found. All families had an electric iron; two families used forks and one family had a gas stove.

Lewis stressed the high expenditure on religious objects, which he estimated at $210 for the entire slum; the expenditure on religious objects was relatively higher among the poorer families. My observation confirms this fact, but it is not due to a higher religiosity among the poorer settlers. The fact is that the prices of images are about standard for everybody; hence the investment in such images represents a higher share of the income among low-income families.

Lewis estimated the total value of all material belongings in the slum at $4730. The value per domestic unit fluctuated between $199 and $937. I have not attempted such estimates in Cerrada del Cóndor, because a high proportion of material belongings are purchased secondhand. This fact should make a considerable difference in their value. To a family earning less than $100 per month, the purchase of a piece of furniture would represent a major investment, irrespective of the price that is eventually paid.

One of the most interesting indicators of economic level in Cerrada del Cóndor is the ownership of electric appliances. Such appliances are normally purchased brand new on the installment plan. This is important because it reveals that the credit of the marginals is considered good by an important urban business sector. Table 4.16 shows that shantytown sales account for a major share of the total appliance market in Mexico City.

Most homes have a radio, usually a portable transistor radio. Roughly one-third of the homes also own a television set, even though there is no legal electrical installation. The television set represents by far the most valuable

TABLE 4.16

Ownership of Electrical Appliances

	Radio		Television	
	Number	Percentage	Number	Percentage
Owners	147	81.6	71	39.4
Nonowners	24	13.3	100	55.5
Unknown	9	5.0	9	5.0
Total number of residential units surveyed	180	99.9	180	99.9

single object in the household. Whenever a family owns another appliance, in addition to the electric iron, the radio, and the television set, this fact represents a relevant indicator of the higher economic level enjoyed by the family.

ECONOMIC LEVEL AND LIFE-STYLES

Summarizing the tables displayed earlier in this chapter, we may conclude that the economic level in the shantytown is correlated with the following factors:

1. *Income.* Most incomes in level A exceed 1200 pesos a month ($98 US) whereas most incomes in level D are below 600 pesos a month.
2. *Occupation.* Occupations that carry a relative job security and income stability are largely found in levels A and B.
3. *Property tenure.* No property owner is found in level D; practically all property owners are found in level A. Four families in level A are paying rent, but these rentals are among the highest in the shantytown (up to 400 pesos a month).
4. *Material belongings.* All settlers in level D live in one-room homes and their belongings are limited to beds, one small table, one shelf, one electric iron, one transistor radio, some religious objects, and articles of daily use. Some also own a television set. Urban-type furniture and appliances, including gas stoves, plastic-covered furniture, food blenders, record players, and the like, are only found among members of levels A and B.

Economic levels are also reflected in the number of people to a room, and in the number of people per bed in the household. Let us now consider two new factors that may have some effect on economic levels as found in Cerrada del Cóndor: alcohol consumption, and the number of economically active persons per household.

According to close informants, usually wives, none of the male heads of households in level A are excessive drinkers. On the contrary, 77% of the heads of families in this category are nondrinkers or light drinkers. In the same survey it was found that level D contains more excessive than moderate drinkers, as shown in Table 4.17.

The most significant change in the pattern of alcohol consumption is found in the intermediate economic levels, that is, in the transition from level C to level B. In the latter level practically no excessive drinkers are found. From a medical point of view, the category of "excessive drinker" includes settlers who may be described as alcohol addicts. I conclude that alcohol addiction in the shantytown is correlated with the lower economic levels (C and D), and that the transition between levels C and B marks a qualitative change in the pattern of alcohol consumption among shantytown settlers.

Let us now consider Table 4.18, which describes the patterns of gainful employment within the households in Cerrada del Cóndor.

In levels C and D, heads of households are regularly the only wage earners, often because they forbid their wives to seek gainful employment. In levels A and B, on the other hand, most households contain two or more breadwinners, a fact that implies a more tolerant attitude toward female work outside the home. Another interpretation might be the presence of adult sons or daughters who contribute to family earnings. These interpretations are not mutually exclusive, and both have decisive consequences in the economic level of the family.

The different attitudes detected in the shantytown concerning alcohol consumption and the gainful employment of wives reflect a change in life-styles as the urban acculturation of the settlers proceeds. Remember that the transition from level C to level B usually occurs at least 10 years after migration. The difference between these levels may be appreciated on simple inspection: As one

TABLE 4.17

Alcohol Consumption of the Head of the Residential Unit According to Family Members[a, b]

Amount of consumption	Levels				Total
	A	B	C	D	
Zero to moderate	77.1	50.0	31.3	25.0	33.2
Average	22.9	49.4	46.9	44.7	43.2
Excessive	0	.6	21.8	30.3	23.6
	100.0	100.0	100.0	100.0	100.0

[a]Based on a survey of 157 residential units, not counting 23 where the information was unknown.

[b]Expressed as percentages.

TABLE 4.18

Number of Working Adults per Residential Unit[a]

	Level A		Level B		Level C		Level D		Total	
	Number	Percentage	Number	Percentage	Number	Percentage	Number	Percentage	Number	Percentage
0	0	0	0	0	2	1.1	3	1.7	5	2.8
1	6	3.3	6	3.3	26	14.5	66	34.1	104	58.0
2	4	2.2	9	5.0	8	4.5	25	16.2	45	25.0
3 or more	4	2.2	2	1.1	7	3.9	12	6.7	25	19.2
Total	14	7.7	17	9.4	43	24.0	105	38.7	179	100.0

[a]Based on a survey of 179 residential units.

TABLE 4.19

Schooling and Economic Level[a]

Schooling of the head of residential unit	Level A		Level B		Level C		Level D		Total	
	Number	Percentage	Number	Percentage	Number	Percentage	Number	Percentage	Number	Percentage
None (illiterate or self-taught)	1	7.2	3	17.5	9	20.9	40	38.1	53	29.6
First to third grade	4	28.5	11	64.9	8	18.6	25	23.8	48	26.8
Fourth to sixth grade	6	42.8	1	5.9	9	20.9	14	13.3	30	16.7
Beyond sixth grade	2	14.3	1	5.9	4	9.3	3	2.9	10	5.6
Unknown	1	7.2	1	5.9	13	30.3	23	21.9	38	21.3
Total	14	100.0	17	100.0	43	100.0	105	100.0	179	100.0

[a]Based on a survey of 179 residential units.

enters a room, the furnishings in level C and D appear as characteristically rural, whereas among levels A and B there is a marked preference for so-called modern furnishings. These utterly different life-styles are believed to reflect real changes in cultural traits brought about by acculturation to city life.

SCHOOLING AND ECONOMIC LEVELS

According to my schooling survey in Cerrada del Cóndor (see Table 3.10), it was found that 76.8% of the heads of families and their spouses, if migrants, had less than 3 years of schooling. In 43.3% of the cases they never went to school at all. Literacy is slightly higher among those born in the Federal District; but the proportion of illiterates is still high. Altogether, fully 35.6% of all heads of families and their spouses in Cerrada del Cóndor have never had any kind of formal education.

There is not much difference in schooling between men and women; however, the number of self-taught literates is significantly higher among men. Self-taught literates are settlers who have taught themselves the rudiments of reading and writing after migration, usually because of the requirements or urban jobs. Similar needs among women are less pressing, since typically female jobs are not deemed to require any degree of literacy.

Because of the generally low level of schooling in Cerrada del Cóndor one might expect to find little differences in schooling between the economic levels of the settlers. (See Table 4.19.) Yet there is some tendency for the economic stratification in the shantytown to be reflected in terms of literacy.

It is also significant that a high proportion of informants in levels C and D failed to reply to the literacy questions. The number of illiterates increases markedly from levels A to D, to the extent that over 75% of the settlers in levels A and B possess some formal schooling. If the lack of an answer is interpreted as a tacit admission of illiteracy, the differences between the two groups of life-styles are even more striking. In conclusion, there appears to be a definite correlation between literacy and improvement in economic level within the shantytown.

AN INFORMAL ROTATING CREDIT INSTITUTION: *TANDA*

Tandas are characteristically Mexican informal credit groups. As seen and practiced in Cerrada del Cóndor, a *tanda* is a club of between 4 and 10 members, each of whom contributes a monthly quota to a common fund. For example, in one *tanda* of 6 members, each member gave 100 pesos every month. The total sum was pocketed by each member by turn; the sequence of turns among the members was initially settled by drawing lots. In this *tanda,* each participant obtained a sum of 500 pesos every 6 months. This institution is quite popular throughout Mexico, not only among poor people but also among groups of the middle-class including housewives and civil service employees. In Cerrada del Cóndor I have found participants in *tandas* among the members of more than 70 families. Most members of *tandas* are recruited among close relatives, neighbors, or companions at work. The amount of each member's monthly assessment fluctuated between 10 and 100 pesos. The *tanda* system may be described as a rotating credit system with a continuously replenished capital fund; it is quite analogous to an institution described in Asia and Africa by Geertz (1962:241–263). Since there is no accumulation of capital, no treasurer is required.

The payment of dues in a *tanda* rests on mutual trust among the members. Since there is no written contract of any kind, payment cannot be legally enforced. Relatives and friends join a *tanda* in a spirit of mutual assistance. Saving money in a group is more practical than attempting to do the same as an individual; also, there are no risks associated with keeping money under the mattress, not to mention the temptation of spending it prematurely. This is the most practical system of savings under shantytown conditions. In Cerrada del Cóndor, *tandas* originate most frequently among members of a network of reciprocal exchange. They represent an important system of economic cooperation and a means of reinforcing the level of *confianza* between the members of a network.

SUMMARY AND CONCLUSIONS

The economics of marginality may be described as featuring a combination of low income and low job security. Following Muñoz, Oliveira, and Stern (1972:336), we may define urban marginals as those workers who earn less than the monthly equivalent of a legal minimum wage, and who fall into one of the following occupational categories: (1) street vendors; (2) unskilled construction workers; (3) unskilled production workers; and (4) unskilled service workers. On the basis of my survey in Cerrada del Cóndor, we should add also the semiskilled workers commonly designated as *maestros,* who are free-lance workers without a stable job. Such *maestros* make more than the minimum monthly legal salary, *provided that they find work;* actually, however, their mean monthly salary is usually less than the equivalent of a full-time minimum legal wage. This shows that the criterion of minimum wages should be used with some caution. The most relevant factor for defining marginality is *economic insecurity.* A schoolteacher may earn less than a construction foreman, yet he cannot be considered marginal because he has job security. The foreman, on the other hand, may be bordering a lower-middle-class level if his life-style changes.

I have shown that there are four objectively different economic levels in the shantytown. These levels are not claimed to be absolute, and they are not necessarily universal for all shantytowns in Latin America or even in Mexico City. There is a certain arbitrariness in using some variables (housing, furniture, and appliances), rather than others. I hope to have shown, however, that the economic levels defined in this manner are self-consistent and correlate with an important set of economic and cultural indicators in the shantytown. This shows that there are definite economic inequalities among the shantytown settlers, since these inequalities are reflected in terms of income, occupation, material belongings, schooling, number of economically active persons per household, and even alcohol intake. I suggest that two different life-styles may be found coexisting in the shantytown, namely a rural-type marginality and an urban-type marginality. The transition between these two life-styles is reflected in terms of economic indicators. My data show that the transition toward the urban life-style takes at least 10 years of residence in the Federal District.

The presence of economic levels in the shantytown shows, among other things, that poverty is not necessarily more homogeneous than wealth. There are economic differences and shadings among the poor as there are among the middle class, though the factors of differentiation may be different in each case. The economic system of the shantytown values security of income above everything else (Stepick and Hendrix, n.d.:14). The highest economic level belongs not necessarily to those settlers who earn higher wages but to those who enjoy a stable income, whether it be derived from an industrial wage or from a monthly rental. Access to employments providing a relative degree of job stability requires a certain amount of knowledge of the urban way of life; hence the upper economic levels in the shantytown are identified with an urban life-style. Rural life-styles are found predominantly among the lower economic levels, recognizable by their use of rustic furniture, earthenware dishes, and rural-type dress including straw hats, as well as by a higher degree of control by husbands over wives and children. There are exceptions, however; two families of economic level A had managed to keep certain rural-type cultural features, including a barnyard with animals, earthenware dishes, and the absence of urban-type implements such as forks.

The occupational histories of settlers in Cerrada del Cóndor indicate that marginals frequently change their occupations within the bounds of marginality. An unskilled laborer may be a construction worker today, a waiter or a carpenter tomorrow. Specialization occurs at the level of *maestro,* i.e., the semispecialized craftsman or free-lance worker. There is no normal access of these *maestros* to the industrial job market (anymore than there is a possibility for a street vendor to become a member of the Chamber of Commerce). There are too many economic, educational, organizational, and social barriers against the eventual incorporation of marginals into the urban industrial economy.

Some of my reported figures for housing and material belongings in Cerrada del Cóndor suggest comparisons with similar studies made elsewhere in Mexico City. Bataillon and Rivière d'Arc (1973) have described a shantytown in which more than 50% of all dwellings had a floor space less than 14 square meters. There were no sanitary facilities, and 10% of all homes had a single bed for five people on the average. Single rooms were used "for sleeping, for cooking, and for living." Another shantytown of Mexico City, described by Pozas *et al.* (1969:19–26), contained 56% of single-room dwellings (against 58% in Cerrada del Cóndor). In that shantytown 92% of the heads of families had monthly incomes below the equivalent of a minimum legal wage, and 95% of the settlers were migrants. Physical, economic, and social conditions were quite similar to those of Cerrada del Cóndor, though conditions of property tenure were perhaps slightly better.

As a whole, the data on shantytown economy reported in this chapter suggest the existence of an *economic system* that is peculiar to marginality. This system meshes, so to speak, with the urban industrial system since it exists on its waste, inefficiency, and occasional surplus. Marginality may be seen as a combination of cultural, economic, and social characteristics pertaining to a specific economic niche, which is interstitially related to urban industrial economy. Anthropologically speaking, marginals are the hunters and gatherers of the urban jungle. A marginal wears used clothing, uses empty cans as buckets for carrying water to his home, and covers his roof with random materials found around construction sites. He takes whatever jobs are available and changes his occupation from one day to the next. The use of waste materials can become a way of life, as in the case of the *pepenadores,* marginals who sort and salvage materials from garbage dumps. Marginal children collect choice bits of garbage for feeding their pigs in the backyard. As a result, the marginal economy is utterly dependent on its host economy. It controls none or almost none of the economic or ecological factors that determine its survival. The basic insecurity of marginal existence can be compensated in only one way: by generating mechanisms of economic solidarity, based on the full mobilization of the social resources of the individual. We shall now explore some of these mechanisms in greater detail.

Family and Kinship

This chapter describes the internal social organization of the shantytown of Cerrada del Cóndor from the standpoint of kinship relations. As we shall see, the basic principles and forms of organization found among the settlers may be understood in terms of a few deeply rooted traditional institutions, and the same is true of the modes of articulation with the national society at large. These traditional institutions have not been weakened by the economic instability of the marginal social structure: quite the opposite. I hope to show that the notable persistence and the characteristic evolution of family–kinship patterns in the shantytown are actually conditioned by imperatives of economic and social survival.

Again, the vitality of family and kinship institutions appears as a key element of Mexican culture. This enduring vitality may be seen as the mainspring of social innovation in the adaptive mechanisms to be described in this book.

MARITAL ROLES

In Cerrada del Cóndor one finds a strict partition of marital roles. This partition goes beyond a male–female division of labor; it also encompasses leisure, friendship, and the domain of the affections. I have observed that shantytown husbands tend to see in their wives mother substitutes, minus the emotional attachments that are a mother's due. Such attachments, and the outlets for related emotional needs, are largely transferred to the husband's circle of male friends. Participation in a male friendship circle implies a special type of relationship, peculiar to Mexican culture, which is called *cuatismo*. The term *cuate* (a Nahuatlism meaning "twin brother") describes a special male friend who may be entrusted with intimate information, and who may be depended upon for mutual assistance and for spending leisure time together. The institution of *cuatismo* may include adventures with other women; such adventures are not viewed by the husband as in conflict with his marital role.

The relatively low emotional content of the husband–wife relation causes a wife to transfer the main burden of her affective life onto her children. However, a strong maternal bond does not always exhaust her emotional needs; one also observes a rich emotional relation between a woman and her brothers. In the shantytown the role of the maternal uncle is endowed with unusually strong affectionate feeling. Perhaps it is the only specific cultural role that allows a man to give free rein to his sense of responsibility without becoming suspected of weakness. Frequently one finds the maternal uncle as protector of his sister and his nephews. In general, a wife's kin network nearly always represents a basic element of security for shantytown families.

As for the female role, its traditional hallmark is a capacity for suffering. This attitude is implicit in the treatment of the female child, as observed in the home from early childhood on. Girls are trained to serve their parents as a matter of course; they spoil their little brothers without expecting any attentions in return. Women grow up to take care of their menfolk and to manipulate them, while stoically submitting to the consequences of the men's callousness and irresponsibility. Shantytown women tend to develop strong, resilient personalities that eventually make them pillars of strength within their social group.

Men, on the other hand, are seen as emotionally immature, overgrown children; this is the female view. A wife knows that her husband's whims and temperamental outbursts are to be suffered patiently or overcome by means of superior wisdom and wiles. The male's arbitrary and inconstant behavior, and his propensity for vice, are attributes of the masculine role and are interpreted by women as such. The sex roles are culturally prescribed; a man must be rash and irresponsible to be manly, even where such behavior is out of character. A real woman must share in the nobility of suffering no matter how cheerful and self-reliant she may happen to be. Incidentally, I have noticed an unusual number of marriages where the wife is older than the husband in Cerrada del Cóndor.

Case Histories

1. Guadalupe Contreras, who makes her living by selling raspados (flavored shaved ice) on the street. She lives with a man younger than herself who drinks and often refuses to give her any household money. Finally Guadalupe decided to throw her man out of the room; she actually started putting her husband's belongings outside the door. However, she reconsidered because her brothers and her husband were *cuates.* In the end Guadalupe conformed to the role of a suffering woman rather than confront her brothers with the painful choice of either siding with their *cuate* or with their sister.

2. A family network centered on two sisters married to two brothers; the husbands work and drink together. Valentina, one of the sisters, welcomed her migrant brother to her home; this brother then joined the kinship network, including the drinking circle of his brothers-in-law. He was introduced to the family trade and became a link of strength in the network.

Several months later Valentina's husband had a serious fight with this brother; it happened in the course of a drinking session and both men actually confronted each other physically. The attitude of the sisters toward this conflict was of unhesitating solidarity with their brother. They hid him, cared for him, and generally interpreted the incident as a confrontation between their husbands' family and their own family of orientation. Apparently neither sister felt a serious loyalty conflict; the brother–sister relationship was stronger than the marital bond. This example is a telling comment on the lack of emotional content of the husband–wife relation, as compared with that of the brother–sister relationship.

The preceding illustrations may be supplemented by some comments on the inherent economic restrictions of the marital relationship. In the shantytown most wives are forbidden to work by their husbands, because it is felt that their place is in the home. In case of need a wife is often forced to earn her living without her husband's knowledge and consent. This attitude may be due to a compound of jealousy, authoritarianism, and plain abuse of the husband's prerogatives. A wife has only the vaguest idea of the total earnings of her *señor* ("master"), since the weekly allowance for household expenses depends entirely on the husband's pleasure. In most cases the wives use trickery and deceit to wheedle money or permissions from their husbands; these are based on their knowledge of "how to handle men." The slightest show of responsibility on the part of a husband is pounced upon as a weakness. The following example illustrates the economic implications of marital roles in the shantytown.

3. Gabriela. Gabriela's husband treated his wife very well. He did not drink and gave her nearly all his earnings. As a result the standard of living of the family improved to the point where the relationship with their network of reciprocal exchange became strained. This network happened to be based on Gabriela's consanguineal kin. Because of her increasing economic ease, Gabriela gradually stopped requesting and granting favors. Eventually the family decided to move away from the kinship network, and found a room beyond the limits of the shantytown.

This situation lasted for about 2 years. Gradually Gabriela's husband changed. With the encouragement of his brothers and friends he started drinking and beating his wife. Their economic situation decayed to the point where Gabriela was forced to go back and seek readmission to her former network in Cerrada del Cóndor. The following interpretation of this story was obtained from Gabriela's sister: The fault lay with the wife for failing to appreciate her husband's qualities. Instead of encouraging his good points she took advantage of them, and despised him for his supposed weakness to boot. In the end the husband "had no choice" but to reaffirm his masculine role by taking up drinking with friends. This example shows that the expected behavior of a husband includes some degree of irresponsibility, which is prized as manliness by his own wife.

I might add that nuclear families in Cerrada del Cóndor are relatively stable. The number of incomplete families caused by desertion by the husband is not large. Whenever a marriage breaks up for any reason, including desertion, the woman takes charge of the children and, more often than not, finds herself another man within a short time. Children from earlier unions are normally accepted by a new husband. Many women have one or more children before marriage; such children are often raised by grandparents or other relatives, particularly when the young mother works as a housemaid. Once she is married these earlier children are incorporated into her family of procreation on equal terms with her later offspring. Whenever a woman goes without a husband for any long period of time she tends to join the household of her children or other close relatives.

In conclusion, conjugal roles in Cerrada del Cóndor may be understood in terms of the structure of the traditional extended family, rather than the ideal of the nuclear family as found in urban Western societies. With the sole exception of the sexual functions, all other marital functions may be discharged indifferently or alternately by close relatives such as the maternal uncle. The predominance of a pattern of separate conjugal roles implies a low emotional content for the husband–wife relationship. Hence, the course of a marriage is strongly influenced by the expected rather than the actual behavior of the partners. These conclusions are somewhat reminiscent of the observations made by Ganz (1965:51) in a lower-class Italian neighborhood of Boston.

The shantytown woman is rugged and accustomed to hardship. She knows her role is essential in the social fabric, especially in the networks of reciprocal exchange on which her economic security depends. Potentially her earning power is on the same order as a man's; this fact may signify considerable economic and emotional independence. It is true that the man is normally cast in the role of breadwinner, but the woman, through her role in centralizing networks of reciprocal exchange, is often the key to survival. Hence there is some measure of factual equality between the sexes in terms of the realities of shantytown life. As a result shantytown women appear to suffer from the "alienation syndrome" to a much lesser extent than, for example, urban middle-class women in Mexico (Acevedo 1973).

THE NUCLEAR FAMILY

The nuclear family in Cerrada del Cóndor should be carefully distinguished from the household. Most households contain an *extended family,* i.e., a social group that comprises two or more mutually related nuclear families, plus other unmarried kin. *Arrimados* or single persons attached to an extended family may also join a nuclear family, as we shall see. Let us first discuss the nuclear family as such.

The quantitative data to follow are taken from a survey of Cerrada del Cóndor that I conducted in 1971. At that time there were 133 nuclear families living as individual households, plus 29 extended families living as households of 2.3 nuclear families each on the average. There were 31 *incomplete* nuclear families (23.4%); the remaining 102 nuclear families were complete. Among the incomplete nuclear families, 17 were made up of mothers with their descendants, childless old couples, orphaned children, or young couples without children. Another 14 incomplete families included in addition one or more *arrimados,* such as grandparents (i.e., parents of a head of household), uncles, cousins, or nephews. In one case the *arrimado* was a renter who was no relation to the family. Sometimes an *arrimado* may partly take over the functions of an absent spouse; in other cases he may share expenses or live as a guest of the nuclear family. Among complete nuclear families the proportion of *arrimados* is much lower: 17 cases, as against 85 without *arrimados.*

Frequently, young couples begin their married life in consensual union. Eventually, after several children and depending on their religious feelings or convenience, they may formalize their marriage through parish, Civil Registry, or both. Table 5.1 shows the distribution of marriages by type of union, from information supplied by heads of households.

Information on heads of extended-family households is included in the table. Considering the fact that the survey cuts across the age spectrum, the number of consensual unions is low. Often the incidence of consensual unions is taken as an indicator of "poverty" (see Roberts 1973:40), but this does not seem to apply to Mexico. Kemper (1971b:93) reports a low incidence of so-called free or informal marriages among Tzintzuntzan migrants in Mexico City, in agreement with the present findings. There are good reasons to believe that the relatively high

TABLE 5.1

Type of Marriage Union of Heads of Residential Units

	Number	Percentage
Consensual union	29	17.8
Civil registry	17	10.5
Parish registry	12	7.4
Both civil and religious	72	44.4
Separated or uncertain	32	19.8
Total	162	100.0

stability of the nuclear family in Cerrada del Cóndor may be culturally conditioned and may be typical of all strata of the Mexican population.

Another important parameter is the number of children per nuclear family. The survey included live offspring of all mothers, irrespective of whether they belonged to nuclear or extended families; the data are shown in Table 5.2. It should be kept in mind that the figures represent a kind of status report on an evolving situation. Because of the large number of young couples in the sample, the expected fertility of a given couple should be higher than the sample median of

TABLE 5.2

Live Offspring per Nuclear Family[a]

Number of children	Number of families	Percentage
0	17	8.5
1	21	10.5
2	25	12.5
3	28	14.0
4	23	11.5
5	26	13.0
6	16	8.0
7	16	8.0
8	14	7.0
9	3	1.5
10	3	1.5
11	1	.5
12	0	0
13	2	1.0
Unknown	5	2.5
Total	200	100.0

[a]Includes nuclear components of extended families.

four children that appears in the table. According to Table 3.16 about 40% of the couples in our sample were below the age of 30. The extremely high fertility observed in Cerrada del Cóndor cannot be attributed solely to cultural preferences but must have economic causes as well (see Chapter 4, on the economic contribution of children).

THE HOUSEHOLD: DEFINITION

A household is traditionally defined as the social group of all individuals who share the same residence and who also share the same entrance or access to a residential unit. This definition is useful in a rural setting where no space limitations prevent the members of a household from clustering together within a common house or plot. Such a rural household, if transferred to a suburban shantytown, may be forced to occupy several neighboring rooms with independent access doors if no other accommodations are available. As a result the former household may be split into nuclear families apparently leading independent economic lives, even though their interaction may actually be more intense than before and the total space occupied by the household may have shrunk as compared to the rural situation.

The point of this discussion is that a revision of the household terminology may be necessary when dealing with new types of settlements that arise under special conditions of land tenure and occupancy, as found in shantytowns. Extreme scarcity of space and severe economic constraints produce new residential patterns and a rearrangement of domestic functions. All of this turns out to be most relevant to an analysis of the social structure in Cerrada del Cóndor.

Let us forgo a theoretical discussion of the concept of household in general; this task has been accomplished, among others, by Bender (1967:493–504) and by Nutini (1968:175). I follow Bender in distinguishing three semi-independent variables in the classification of households: kinship, residential proximity, and domestic function. Each society may feature a characteristic combination of these variables; hence the concept of household may acquire different connotations and meanings depending on the social context.

In Cerrada del Cóndor one finds households that comprise one or more kinship-related nuclear families; they may dwell either in a single residential unit or in several adjoining units; and they may share certain domestic functions and not others. Keep in mind that the spectrum of shared domestic functions may be quite broad: preparation and consumption of meals, child care, leisure activities, ritual duties, and a wide range of acts of kindness or mutual cooperation.

Thus, in the shantytown a cluster of seemingly independent one-room dwellings may contain a single household. Conversely, a set of rooms with a single entrance may contain several households. This is the case of the so-called *vecindades* or courts, a double row of one-room apartments that face on a narrow lane. The access to this lane and hence to the rooms is through a gate controlled by the owner of the court; the families renting rooms are usually unrelated. Thus, the residential pattern is determined by property conditions that tell us little or nothing about the social structure in the shantytown. The real-estate system of the shantytown operates according to the random occurrence of vacancies. Total strangers may be forced to live together in the intimacy of a *vecindad* and households may be broken up for lack of joint accommodations. The formation of a household in Cerrada del Cóndor is a dynamic process involving many random factors, such as the availability of vacancies or the availability of kin ready to move in when a vacancy develops. The different types of households to be described should be seen as resulting from the interaction of these random factors with the three basic variables, namely kinship, residential arrangement, and domestic function.

TYPES OF HOUSEHOLDS

The following classification of households is proposed for Cerrada del Cóndor (see Figure 5.1):

1. According to *kinship,* the household may be either nuclear or extended. A nuclear household contains a single nuclear family, and an extended household contains an extended family.
2. According to *residence,* the household may be one of three types: *single roof, single plot,* or *jointed.* A single roof household shares the same residential unit. In the single-plot type, a series of dwellings share the same plot of land; in the jointed type, the household occupies two or more adjoining residential units not originally built for one household.
3. According to *domestic function,* the household may be classified as with or without expense sharing.

Households that contain a single nuclear family are in the minority. About half of these were waiting for a vacancy so that they might settle in the proximity of relatives who had become established elsewhere in Cerrada del Cóndor. To a marginal family the luxury of living alone is fraught with hazards. Indeed, nuclear households are generally short-lived and may be regarded as transitional states between more stable arrangements of the extended type. The incidence of the various types of households in Cerrada del Cóndor is shown in Table 5.3.

As Table 5.3 shows, the extended family prevails in the great majority of households. Only 30 households live as nuclear families by themselves, without any relatives in the shantytown. However, as we shall see, even these minority households are incorporated in neighborhood-type networks.

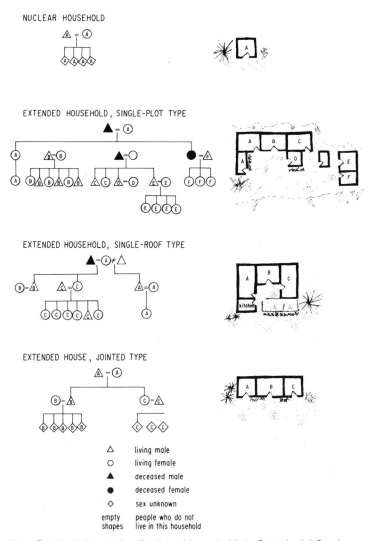

Figure 5.1. Residential-type classification of households in Cerrada del Cóndor.

A major segment of the social structure in the shantytown is represented by the jointed-type household. This household type does not feature any sharing of cooking duties or household expenses among the components of nuclear families. Each family leads a separate economic life. On the other hand, there is an intense reciprocal exchange including a wide variety of domestic functions. Nuclear families tend to share a common outside area used as laundry,

TABLE 5.3

Types of Households[a]

	Number	
	Subgroup	Total
Nuclear		
With relatives in the shantytown	28	
Without relatives in the shantytown	30	58
Extended		
Single roof		
With expense sharing	13	
Without expense sharing	6	19
Single plot		
With expense sharing	3	
Without expense sharing	7	10
Jointed[b]	68	

[a]The figures refer to nuclear families except for extended households living together on a single plot or under a single roof, which comprise a total of 29 households including an estimated 80 to 85 nuclear families.

[b]Total number of nuclear families living as part of jointed households.

kitchen, and children's playground. Thus, a jointed household has a broad base of security resting on the cooperation between close kin with a certain amount of autonomy and privacy for each component nuclear family.

The majority of the population in Cerrada del Cóndor lives in extended households of the single-roof or single-plot types. Such households usually contain three generations: husband and wife, their descendants, and the latter's nuclear family of procreation. As a household lives under one and the same roof its members frequently share household and cooking expenses; yet among almost one-third of the one-roof households, no expense sharing is found. The converse is true for single-plot households, where the cases of expense sharing are in the minority.

On the whole, it may be said that the pattern of household formation in Cerrada del Cóndor is extremely fluid. When a nuclear family moves it may easily adopt a different household arrangement. Newly married couples tend to participate in an extended single-roof household; eventually, however, they may become integrated into a jointed-type household, after going through other stages such as the nuclear household. A nuclear household, by incorporating other nuclear families, becomes an extended household (see Table 5.6). This dynamic process of change in household types without necessarily implying a change in residence represents one of the most relevant features of marginal social structure.

Case Histories

1. A nuclear-family household. Señor Pastrana is from Villela, San Luis Potosí. He came to Cerrada del Cóndor years ago, among the earliest Villela migrants, and found work in the brick factory. His present age is 45; his wife Albertina, 42, born in Guanajuato, has been living in Cerrada del Cóndor with her parents since 1948. Her family owns a little plot of land and her father also used to work in the brick kilns. Albertina met Señor Pastrana in the shantytown. For the first years of their marriage, the couple lived with Albertina's parents. After the birth of several children, they moved into a rented room in the shantytown. They later moved to another rented room and ultimately to their present plot. They are paying a monthly rent of 80 pesos for the plot. On this plot Señor Pastrana, with the assistance of his Villela friends, has built the dwelling they live in today.

They have been living in this residential unit for 3 years. The dwelling is relatively spacious; it contains two rooms and a fenced-in patio. The patio has laundry and washing facilities; they also keep a pig. The household is made up by the couple, their eight children, and Señor Pastrana's widowed father. Formerly there was also a cousin of Señor Pastrana with his bride, living in; but they got married and went to live elsewhere.

Señor Pastrana is a carpet layer who earns 45 pesos a day. He has also been a brickmaker and trucker's helper. He does not allow his wife and his eldest daughter to work for a wage. He was introduced to the carpeting trade by his *cuates* from Villela. He claims to earn about 500 pesos a fortnight, but his actual income is extremely variable. The family owns a television set, a record player, a dining-room set, two double beds, two twin beds, and a gas range. Their economic level is rated B. Albertina supplements the family income by raising pigs.

This household functions separately and independently of others; however, it participates in an exchange network a few blocks away that includes the parents and brothers of Albertina. Albertina visits with her parents every day and regularly uses their bathroom. In addition Albertina has several married sisters living in Cerrada del Cóndor, who maintain a very active mutual exchange. This exchange supplies her occasional needs. Señor Pastrana also maintains excellent relations with his in-laws and there is a great deal of mutual help.

Señor Pastrana has his own group of friends—the Villela group—including some relatives such as a brother who lives in Cerrada del Cóndor. They drink together every weekend. He owes them his current job, as well as assistance in building his present home. The Villela men are *com-padres* and help each other. Most of them live close by. Thus, this nuclear household is only apparently detached since it actually participates in old, solid networks of reciprocal exchange within the shantytown.

    2. *An extended single-roof household with expense sharing.*   The Cuevas–Santoyo family lives in a residential unit containing three rooms

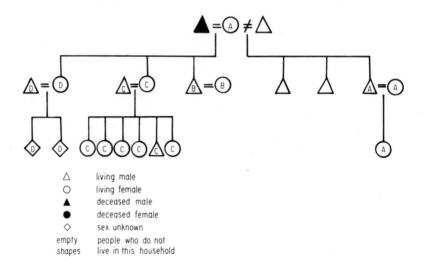

△	living male
○	living female
▲	deceased male
●	deceased female
◇	sex unknown
empty shapes	people who do not live in this household

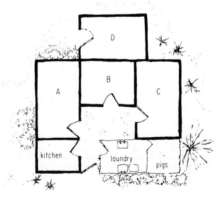

Figure 5.2.   An extended family that lives under a single roof and shares expenses. (Note that room D houses a nuclear family that does not participate in expense sharing.)

plus kitchen (Figure 5.2). Essentially it is an extended family built around a widowed mother with her six children and their descendants.

Three of Estela Santoyo's six children are issues from the Cuevas marriage; three belong to a later union. The sixth child, a daughter, does not actually live under the same roof, but inhabits an adjoining room that has a separate entrance. Her nuclear family is part of the household but does not share the cooking arrangements and the expenses to be described. Strictly speaking, we may say that this household is a jointed arrangement featuring an extended single-roof household plus a nuclear-family household.

The extended family has an expense-sharing arrangement, which comprises all domestic expenses: light (10 pesos a month), rent (150 pesos), and food. All wage earners surrender their cash to the grandmother—Doña Estela. This strong, dominant woman is about 65 and coordinates the economy of the household. Doña Estela was born in Mixcoac, Federal District, at a time when this township was still a rural village. About 45 years ago she married a migrant from Guanajuato and went back to Guanajuato with him. Ten years later she was widowed and returned to the Federal District with her three children. There she met a man 15 years her junior, and had three more children by him. The second husband abandoned her. The family has been living in Cerrada del Cóndor since 1964. At the time of my survey the extended family was constituted as follows: Doña Estela herself, one married daughter, two married sons, two unmarried sons, and the respective nuclear families of the married descendants. None of the sons had any children, but the daughter already had five children. Doña Estela's daughter and daughter-in-law take care of the washing for the whole extended family and prepare the food under Doña Estela's direction. The children are looked after by any of the women. When the nopal cactus is in season, all three women go out with the children to pick nopal leaves; the women clean them and sell them. Magdalena, the married daughter who lives in a separate room in the back, sells food at a stand. Her husband drives a tractor. The domestic functions shared by this couple are much more limited; Magdalena's children are not under the authority of her sisters-in-law; i.e., the sisters-in-law are not authorized to scold them. Although there is no expense sharing there is economic assistance in case of need, including daily loans of food and the reciprocal care of children and the sick when their parents are away. Magdalena visits with the extended family every day and maintains intense personal ties, particularly with her mother. The total income of the extended single-roof family is rather small. The son-in-law is a trucker's helper who earns a minimum wage when there is work. The eldest son is a truck driver, a trade he learned while spending 5 years in jail. The three eldest sons work in a printing shop. Doña Estela sells *nopales* or vegetables in the market of Mixcoac, but she does not own a stand there. The daughter sells *raspados* (shaved flavored ice) in Cerrada del Cóndor. Each nuclear family buys its own clothing, but clothing is borrowed or exchanged within the extended family. The oldest son buys shoes and clothing for his mother, when she is in need. Each man contributes to the household expenses and keeps some spending money for himself. Doña Estela's control is rather strict. She has no authority over her son-in-law, who earns little, has five children, and regularly contributes 100 pesos a week to the household as his share in the rent and other minor expenses. In other words, the extended family has a mixed economy where each man handles his own money and contributes his share of the household expenses to the matriarch instead of to his own wife.

All food is cooked in the kitchen; there is a rural-type wood-burning stove. The women eat as they cook, and the men and children drop in and serve themselves at any time. The economic level is rated D but they own a television set and everyone contributes to the monthly payments. Magdalena and her family view television with the other members of the extended family. But Magdalena's husband has his own mother and brothers in Cerrada del Cóndor; he prefers to drink with his brothers rather than with his brothers-in-law.

The management of this household is economical because of expense sharing, but this depends critically on the centralizing role of an authoritarian woman. Because of Magdalena's husband's preference for a separate expenditure arrangement, there is a modified residential pattern (jointed household), to include the nonparticipating family.

3. An extended single-roof household without expense sharing. Señor Gutierrez, a former charcoal maker from the State of Guanajuato, migrated to the Federal District in 1947 with his family. Some time earlier, however, one of his married sons had gone to the city because his wife had relatives in Puente Colorado. In view of the fact that this son had stopped writing and had practically "become lost," another son left home to look for him. This son not only succeeded in locating his lost brother but sent money home to get his parents to join him, "as life was easier and more comfortable here." Upon arrival the family was put up at the home of their first son in Puente Colorado; then they spent 10 years as caretakers of a vacant lot in Colonia Pilares (southern metropolitan area). When the lot was sold they found their present quarters in Cerrada del Cóndor, where they have been living for 14 years.

The household I am about to describe (Figure 5.3) includes the elderly couple, a married son with his wife and two children, and an unmarried son. One room houses the son who had caused them to come to Mexico City, with his second wife and two children. The oldest boy, an issue of his first marriage, shares the same room with his grandparents. There is also a married daughter now living in Puente Colorado. Another seven sons and daughters are deceased. Altogether the living arrangement includes

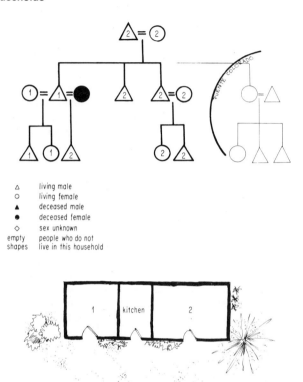

△   living male
○   living female
▲   deceased male
●   deceased female
◇   sex unknown
empty   people who do not
shapes live in this household

Figure 5.3.   An extended family that lives under the same roof but does not share expenses.
The married daughter lives in another shantytown, within walking distance from her parents.

two one-room dwellings with separate entrances; one room housing an
extended family and the other a nuclear family.

This household is extremely poor (level D). Señor Gutierrez is a water
carrier who makes about 10 pesos a day servicing neighboring homes in
Cerrada del Cóndor. Jesus, his eldest son, is a painter's apprentice without a steady income. Armando, the second son, used to be a bricklayer.
One weekend some people came to the shantytown looking for the carpet
layers who lived there, but most of them were drunk and they did not find
anyone willing to work. According to his mother, Armando "decided to go
along and I suppose they liked his work because they offered him a job."
He has been working as carpet layer ever since. His earnings are unknown but he gives his wife 100 pesos a week for household expenses.
His wife does not work for a living. The youngest of the Gutierrez brothers
is only 12 and has no steady job.

The rooms have a dirt floor, brick walls, and zinc roofing. In between the rooms is a small kitchen shared by the members of the household. Rent is separately paid for each of the rooms; the room that houses the old couple costs 50 pesos a month. Martha, wife of Señor Gutierrez, cooks for her husband, her unmarried son, and her oldest grandson. Her husband gives her 8 pesos a day, and she also receives "whatever Jesus hands her," in return for feeding his son. Armando's wife cooks separately for her nuclear family even though they all live together in the same room. This wife does not get along with her sister-in-law, Jesus' wife, who lives next door and has no relatives in the Federal District, as she originally migrated with some girl friends to take up a job as a housemaid. Jesus' wife is closest to her mother-in-law and helps her when she needs anything. On the other hand, Armando's wife is less dependent on her affinal kin; her own mother and two of her sisters live in Cerrada del Cóndor. Domestic functions in this household are less widely shared than in the preceding case. The women do not cooperate in the cooking or in the household economy. Assistance is largely limited to loans (in money and kind), food, and services. As an example, when Jesus remarried his parents adopted his small son on a permanent basis. Armando pays the rent because his old father is earning less these days, and Jesus contributes to the food expenses. Everybody uses the kitchen, the laundry vat, and the outside space. Sons and daughters-in-law exchange assistance with the old couple, and the brothers help each other even though their wives do not get along. Armando's wife maintains an active exchange with her mother and her two married sisters who live nearby and who are handy for her minor needs. The present case suggests that the structure of the household is largely determined by the social relations between the women. The unfriendly relations between daughters-in-law exclude the possibility of expense sharing.

4. A single-plot household with expense sharing. The Gonzalez S. family is a four-generation extended family living together on a single plot (Figure 5.4). The group includes six nuclear families, five of which share expenses; the sixth shares the plot and use of the privy but keeps its own economy separate. The five families sharing expenses have a kitchen of their own.

The family group originates from the state of Michoacan. Don Francisco, the earliest migrant, was a crew member of a fruit truck; he reached Mexico City at age 16. Eleven years later, in 1939, Don Francisco brought his parents and his three smaller brothers to the city. The family first settled in Olivar del Conde and moved later to Merced Gómez, from there to the Tarango cemetery and finally to Cerrada del Cóndor (about 1958). There they rented a plot on a small natural terrace adjoining the bottom of the gully. Everybody shares in the rent payments, which currently amount

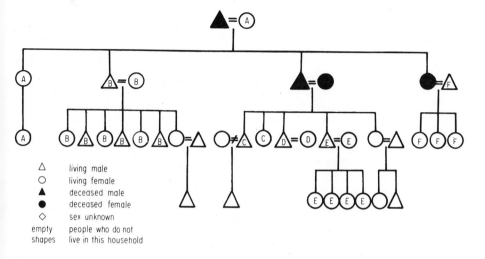

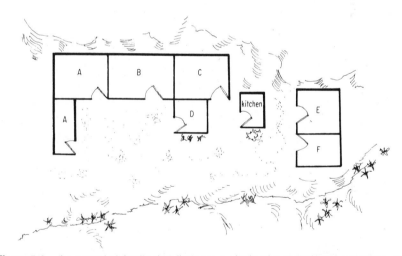

Figure 5.4. An extended family that lives on a single plot and shares expenses. Note that room E contains a nuclear family that does not participate in expense sharing.

to 200 pesos a month. As the family group grew in size additional rooms were built on the plot. The topography is such as not to require a fence around the plot.

The father is now dead and Doña Maria (Don Francisco's mother), aged 68, was the head of the household in 1972. Her sons had gotten married and lived together on the plot with their families, according to the distribution shown in Figure 5.4. Don Francisco and Albertina, two members of the original sibling group, are dead but their descendants still live in the plot. Rosa, one of Doña Maria's daughters-in-law, is originally from Cerrada del Cóndor and therefore maintains active exchange relations with her former family network. She has six unmarried sons and one married daughter; the married daughter lives in Cerrada del Cóndor with her husband's network, though she also maintains active exchange relations with her orientation family.

Doña Maria, the matriarch, lives in one room with her daughter (an unmarried mother) and the latter's young daughter who has been raised by Doña Maria like a daughter of her own. Another room contains the single surviving son with his wife (Rosa) and their six unmarried sons. Three further rooms contain the descendants of Don Francisco and his wife, both deceased; one room contains two unmarried sons and one married couple without descendants, another room contains a son, Concepción, his wife Soledad, and four children. This is the nuclear family that does not share expenses with the rest. The third room contains another of Don Francisco's sons, his wife, and three children.

Albertina's widower lives in another room with his three sons. Altogether there are 25 people sharing this plot; 19 share all expenses. This economic community embraces all aspects of life up to and even beyond death: Albertina's widower still shares all expenses with his late wife's relatives. Similarly, one granddaughter of Doña Maria has entrusted her little daughter to her care, and the entire family group now shares in the upbringing and socializing of the little girl.

Preparation of food is in the charge of Doña Maria and her daughter-in-law, Rosa, with the assistance of other available women or girls. Doña Maria makes breakfast and dinner for all those who participate in the expense-sharing arrangement. All members who are currently earning contribute to food expenses; there are no fixed quotas and everyone who is laid off may stop contributing. Each nuclear family also has additional foodstuffs bought with their own money, and these are not generally shared. Whenever such private food is offered for common use, the contributing member has the right to reserve the choice part for himself or for members of his nuclear family.

Rosa (aged 33 in 1972) cooks the midday meal. For this purpose Doña Maria gives Rosa whatever she requires to buy the ingredients; the daily lunch expense is quite variable. Soledad, wife of the grandson who does not participate in expense sharing, buys her own food though some of the other women will often keep her company. She never sends other women on food errands. She buys her tortillas from Rosa (who makes tortillas for sale in the shantytown). Rosa's daughter, married in Cerrada del Cóndor, quite often takes her child along to spend the day and eat at her mother's while her husband is away from home. She will usually bring a little something to contribute to the food.

Bathing the children is a communal affair, handled by two or three women who heat the water in buckets; the children help carry water and firewood.

Most daily activities are centered around the patio of the plot. This is a place for eating, for cleaning and peeling vegetables, for doing laundry and washing dishes, for gossiping, and for supervising the play of the children. Rooms are used only for sleeping or for keeping out of the rain. When one of Don Francisco's sons bought a television set, his room became a gathering place for television viewing, particularly the evening movies.

Twice a week all available members of the family group gather firewood. However, Soledad's family does not share in this work since they use an oil stove. There are similar expeditions for gathering wastepaper, cement, glass, and scraps of metal or empty cans for sale. Everybody cooperates in joint activities such as mending roofs, building a room, carrying heavy objects, and so on. All take responsibility for the children, giving them a hand or letting out a shout in case of danger. Among adults there are frequent loans of clothing and other belongings of nuclear groups; children and youngsters help themselves without asking permission. Everybody enters any room as if it were their own.

Soledad is less active in the general exchange; she is found more often with her own brother and sister-in-law who live nearby, and who share many goods and services with her. However, her nuclear family contributes to paying the rent and the light bill (20 pesos a month). Everybody helps keep the patio clean; the care of the sick and the ritual expenses (burials and so on) are also shared by all.

The economy of this extended family is financed as follows: (1) Doña Maria washes stairs in Mixcoac three times a week (15 to 20 pesos a day), and takes home old tortillas and stale bread for the pigs, which are raised on the plot as a joint project of the family group. She participates with the other women in the sale of tortillas. If there are no pigs at the moment, the stale bread and tortillas are sold to other pig-raising families in the shantytown. (2) Antonio, Rosa's husband, is a trucker's helper or bricklayer or driver of a sand-hauling truck. He makes 280 pesos a week and he eats at home. (3) Ricardo, grandson of Doña Maria, is a trucker's helper or truck driver (40 pesos a day). (4) Francisco, son of the deceased Don Francisco, is a locksmith's apprentice (30 pesos a day). (5) Albertina's widower looks after cows in a dairy (his earnings are unknown). (6) Rosa makes tortillas for sale. (7) One of the children sells newspapers in the mornings (10 pesos a day) and goes to school in the afternoon. (8) One granddaughter takes in washing two or three times a week (35 pesos a day). (9) Another granddaughter is a daytime housemaid (25 pesos a day). (10) Wastepaper, cans, and animals raised (pigs; at one time they also had 30 sheep) are sold.

The family group is self-sufficient and has no contact with neighbors. The men claim that they socialize only within the family; they drink together at home on Sundays. Rosa gets along very well with her married sisters, who visit her every day and buy their tortillas from her. She goes every day to her mother and takes 5 kilos of tortillas along. As we saw earlier, Rosa's daughter is following the same pattern and relying on her family of orientation for many aspects of daily life. Finally, Soledad maintains exchange relationships with her family of orientation. With these exceptions in mind, the family group is autonomous and self-sufficient. There is intense mutual assistance and great personal trust among all components of the network. In general, single-plot households with expense sharing tend to form compact residential arrangements, where the original parents are usually the owners of the plot. The household coincides with the extended family and with the residential unit, forming a single reciprocity network. The only difference with single-roof households lies in the residential pattern of several rooms with separate entrances on a common plot.

5. A single-plot household without expense sharing. Don Bernardo Cáceres and his wife Zoilita migrated to Mexico City in 1945. He was a sharecropper in a hacienda that was expropriated, and "he was not awarded any land, apparently having supported the former owner." Don Bernardo was 38 at the time and his wife was 30; they had three children. After changing occupations and residences in Mexico City several times, they bought a little plot in Cerrada del Cóndor in 1948. Don Bernardo worked at first in the brick kilns. When they closed he became a bricklayer until he tore a ligament in his shoulder. Then he set up a fruitstand in front of his home.

The couple had 13 live children and 6 who died, plus an adopted son. Five children and the adopted son live together with their parents in the same plot (Figure 5.5). The remaining children are all married daughters, two of whom are now living in Cerrada del Cóndor. Their economic standard is rated A but their style of life is rural. The rooms are grouped around a central lane in a U-shaped pattern. Room 1 contains the head of the household, Don Bernardo, his wife, a 17-year-old son, two daughters aged 16 and 22, and the 3-year-old adopted son. Next is the kitchen, which also houses a duck, a rooster, and some chickens; there is also a privy. Room 2, housing Alberto and his wife Juanita (age 25 and 23), occupies the far end of the plot. It also houses their two children plus two orphaned siblings of Juanita's. One of them, a 12-year-old girl, shares a bed with their daughter; the parents let their son share their own bed.

Juanita's orphaned brother, aged 17, sleeps in a little oratory where

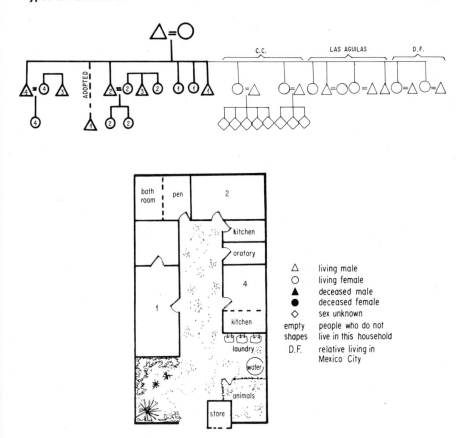

Figure 5.5. An extended family that lives on a single plot but does not share expenses. Two married daughters live in Cerrada del Còndor; other sons and daughters (married as well as unmarried) live elsewhere in the urban area. D.F., Federal District.

images and relics of saints are kept. Finally there is the room of son Martin, his wife Julia, and their son. There is a brother of Julia's who also sleeps in the oratory but who eats his meals at his sister's home. Don Bernardo's fruitstand is merely a table and a seat for Don Bernardo and sometimes for his wife. He sells oranges, onions, candies, cookies, all in very small amounts. The patio of the plot houses pigs, rabbits, pigeons, chickens, turkeys, and one goat, all enclosed in a small pen. In the middle of the plot there is a wood stove where the women make their tortillas in the mornings, because they do not care for the ones that can be bought at the local tortilla mill. On one side they have planted a little tree for shade.

All members of this extended family help in the maintenance of the plot and share the outside facilities. However, each room has its own little kitchen where food is prepared for each nuclear household. The oratory, the laundry, and the privy are shared by all. There is also a little water tank, which is shared by all and is jointly filled every night. The family group spends much of the time in the patio; rooms are mainly used for sleeping.

Don Bernardo earns very little and his sons give him some money every week or every other week. The 22-year-old daughter is a maid and hands practically all her earnings to her father. Both married sons, Alberto and Martin, give their wives a weekly household allowance and keep the rest for their entertainment as well as for their father's allowance. The women go together to church or shopping; they borrow food, money, and other articles from each other. The children are jointly raised by all. The two married daughters live about two blocks away and are members of the exchange network. They visit their parents every day, and send their children to stay and use the privy. Two sons and two daughters live in Las Aguilas and visit their parents' household once or twice a week. Two married daughters live farther away in the city (one in Colonia Aurora and another near the Women's Jail); these come to visit every other month on the average.

The younger married men of the household, including the two married sons and the sons-in-law of Don Bernardo, work together as mechanics in the same shop. They have helped each other in finding work together. Each time a member got married, the others helped in building a new room. The economic assistance given to Don Bernardo is in compensation for the use of his plot. The two brothers of daughters-in-law who are of working age give an allowance to their sisters; if they have no work they do not need to pay. The main feature in this household is the fact that each nuclear family has its own separate economy. However, the head of the household centralizes social activities and remains the dominant element in the structure of the household, both as father and as owner of the plot. Likewise, Don Bernardo's wife is the dominant element in the group of the women, all of whom cooperate and get along well together.

6. An extended household of the jointed type. The Carrera family group includes five nuclear families living in adjoining rooms that have separate entrances (Figure 5.6). The unifying element of the household is kinship: two brothers, one sister, one nephew, and one cousin, with their respective consorts and descendants. The Carreras come from the state of Zacatecas and are related through affinity with two other family groups from the same state living in Cerrada del Cóndor. However, their current direct relationships with these two families are negligible. The history of their migration goes back to Melchor Carrera, who arrived in 1966 and joined the home of an uncle living in Cerrada del Cóndor since 1954. This

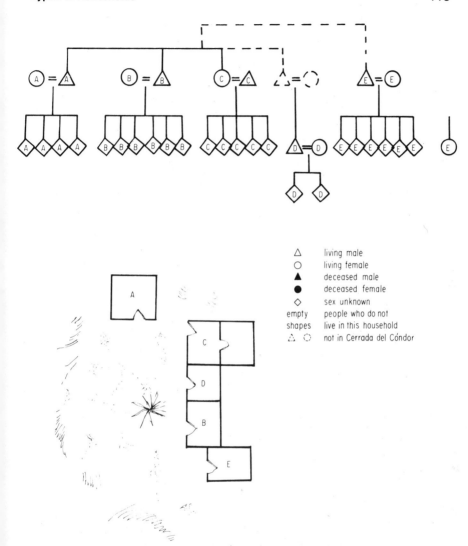

Figure 5.6. An extended family household of the jointed type. The dashed lines have been added to show the relationship between network E and the rest.

uncle was a bricklayer who got Melchor a job in the construction site where he himself was currently working. A few months after this Melchor brought his wife and two sons to Mexico City. Two more children were born later. The family rented a room in Cerrada del Cóndor; later they rented a plot where Melchor built his home. The rent of the plot is 80 pesos a month.

Melchor has learned the trade of bricklayer and has now become a foreman, thanks to his uncle's coaching. As a foreman he has included all male members of his present household into his bricklayers' gang. He insists on working only with his own relatives. In 1970 he became seriously ill and lost his job; hence the brothers in the household were all jobless at the time of the survey.

After Melchor had settled in the shantytown he first encouraged his nephew Soledad to join him. Soledad arrived in Mexico City and joined his uncle's household with his wife in 1968. They now have two children. His brother Natividad, married, with six children, migrated in 1969 and initially lived in Soledad's room. In 1970 they moved into an adjoining room that had formerly been occupied by a cousin. This cousin became separated from her husband and went to live with her parents in the shantytown. A few months after the arrival of Natividad they were joined by their sister Roberta, with her husband and five children. During the first 4 months they lived with Melchor; then the men of the family jointly built another room on a rented adjacent plot. Roberta's husband also found work under Melchor. Finally the group was joined by Señor Serrano, a cousin to the Carreras, who had migrated to Mexico City in 1962. The Serrano family had been moving from place to place within the southern part of the city for 9 years. In 1971, during a visit with Soledad Carrera, Soledad encouraged them to move into a neighboring room that had just been vacated, "so as to stay close to the family." The Serrano family has six children and a niece who lives with them. The man is a bricklayer. They pay 135 pesos a month in rent.

Here we have an extended family made up of five nuclear families. Each nuclear family lives in its own residential unit and maintains its own economy. Prior to their reunion in Cerrada del Cóndor, the Carrera brothers had been in touch through letters, and through occasional trips between the province and the city in both directions. The men of the household are also a single labor unit under the leadership of Melchor. Roberta works as a daytime maid and makes 350 pesos a month; she works from 9 A.M. to 3 P.M. In the evenings she makes dresses, which are ordered by her neighbors in the shantytown. Her 17-year-old daughter also works as a maid and also makes 350 pesos. Her older boys go to secondary school and occasionally work with their father. In the other nuclear families the husband is the only breadwinner. All earn a minimum salary except for Melchor who earns as a foreman.

Each nuclear family pays rent, prepares its own food, and educates its own children. All share the same outdoor facilities, including the laundry vats. There is a continual exchange of mutual assistance: money loans, loans of tools and artifacts, services such as the care of children and the sick, assistance in building new housing facilities, job assistance, migration assistance, and so on. They presumably also share ritual expenses, though no instance arose during the time spent on the study. There are some indications that the reciprocity network based on this household might extend to a woman who lives next door to Soledad Carrera and who has no relatives in the shantytown. This neighbor exchanges mutual assistance with Soledad's wife. If this relationship were to become consolidated, the neighbor might be included in the reciprocity network and this fact could be acknowledged through *compadrazgo*. At present there are *compadrazgo* ties among all member families of the household; three of the *compadrazgo* ties already existed in the province prior to migration.

SOME COMPARISONS OF HOUSEHOLDS

The kinds of households we have described for Cerrada del Cóndor are mainly based on the extended family. This is not unusual; on the contrary, it appears to be normal among marginal populations of Mexico and Latin America.

Among the Tzintzuntzan migrants in Mexico City (Kemper 1971b:85–86), one finds what Leeds (1969) has called an *extended-family enclave*. As he describes it, this type of settlement corresponds to our nuclear household; however, most of these migrants belonged to the lower middle class or to the industrial proletariat. Marginals made up most of the remainder of the sample; 8.1% of these families were found to constitute extended single-roof households whereas 33.8% lived in jointed-type households. Ward (1976:336) found that the number of nuclear families per plot increased from 1.2 in the youngest shantytown (Santo Domingo de los Reyes) to 4.2 in the oldest (Colonia Popular), all in Mexico City. This seems to show that the number of extended-type households increases during the process of consolidation of a shantytown.

The household pattern of Cerrada del Cóndor is quite similar to one described in two slums of Cali, Colombia (Ashton 1972:177–194), where 79% of the families lived in extended households. In a Puerto Rican shantytown investigated by Bryce-Laporte, "the dominant form of family organization was not the separate household or the nuclear family but certain modified forms of extended families featuring neighborhood or closeness of residence. At the same time, the households were related through kinship with three or four similar groups within 'El Arrabal' [1970:88]." And according to Ganz, "the households are of the nuclear type but the family itself tends to the extended type. Even when they are not an economic unit, they function as if they were extended . . . preferably as a social circle . . . members of the family circle also practice advice and assistance in daily problems [1965:45–46]." Finally, Lewis (1959a) described three different slums in Mexico City. In the first slum, "nine of twelve residential units are related through kinship and represent three extended families . . . but in only one case they live together as a true extended family consisting in a married couple with their married daughter and their grandchildren [p. 27].'' In a second slum, "more than one third of the residential units had people with kin in the same slum and about a quarter of them were related through consanguinity or compadrazgo [p. 68].'' In the third slum, "nine of twelve residential units were related to each other through consanguinity or affinity, and all of them were related through compadrazgo. Loans were frequent and the residents went in and out informally of any of the rooms [p. 125].''

THE RESIDENTIAL PATTERN

The preceding case histories show that the residential pattern in Cerrada del Cóndor depends on spatial, economic, and kinship factors. In this section I shall present additional data obtained from a special survey on residence conducted in the shantytown during the year 1971.

When a new couple has no relatives in the Federal District, it will settle as a neolocal household. In the case of nuclear families having neither relatives nor other resources in the Federal District, the man usually migrates in advance of the remaining members of his household. He stays with friends until his economic situation permits his family to join him. In all other cases one observes a strong tendency for migrants to settle with relatives in the city; this tendency is bilocal with some predominance of patrilocality over matrilocality. In other words, the migrants favor staying with relatives of the husband's rather than of the wife's. Similar results have been found in a sample of marginal migrants in Monterrey; about 70% of these migrants joined households of the husband's kin (Browning and Feindt 1971:63). These results may be contrasted with the findings of Young and Willmot (1957:35), in a low-income neighborhood of London, where most young couples tended to join the households of the wife's kin.

Table 5.4 describes the residential pattern found for the shantytown of Cerrada del Cóndor. This table quantifies the initial residence after migration or (for nuclear families formed in the city) the initial residence of the couple. Only 13 households were authentically neolocal at the outset; these couples were either born in the Federal District or migrated at a very early age, which means that they presumably knew the city and could fend for themselves. A dominant pattern of initial residence with relatives has been widely reported among migrants in many parts of the world. One recent example is the pattern of rural–urban migration in Yugoslavia as described by Simic (1970:200–201).

Most of the families in Cerrada del Cóndor do not stay at their initial place of residence for long. The trend is toward a sequence of residential changes, as described in Chapter 3. Table 5.5 summarizes the pattern of changes in locality

TABLE 5.4

Initial Residence of the Couple in Mexico City

	Number		Percentage	
	Subgroup	Total	Subgroup	Total
With wife's relatives	16		9.8	
Near wife's relatives	21		13.0	
Total matrilocal		37		22.8
With husband's relatives	48		29.6	
Near husband's relatives	13		8.0	
Total patrilocal		61		37.6
With sons	8		5.0	
With job givers	6		3.7	
Alone	13		8.0	
Total neolocal		27		16.7
Near relatives of both	13		8.0	
With friends or countrymen	8		5.0	
Total others		21		13.0
Unknown		16		9.8
Total		162		99.8

as observed in the shantytown. This table is given as a transition matrix; i.e., each figure represents the number of cases beginning their residence as the column heading and ending up according to the row heading. For example, nine cases (5.6%) corresponded to the number of nuclear families initially matrilocal but neolocal at the time of the survey. The large number of unvarying preferences as to residential locality reflects the high proportion of young couples in Cerrada del Cóndor. Many of these couples were still living at their initial place of residence. In conclusion, patrilocality is predominant in the shantytown, though the proportion of patrilocality to matrilocality dropped from an initial 5:3 to 4.5:3 at the time of the survey.

The residence pattern and the related pattern of family organization must be viewed as the results of a dynamic process that strongly depends on economic circumstances, stage in the life cycle, availability of residential vacancies, personal relationships between relatives, and many other factors. The initial selection of a residence is often governed by economic considerations. Eventually, living conditions in the extended-family household may prove too crowded or taxing because of other problems, such as conflict between linear and collateral kin. This explains the tendency for new couples to seek an independent or neolocal residence. Still later there arise a series of new difficulties in the grow-

TABLE 5.5

Trends in Change of Residence

| | Initial residence | | | | | | | |
| | Patrilocal | | Matrilocal | | Neolocal | | Total | |
Current residence	Number	Percentage	Number	Percentage	Number	Percentage	Number	Percentage
Patrilocal	50	31.1	2	1.2	5	3.1	57	35.4
Matrilocal	4	2.5	35	21.8	1	.6	40	24.9
Neolocal	19	11.9	9	5.6	32	20.0	60	37.5
Total	73	45.5	46	28.6	38	23.7	157	97.8

TABLE 5.6

Evolution of Extended Households

Current residence	Initial residence							
	Patrilocal or matrilocal				Neolocal		Total	
	Single roof or lot		Jointed					
	Number	Percentage	Number	Percentage	Number	Percentage	Number	Percentage
Single roof or plot	37	23.1	2	1.2	1	.6	40	24.9
Jointed	16	9.9	36	22.4	5	3.1	57	35.4
Neolocal	22	13.7	6	3.8	32	20.0	60	37.5
Total	75	46.7	44	27.4	38	23.7	157	97.8

ing family: succeeding childbirths, economic problems, loss of job, or defection of the husband. Such difficulties often force the nuclear family to seek the shelter and protection of relatives. Table 5.6 shows how this process involves an increase in the number of jointed households as compared to single-roof or single-plot households.

The evolution of households, as the table shows, favors the jointed household, which increased from 27.4% to 35.4% in the sample. On the other hand, as many as 46.7% of nuclear families began their married life in the city as members of an extended household of the single-roof or single-plot type; yet only 24.9% of nuclear families were still members of such households at the time of the survey. This is particularly significant because of the large number of young couples in the sample. Many of these young couples were still members of extended-family households or were temporarily going through a neolocal situation. If I could have followed up the evolution of the neolocal households, I should probably have found that most of them evolved toward households of the jointed type.

In conclusion, the typical couple in Cerrada del Cóndor begins married life in the shelter of an extended household formed by relatives of the husband. They may be the husband's parents, though brothers, uncles, or cousins are also frequent options. Later the couple may pass through neolocal stages and may end up by becoming affiliated to a kinship group within an extended household of the jointed type. This pattern is not overwhelmingly dominant, however; there are many variations depending on circumstances of kinship, economy, and other factors. The cases in this chapter provide an insight into the complexities of the mechanism of household formation in the shantytown.

Urban industrial culture features an implicit ideal of neolocality, which is transmitted through the mass media. This ideal can rarely be fulfilled under the strained circumstances of marginality. The extended household of the jointed type may perhaps be viewed as a compromise between the rural-type extended family (sharing one and the same roof or plot) and the urban-type neolocal family. The jointed household is a typically urban solution adaptive both to the self-help and mutual assistance required of marginals and to the system of housing and real-estate property.

In somewhat analogous fashion, there is a prevailing cultural ideal of patrilocality, which becomes modified by the circumstances of migration and its sequel of widely scattered kinship groups. Relatives of the wife are preferred whenever the husband has no relatives in the city, or his relatives are not in a position to grant the required shelter. It sometimes happens that a wife's relatives can offer space in a plot or other facilities that are particularly attractive to a newly formed household.

It is also worth remembering that the patrilocal situation contains an element of potential friction between mother-in-law and daughter-in-law, which is not present to the same degree in matrilineal households. Women live together in the same household all day long and sleep in the same residential unit; the father-in-law and the son-in-law not only spend less time together but also may avail themselves of conflict-solving mechanisms through the institution of *cuatismo* and the use of alcohol. Hence matrilocality can be somewhat more stable than patrilocality and this tendency appears to be reflected in Table 5.5.

KINSHIP

In Cerrada del Cóndor the kinship system is bilateral. The descendants inherit the family names of both father and mother, though the father's family name is used first. An unmarried mother's child may use his mother's family name. However, in the vast majority of cases there is a continuity of kinship through both the father's and the mother's lineage, which is expressed by the use of both family names.

The community identifies an individual as a member of both families that appear in his name. From the point of view of the individual, there is a social group that includes all persons identified by him as relatives; this is the individual's kindred. Take as an example the kindred from Zacatecas shown in Figure 5.7. This kindred is related to a jointed-household network to be described in Chapter 6. The kindred is centered about a woman whom we will call Doña Chela.

Case History

Chela Villaseñor Esparza arrived in Cerrada del Cóndor in 1954; one of her sisters was an old-time resident of the shantytown, the wife of one of the original owners of the property. Doña Chela set up a small grocery store in the shantytown and her husband worked in the building trade. As time went by and with the help of her kinship relations with the shantytown owner, Doña Chela was able to assist in the migration of a large number of her kin. All such relatives, whether her own or her husband's, received lodging, housing, job-finding assistance, and credit in her store. For this reason, the kindred is centered about the Esparza–Villaseñor family. Actually the Esparzas are practically indifferent to the Villaseñores; however, all members of the kindred actively socialize with Doña Chela and with her husband.

The kindred may be grouped by six reciprocity networks, as shown in Figure 5.7. Network A includes the Esparza–Villaseñor family, one unmarried son, and a married daughter with her husband and five children. This network lives in an extended-household arrangement of the single-roof expense-sharing type. Network B is centered on Don Beto, a nephew of Doña Chela. (This network is described more extensively in Chapter 6.)

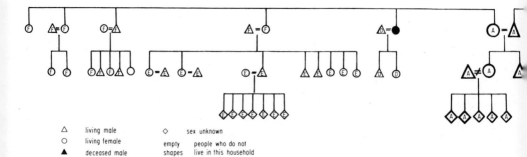

△	living male	◇	sex unknown
○	living female	empty	people who do not
▲	deceased male	shapes	live in this household
●	deceased female	△ ○	not in Cerrada del Cóndor

Figure 5.7. The Esparza–Villaseñor kindred, showing only that part of the kindred living in Cerrada del Cóndor. Network A, single-roof household; B, C, and F, jointed households; D, attached to another network; E, two households, one single-roof, one jointed.

It is an extended household of the jointed type and includes four generations. This is a very exclusive network whose members socialize only with Doña Chela and her husband.

Network C has already been described in this chapter as an example of a jointed-type extended household. The members of this network all descend from two deceased cousins of Doña Chela's husband. They socialize mainly with network A and, through Doña Chela, with members of network E.

Network D is not shown in Figure 5.7 in its entirety, because some of its members are relatives of Doña Chela's brother-in-law. This brother-in-law, currently widowed, has already been mentioned as the original owner of the shantytown property and as a prime source of Doña Chela's influence and power. Differences in economic status between networks A and D have prevented a reciprocal exchange relationship between these networks. Actually the relation may be described as a dyadic exchange between Doña Chela and her brother-in-law and nephews; there is no relationship with the remaining members of network D. Doña Chela pays rent to her brother-in-law and receives favors from him; it is an asymmetric relationship of the patron–client type.

Now, before I describe networks E and F, let me state that there is a great deal of contact between the members of these two networks. Doña Chela, her sisters, and her brother are close to their aged parents, who live downtown with another daughter. Doña Chela sees them about once a month, and her sisters and brother also visit with them quite regularly. Another brother lives in Puente Colorado and Doña Chela sees him frequently; there is also a brother who lives at the other end of town and whom she sees only when they meet at her mother's.

Network E includes Jacinta Villaseñor, her husband Ismael Rodriguez,

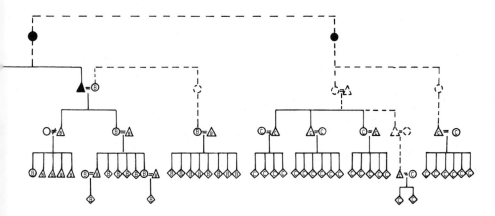

and their direct descendants. Ismael has no relatives in Mexico City. His parents live in their village in Zacatecas, with another son and his family of 10. A further brother of Ismael's, with his descendants, has settled in Torreón, Coahuila; a married daughter with five children lives in Durango. Ismael never travels and never visits with any member of his family.

The Rodriguez–Villaseñor family has 15 children, 5 of whom are deceased. That part of the family living in Cerrada del Cóndor shares an extended household, partly single-roof and partly jointed; there is no expense sharing. The household includes all sons and daughters except for a married son in Zacatecas (three sons), and a married daughter in Durango (three sons).

One large mutual assistance network includes all family members living in Cerrada del Cóndor. An important though less intense relationship of mutual assistance exists with Jacinta's parents, who live in Mexico City. There is contact by correspondence with her son, who lives in Zacatecas, thus leaving open the possibility for more relatives from Zacatecas to migrate to Mexico City with the assistance of their relatives there.

Enrique, the eldest son of the Rodriguez–Villaseñor family, is married to Juanita Dominguez, who comes from the Rodriguez's hometown in Zacatecas. Her parents and most of her relatives are still living there. One of her cousins has married one of her brothers-in-law; they were married in Zacatecas but live now in Cerrada del Cóndor. At first Juanita was reluctant to migrate and leave most of her family behind; however "she had no choice" but to abandon the village because 2 successive years of drought had spoiled the harvest. There was nothing to eat, and all the time her mother-in-law (a 6-year resident of the shantytown) was writing letters urging them to migrate to the city. Enrique and one of his brothers finally decided to move; they stayed in the shantytown for 3 months and then fetched their respective families. A room near Enrique's parents became vacant at that time; his mother quickly held it for them. This happened in 1970; Juanita has since returned only once to the village and her husband has forbidden her any further visits. Both Enrique and his brother are members of the extended-family network headed by their parents in Cerrada del Cóndor, which includes their wives (who are first cousins) and their descendants.

The last of the Rodriguez–Villaseñor daughters living in the shantytown is also married to a man of the same Zacatecas village. Four years ago they migrated directly to stay with a half-sister of Jacinta. Her husband's relatives are still in Zacatecas, except for a sister who is living in Mexico City (though they do not see each other). This home has just broken up and the woman with her three children is now living with her parents.

Finally, network F is an extended household of the jointed type, which includes two nuclear families plus an unmarried sister.

The present example affords a panoramic overview of kindred formation in Cerrada del Cóndor. It confirms that contact among kin is conditioned to spatial proximity and to closeness of kinship in terms of the nuclear family of procreation or of orientation. As a nuclear family is scattered through migration or death, contact with more remote kin tends to become confined to those relatives who live in proximity to each other. For relatives living in Mexico City, real contact is limited in practice to those who live in the same shantytown or within walking distance. Regular visiting over greater distances is largely limited to first-degree relatives, particularly a mother with her sons and daughters. Even brothers living in the same city often lose contact with each other except for occasional meetings at the mother's home; if the mother dies they may stop seeing each other altogether.

This kinship system is characteristic of much of Latin America (Foster 1965), and of other societies particularly of Latin Catholic background. Among the examples found in the literature are urban French Canadians (Garigue 1970:123–135) and Italian migrants in Boston (Ganz 1965). Thus, among the Italian migrants there was a tendency toward the formation of peer groups that included collateral relatives (such as brothers, cousins, and brothers-in-law). These peer groups were based on mutual compatibility and tended to function as intimate kindreds during the lifetime of the participants. On marriage, "each of the spouses is centrifugally attracted by their respective family circles, unlike the middle class where usually the effects are centripetal and tend to bring the couple closer together [Ganz 1965:45–46]."

The structural pattern among extended families that span two or three generations in Cerrada del Cóndor differs in no essential way from the one described by Foster (1965:6) in Tzintzuntzan. After an initial disorganization produced by migration, the kindreds are regrouped and reconstituted in the shantytown. Where the parents have died or do not live in Mexico City, we observe fraternal extended families such as the peer groups described by Ganz. There are eight examples (27% of all extended families) in Cerrada del Cóndor. Most extended families include up to three generations; in one case an extended family included four generations.

A nuclear family that decides to live with a certain group of relatives thereby expresses a definite priority of preferences. First preference usually goes to parents and brothers; uncles and cousins come next. The more distant a kinship relation, the greater is the role played by congeniality and economic convenience. The availability of vacancies is rarely the controlling factor since families will settle for whatever space is available, sleeping on the floor until a vacancy develops. When a migrant has relatives of comparable rank in different parts of Mexico City the decision will depend on economic factors and congeniality. Once his lot has been cast with a given group of relatives the area of his future residential moves is usually circumscribed to his initial neighborhood of residence.

It may happen that the nuclear family has no relatives at all in the shantytown. There are 30 such families (18% of surveyed households; i.e., less than 10% of nuclear families) in Cerrada del Cóndor. The distribution of these families as to closest of kin is shown in Table 5.7.

These families fall in two main groups. Either they enjoy a greater occupational stability than the average family of the shantytown, a fact that makes them less dependent on mutual assistance based on kinship, or else they are elderly people, or families abandoned by their relatives (and in this case they are usually very poor). In either case the lack of nearby relatives may indicate an unusual economic or social situation within the norm of marginality.

Many settlers in Cerrada del Cóndor have relatives in neighboring Las Aguilas or in Puente Colorado (see Figure 3.1). The latter is a nearby shantytown quite similar to Cerrada del Cóndor. There is some moving of families back and forth between the two shantytowns. With more distant shantytowns the social contact

TABLE 5.7

Nuclear Families without Relatives in the Shantytown

	Number	Percentage
Relatives near Cerrada del Cóndor	6	20.0
Relatives elsewhere in the metropolitan area	17	56.6
All relatives outside of Mexico City	5	16.6
No relatives	1	3.3
Unknown	1	3.3
Total	30	99.8

TABLE 5.8

Geographical Distribution of Relatives in the Federal District[a]

	Number
A. In nearby *colonias*	
Puente Colorado	25
Olivar del Conde	6
Las Aguilas	15
Merced Gómez	12
Mixcoac	2
Copilco	2
Tizapán	4
Tlalpan	3
Los Alpes	3
Tlacopac	2
San Angel, Contreras, and San Jerónimo	3
B. In more distant *colonias*	
Tacubaya	3
Tacuba	3
Narvarte	2
Del Valle	2
Piloto	2
Aurora	2
Capulín and Calzada de Puebla	2

[a]See map, Figure 3.1.

is much less, though some contact may exist. Table 5.8 affords an idea of the distribution of relatives within the Federal District.

Whenever a settler is asked a question about his relatives, he tends to name first all the members of his nuclear family of orientation or of procreation. Next he will usually name the relatives who live close by. If the parents live elsewhere in Mexico City with other relatives, such relatives may be counted as part of the close kin group because of the frequency of visits. On the other hand, after the parents die the relationship with such relatives (as with uncles or more distant cousins) tends to fade. *The effective community for the individual is made of relatives living nearby.* Special congeniality between relatives living in other parts of the urban area may induce a sequence of residential changes, until the group of congenial relatives is finally reunited in one and the same neighborhood.

Among the distancing factors between relatives, socioeconomic mobility is foremost. A relative whose status is rising becomes less dependent on the need for economic exchange with members of his family network. He stops asking for assistance and eventually he moves away unless patron–client relations develop that might become important for both (see Chapter 6, on networks). The frequency of personal contact between such relatives, even among brothers, decreases drastically.

As a rule, relatives who live in Cerrada del Cóndor see each other every day. If they live in Las Aguilas they may see each other once a day, and if in Puente Colorado once or twice a week. Close relatives living in Merced Gómez, Barranca, or Mixcoac visit each other once or twice a month. Visits that involve a bus ride are still less frequent. Such relations become important, however, when a family is thinking about a change of residence.

RELATIVES IN THE COUNTRY

No matter how rapidly the migrants adapt to the urban environment, they tend to maintain rural contacts for quite a long time. The relationship with country relatives is semivoluntary in the sense that the element of personal preference becomes important. This new type of relationship is typically maintained through a constant exchange of visits. Brandes in Spain (1975:126–128) and Simić in Yugoslavia (1970:215–217, 220) have described a kinship pattern between country and city relatives that greatly resembles the one in Cerrada del Cóndor. Such a relationship is advantageous to relatives in the city and in the countryside alike.

Some migrants maintain economic interests such as animals or inheritance rights to a property in their place of origin. This is possible as long as these interests can be entrusted to a close relative in the village. A migrant will often see this tie to the place of origin as a source of psychological and economic security. In case of hard times he can always go back to the countryside. The peasant relative who remains behind sees his city kin as a resource for possible future migration (to himself or to his descendants), as well as a source of assistance in money and in kind. In Yugoslavia it was found that "continued kinship ties between the countryside and the city represent a material and psychological security against hard luck [Simić 1970:220]."

An example of such continued kinship ties is Guadalupe, who regularly sent money orders to her mother in the country. She worked in a home as a maid, but then she had a baby. She left the baby with her mother, who agreed to raise her until the little girl would be big enough to stay with her mother or to be acceptable to her patrons. Then Guadalupe got married. Her brother became a seasonal migrant to Mexico City during the slack season in the countryside. Whenever he was in town, he stayed with his sister for months at a time. Guadalupe became pregnant again, and her doctor ordered rest; she then packed up and stayed with her mother for 2 full months.

Such characteristic two-way exchanges between city and countryside are clearly beneficial to both parties. Yet this interaction becomes weaker as the village-based family is scattered by the migration process. The second generation born in the city is often completely devoid of rural ties.

The frequency of visits to the village depends on the relative distance and on the closeness of relatives (parents, brothers, sons, uncles) in the countryside. Unmarried men or women travel a great deal back and forth; they often induce new migrants to come along to the city where they will help them find a job. Married migrants who maintain an interest in a joint property with some relative in the village may return once or twice a year for visiting or helping with the harvest. Visits often coincide with ritual occasions, such as the fiesta of the village patron saint, Mother's Day, or All Saints' Day.

Between visits contact is maintained through money remittances, correspondence, and word-of-mouth news transmitted through fellow villagers. During the early years of urban residence in particular, a migrant keeps an interest in village gossip and other details concerning the native place. Gradually, however, migrants are assimilated into the city and form their own little community of relatives and former countrymen in the urban environment. As the stream of relatives decays so does the interest of the settler in the affairs of his former village. The following comments are extracted from interviews with informants representing about one-fourth of the heads of families and spouses in Cerrada del Cóndor:

> "I have not been to the village since my parents and grandparents died. I used to go before and I used to send money."

> "I have not seen my parents in 18 years, that is, since I got married and came to Mexico City to live with my husband."

> "I have lived in the Federal District for many years, I have not been back and I have lost touch."

> "Since my mother died I have not returned; my dad has gotten married again and I do not get along with my stepmother."

> "All my brothers now live in town; I used to go and bring them some money; I don't go anymore."

In conclusion, as Firth and Dyamour (1970:145) have pointed out:

> Any investigation of kinship in an urban environment soon brings out the great degree of variation in relations with kin. . . . Among the correlates of the varying recognitional maintenance of kin ties would appear to be the following: residential accessibility; common economic interests, as in occupation, or in property holding; composition of household; composition of elementary family, especially as regards that of the sibling group; the biological range of persons available for kin recognition; the existence of key personalities in the kin field to take the initiative of kin contacts; and the phase of development in which any given family finds itself. Through these combinations of circumstances runs the element of personal selection, leading again to the question of what regularities can be discerned.

These factors all contribute in defining kinship relations in Cerrada del Cóndor.

Networks of Reciprocal Exchange

A social network is a field of relationships between individuals (Barnes 1954:98–99). The term *field* is an abstract descriptive concept; it refers to a space, such that each point in the space is associated with a value of some physical or social variable. For example, a magnetic field in physics is a three-dimensional space, each of whose points is associated with a value of the magnetic intensity; or the gravitational field of a planet is the set of all gravity values in space centered about that planet. Similarly, a social field is a set of individuals who are related through some suitable variable, which must be specified for the purpose.

In the anthropological literature one also finds a more general use of the term *network:* According to Radcliffe-Brown, the "set of social relations which exists in reality [1968:190]." Such general networks constitute the principal object of study of social anthropology. However, in recent years the term *network* has increasingly been used in the more specialized meaning assigned to it chiefly by British anthropologists (e.g., Barnes 1954; Dirks 1972; Mitchel 1969; Mayer 1968; Wolfe 1970). The variable used to define the social field may refer to any aspects of a social relation (kinship, information, economic exchange), and it is up to the anthropologist to define it in each particular case. A field may be diffuse, or it may be centered about a given individual just as the terrestrial gravity field is centered about the earth. In the latter case, the underlying variable is correlated with the physical and social distance of each individual to the center of the network. Each individual in turn may be thought of as the center of another network, or he may belong to several networks at once.

I propose to use the concept of social network much as the concept of field is used in physics. Both are scientific abstractions used to facilitate a compact description of a set of more or less complex relationships between points or individuals in a space. The question about the "real" existence of a social network is meaningless; it is an abstract category defined at the convenience of the anthropologist. It is not a native category. The response of an informant to questions about his "reciprocity network" would be blank; the field-worker has to discover the network structure in terms of information on the exchange of goods and services.

For the purpose of studying marginal populations in large urban centers of Latin America, I propose to discuss a type of network defined by the flow of reciprocal exchange of goods, services, and economically valuable information. It is convenient to use a variable to be called *intensity of exchange* as the underlying variable of the networks described in this book. Intensity of exchange is defined as the relative measure of the reciprocal flow of goods and services, in quantity, frequency, and social value, within a conventional time interval. Thus we may speak of a relatively *intense* exchange among close relatives who live together in a household in Cerrada del Cóndor. I shall interchangeably refer to such exchange networks as *reciprocity networks,* because the type of exchange observed in these networks is reciprocity. This choice of an underlying variable for the networks is not altogether arbitrary; it corresponds to the demonstrable importance of reciprocal exchange of economically meaningful goods, services, and information in the process of migration and survival in the city. The fabric of reciprocity networks in the shantytown is closely interwoven with patterns of traditional institutions such as the family, fictive kinship, and friendship, jointly constituting the social structure of a shantytown.

Dyadic (one-to-one) reciprocal exchange of goods and services can occur between any pair of settlers, neighbors or otherwise. However, the anthropologist quickly realizes that the intensity of giving and receiving is not uniform throughout the shantytown. There are localized knots or webs of high flow of reciprocal exchange, where several families of neighbors have banded together as it were to form reciprocity networks in the present usage of this term. These networks are distinguished from the ego-centered network of a given settler by the fact that they are *exocentric;* i.e., each participant exchanges goods and services with all other participants. Participation in such an exocentric network does not exclude dyadic relations of reciprocity outside the network; in other words, the exocentric network overlaps, but does not contain, the egocentric networks of each of the participants. What distinguishes the exocentric network is the high intensity of flow of reciprocal exchange, so that by far the largest number of reciprocal transactions in the shantytown takes place between members of such networks.

CLASSIFICATION OF RECIPROCITY NETWORKS

Consider first the *egocentric* network—the set of all individuals who maintain some reciprocal exchange of goods and services with ego. The term *reciprocal exchange* excludes all casual, once-and-for-all transactions as found in commercial exchange. Reciprocity is a type of exchange that occurs only in the context of a long-term social relation, which is conditioned, or at least promoted, by an equality of economic wants between partners.

In an egocentric network each individual dyadic relationship may be described by its intensity of reciprocal exchange. This intensity of reciprocal exchange depends on four factors: (1) formal social distance, (2) physical distance, (3) economic distance, and (4) psychosocial distance, which will be discussed next.

Formal Social Distance. In Cerrada del Cóndor the economic relations of reciprocal exchange of goods and services are intertwined with and partly camouflaged by kinship relations. In most extended families, the household also functions as a reciprocity network. It may be of some interest to distinguish between networks, social groups, and households. The social group is a recognized category within the culture, with its norms and values, its membership attributes, its boundary, its objectives, and other cultural forms that may serve to identify it. The family may be a social group. A household is a kinship group that shares a residential unit plus certain domestic functions (see Chapter 5). A reciprocity network, on the other hand, frequently contains nonkin neighbors as well as kinship groups.

Every social group prescribes a set of norms for reciprocal exchange; e.g., the relationship parent–child normally implies a deferred reciprocity arrangement, based on the sustenance and protection provided by parents during the childhood period. In rural Mexico one finds prescribed forms of reciprocity for each formal social distance: between brothers, between *compadres,* between friends, and so on. Such basic reciprocal norms continue to be observed among urban marginal populations in Latin American cities, as has been often pointed out (e.g., Bryce-Laporte 1970:70, 89, 92, 94; Butterworth 1962:98–113; Lewis 1966, 1969a:12; Mangin 1970; Roberts 1973).

Physical Distance. Social closeness, such as consanguinity, is not enough to guarantee a high intensity of reciprocal exchange in the urban marginal situation. The longer it takes to walk or travel to visit a partner, the smaller is the likelihood for a sustained contact. Where one or more bus rides are involved, the flow of reciprocal exchange may drop to zero even between brothers. The daily interaction between close neighbors can, and frequently will, generate intense relations of reciprocal exchange between erstwhile strangers; such relations may eventually become consecrated through *compadrazgo*. Thus kinship by itself may not be enough to overcome the hurdle of physical distance, and physical closeness between strangers does have the power to create a basis for exchange relations.

Economic Distance. The momentary needs of shantytown settlers are determined at all times by their balance of resources and wants. Whenever the needs of two partners are uneven the exchange tends to become asymmetrical between them; this generates differentials of power between the participants (Blau 1964:112–113). Whenever power differentials occur within a reciprocity network the network eventually splits or disintegrates. Reciprocity as such is based on an equality of wants; otherwise the relationship either becomes severed or converts to a patron–client relation.

Psychosocial Distance. The preceding objective factors are subjectively translated into a complex psychosocial variable that I have called *confianza* (Lomnitz 1971:100). As utilized by Latin American informants, the term *confianza* denotes a kind of trusting relation established between two individuals. It implies a mutual desire and disposition to initiate or maintain a relationship of reciprocal exchange. Thus *confianza* presupposes simultaneously a certain amount of familiarity (social proximity), opportunity (physical proximity), and compatibility of needs (economic proximity). The rare ethnographic references to psychosocial distance in Latin America have not done justice to the considerable importance of this universal variable in social life.

These four factors regulating the flow of reciprocal exchange in networks are not to be conceived as static. They fluctuate in time according to the ups and downs of the life cycle and the emergencies inherent in shantytown life. Important variations in basic reciprocity patterns may be found in other socioeconomic strata; thus, daily face-to-face contact, which is essential in the shantytown networks, may be substituted by frequent and lengthy telephone conversations in the urban middle and upper classes (Lomnitz 1976:4). The use of modern means of communications allows the growth and expansion of reciprocity networks, which may thus be extended beyond the average four to six families participating in a network in Cerrada del Cóndor.

Exocentric networks, or reciprocity networks for short, are local knots of high-intensity exchange in the web of reciprocity relations that covers the shantytown. Each cluster of high-intensity exchange comprises only two to six nuclear families. A characteristic aspect of these networks is the fact that exchange is not centered on one individual but is practiced by all partners alike. Often an exocentric network is a formally constituted social group such as an extended family; in other cases, it is a group of relatives or neighbors whose social relation is one of economic cooperation. Each member of an exocentric network may maintain additional dyadic reciprocity relations with individuals beyond the network; such relations tend to be less intense and less stable than those practiced within the network.

Shantytown networks evolve in time according to the flow of reciprocal exchange of goods and services. There is a feedback between the individual act of exchange and the increase of *confianza,* which promotes future exchange. In extended-family networks, the network may remain stable for many years or as long as internal conflict can be minimized. Such networks grow to a size where they may become self-sufficient, so that dyadic relations of reciprocal exchange outside the network drop to a minimum. In general, however, there are frequent changes in composition of the networks due to arrivals of migrants from the country, marriage of offspring, new descendants, conflict between in-laws, internal disputes, forcible eviction, and the physical destruction of housing units, as well as the lure of better opportunities or more congenial kin elsewhere. Accordingly, the majority of networks have a fluctuating membership, and their stability is constantly threatened by internal and external factors.

NETWORKS IN CERRADA DEL CÓNDOR

In the course of my fieldwork in Cerrada del Cóndor I identified 45 exocentric networks among relatives who practiced a system of reciprocal exchange. The social composition of these networks was as follows: Thirty networks were formed by consanguineal and affinal kin; 8 networks were based on kinship but included at least one nonkin member family, and 7 networks were formed by nonkin neighbors. The distribution of networks by type is seen in Table 6.1.

The size of a network fluctuates because of the processes of growth, division, regroupment, and disintegration. According to Table 6.1, the 45 known net-

TABLE 6.1

Nuclear Families per Network

Number of nuclear families	Relatives only	Mixed network	Neighbors only	Total
2	5	0	4	9
3	7	3	3	13
4	9	1	0	10
5	4	2	0	6
6	3	2	0	5
Unknown	2	0	0	2
Total	30	8	7	45

works include a total of 157 nuclear families, which gives an average of 3.65 families per network. Notice also that networks of nonkin neighbors tend to be relatively smaller; they include 3 nuclear families at the most.

The case histories described in this chapter illustrate the presence of a continuum of stability, autonomy, and intensity of reciprocal exchange within the networks. I intend to show that the gradations within this continuum are correlated with variables governing the internal structure of the networks. The highest intensity of exchange is found in extended family networks that practice expense sharing, the practice of authentic pooling of resources. One such case has already been described in Chapter 5. The networks of nonkin neighbors represent the opposite extreme; here the exchange tends to be dyadic (one-to-one relations dominate), and the exchange tends to be less stable and less intense.

Case Histories

1. A jointed family network.   Don Beto Z., a miner from Zacatecas, widower, migrated to Mexico City in 1963, entrusting his five children to the care of his elderly mother and one of his brothers. His destination was the home of a cousin (female) in Cerrada del Cóndor. This cousin had become related through marriage to one of the earlier settlers and owners of the shantytown, who had helped her install a small grocery and variety store in the shantytown in 1954.

Don Beto found work in the construction of the subway. As a start, he succeeded in getting his brother-in-law from Zacatecas to join him; both worked in the subway and both eventually brought the remainder of their respective nuclear families to Mexico City. Initially Don Beto rented a room adjoining his cousin's store; his brother-in-law rented another room one block away. However, after their families joined them the two households began a relation of mutual reciprocal exchange through Don Beto's sister, who visited her mother, Doña Lupe, every day (Doña Lupe lived with Don Beto). Two years later the two households joined in the purchase of a group of one-room dwellings belonging to an extended family that was leaving the shantytown. Ownership extended to the construction itself, since both Don Beto and his brother-in-law are paying rent for the property on which the shacks are erected. The owners of the plot are distant relatives through Don Beto's cousin.

The arrangement of the dwellings is shown in Figure 6.1. There is an open yard, which is used in common for purposes of doing the laundry and raising chickens and other animals. Also there is a common outhouse. Each family owns its housing unit, and the household economies are separate. The social structure may be described as a network of two nuclear families held together by a common matriarch. The exchange

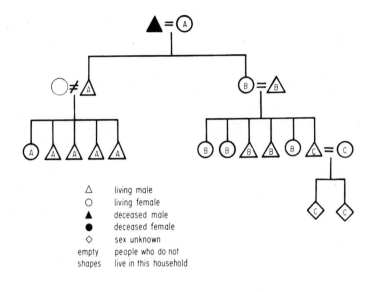

△ living male
○ living female
▲ deceased male
● deceased female
◇ sex unknown
empty people who do not
shapes live in this household

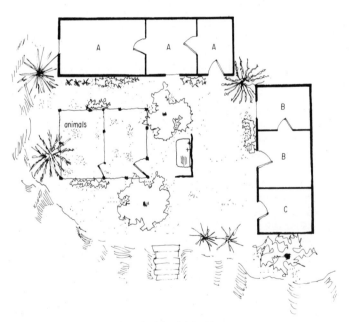

Figure 6.1. An extended household of the jointed type.

within the network is very intense. Doña Lupe, the matriarch, is in charge of the household for Don Beto but is very close to her daughter. Children of both households "are like brothers." The daughter does the shopping for her mother. There was a time when Don Beto was out of work; all that time he received economic support as a loan from his brother-in-law; also, his sister did the cooking for his children, and his cousin sold him merchandise on credit from her little store.

In 1972 Doña Virginia (Don Beto's sister) married off one son and one daughter. Both married into Cerrada del Cóndor families. The son's bride joined her husband's home in the extended-family pattern. When their first child was born, the new grandfather built a one-room dwelling adjoining his own for the new nuclear family. On the other hand, the married daughter moved away to live with her own in-laws in Cerrada del Cóndor.

The year 1973 saw the arrival from Zacatecas of a niece of Don Beto's with her husband and her eight children, "all of them starving because there is no water and no work." They arrived as refugees and stayed first with their cousin Doña Virginia, deeply impressed with the relative opulence of their city relatives. Thus they lived for 2 months on the generosity of their kin. Doña Virginia's husband took her cousin's husband to a job at the construction where he was working at the moment. At the time of my last survey they were planning to add another one-room structure, in which case the network would have grown to four jointed nuclear families.

Reciprocal exchange within this all-kin network is very intense at all levels. The men help each other in finding jobs; the wives exchange food, money, information, and gossip. There is mutual cooperation in building new housing units and in the upkeep of each others' property. Exchange relations have been formalized through *compadrazgo*: Doña Lupe and Doña Virginia are godmothers of two of the children. But each nuclear family carries on its own economy.

Several of the older boys are also working, in addition to their fathers. The older girls have no jobs, but they have been allowed to participate in a short course for health workers in the shantytown health center; at the time of the survey they were doing volunteer work as assistants of the medical intern. Don Beto's eldest son and his cousin (Doña Virginia's son) were both working in a small rubber factory in Las Aguilas; at the time of the survey they had both lost their jobs. The small children did odd jobs for tips, such as taking care of tombs in the local cemetery or watching parked cars; their average daily earnings were about 5 pesos each. At the time of the survey they were earning from 10 to 20 pesos a day carrying packages for customers at a supermarket. On school holidays they make a little more. Don Beto works in an industrial plant for 50 pesos a day, and his brother-in-law is a bricklayer who makes about the same amount.

The network has made no attempt to socialize with another network of relatives from the same part of the country who live in the shantytown, relatives of the cousin who helped Don Beto get established in the shantytown. Members of the two networks are acquainted but have little contact with each other, because Don Beto and his brother-in-law "do not drink" and therefore have no opportunities to socialize. Whenever the assistance of one of these relatives is desired (perhaps in relation to a job problem), Don Beto's cousin acts as a go-between. This cousin has adopted children who live with her in the shantytown, but the network members do not relate to them either.

Doña Lupe, the matriarch, has a brother in the Federal District, who lives in a remote part of town; they very seldom see each other. Once a year Don Beto gets together with other migrants from his village to participate in the festivity in honor of the Virgin, who is the village patron saint. At that time he meets many other migrants and they all dance for the Virgin. The rest of the year he never sees anybody from his home village. His brother is still living in Zacatecas, and Don Beto maintains some active contact through him. This brother occasionally comes to Mexico City for visits; he has been helpful to Don Beto in obtaining certain documents, such as his birth certificate. Don Beto's children who were born in Zacatecas have godparents who still live in the village.

On the whole, this network is nearly autonomous and self-sufficient. All its members are relatives. The daily reciprocal exchange of favors represents the basic fact of life within the network; this includes ritual occasions such as baptisms, which are financed and celebrated in common. Reciprocity covers all the minor and major emergencies of marginal life: illness, loss of job, migration. The absence of expense sharing is a major difference between this type of network and some of the extended networks described in Chapter 5.

2. A mixed network of kinsmen and neighbors. This network is centered about the Contreras family, originally from an *ejido* in the State of Guanajuato. First to migrate was Juan, whose in-laws were living in the shantytown of Puente Colorado. Juan took his family to live with his in-laws; there he learned the craft of tombstone polishing. He moved to Cerrada del Cóndor, where he rented a room. Several years later Juan Contreras brought his parents, who were also landless peasants; his father became a tombstone polisher. An unmarried brother, today also a tombstone polisher, came with his parents at that time; two married brothers and one married sister still remained behind in the village.

A few years later, the two married brothers also decided to migrate to Cerrada del Cóndor. Initially they lived with their father; both brothers were introduced to the tombstone polisher's craft, like the other men in the family. Either their father or their brother would take them to the shop, teach them the trade, and share their salary with them until they were able to fend for themselves. The two brothers' wives happen to be sisters. They in turn began to bring their own relatives to the shantytown.

The wives' kindred in Cerrada del Cóndor included (by order of arrival): an unmarried sister, a married niece with her nuclear family, and another niece who was unmarried. The two unmarried women found work as housemaids living in with their employers. They would regularly visit with their relatives on their days off, or stay with them whenever they lost their jobs. The married niece, by name Josefa, was joined by her unmarried brother from Guanajuato; he slept on the floor and worked together with her husband. Some years later, the two wives' only brother took to spending the off-seasons in Mexico City; those were the months when there was no work to be found in the village. He had been a sharecropper for his in-laws and rented a pair of oxen, but had no land of his own. While living at his sister's he polished tombstones, with his brothers-in-law.

At the time of my initial survey the situation was as follows: One reciprocity network had formed around the two sisters (Valentina and Gabriela), the married niece (Josefa), the two unmarried girls who worked as maids, and the two unmarried men who were seasonal migrants. An adjoining room was vacated, and the husbands of Valentina and Gabriela decided to bring in a friend, a companion at work who was not a relative at the time, but later became related to Valentina's family through *compadrazgo*. Let us call this network A. About half a block away one finds network B, which includes the Contreras family including Juan's parents and an unmarried brother.

Now Meche, the unmarried sister of Valentina and Gabriela, had a baby girl who was sent back to the village in the care of Meche's mother. Two years later she had another child, a boy, who was entrusted to the care of her sisters in the shantytown during the daytime. A year later she went to live with the boy's father, in consensual marriage. At that time Meche was able to take charge of her first baby as well. She visited with her sisters every day. Marcela, the unmarried niece, began to stay with Meche on her days off. There she met the brother of one of Meche's neighbors; they got married and moved in with the neighbors. This was the beginning of a third reciprocity network.

Meanwhile, brother Miguel who used to come to Cerrada del Cóndor during the off-season made longer and longer stays in the shantytown. However, he has until now been prevented from making the move to Mexico City by the fact that his mother and wife refuse to leave the village. When last heard of, Miguel was sleeping at Meche's, and his family as well as his oxen were being taken care of by his sister and brother-in-law in the village.

Here we have a complicated interaction between three reciprocity net-

Courtyard used by the household of Valentina and Gabriela. Notice the large tub and assorted laundering gear. People in Cerrada del Cóndor love potted plants.

Another view of the preceding housing arrangement (see also Figure 6.2). Each door gives access to a room, entailing a separate rental fee. Such courts are called vecindades *and normally belong to a single owner.*

works, one of which (network A) includes a nonkin neighbor. The general situation is fluid because of the coming and going of migrants and the various events and disasters in the life of the marginals. Thus, for a while Gabriela's husband stopped drinking and his economic level began to rise. Gabriela acquired a number of household items, such as a food blender, a set of plastic-top dining-room furniture, a television set, and a record player. By that time Gabriela began to reduce her participation in the reciprocal exchange. For example, if a brother-in-law came in from the village to raise money for some family emergency, she was the only member of the network who would not contribute. Soon there was gossip among the other members of the network, and the social relations cooled. Finally Gabriela and her husband moved away to an urban-type room two blocks beyond the shantytown limits.

Two years later, the roof fell in on two of the rooms and it became necessary to vacate them, thus altering the composition of the network. Josefa's family moved to Puente Colorado, where her husband had an aunt who owned a plot of land; there they built a shack of their own. Teófila, the nonkin neighbor, moved with her family next to her sister-in-law, who also lived in Cerrada del Cóndor and who was a member of the macronetwork of migrants from Villela. Meanwhile Gabriela's husband had taken up drinking again, yielding to the influence of his father, his brothers, and his brothers-in-law; he stopped giving money to Gabriela and started to beat her, thus forcing her to seek shelter with her earlier network. Valentina was happy to welcome the stray sheep back to the fold. A nearby room became vacant and Gabriela moved in with her family; her sisters helped and took care of the family when Gabriela fell ill. Sometime later Gabriela had a baby and her sisters paid the maternity bill. Thus they took care of their sister and her family until Gabriela's husband got back in line.

At the time of my last survey, Valentina's husband had bought a plot of land jointly with his brother Juan. Meche had put some money of her own into this operation and Valentina has asked her to join them whenever she liked.

Reportedly Gabriela will move in with network B, specifically into the room that is to be vacated by Juan Contreras whenever he joins Valentina's family. Thus there will be a new network, which is likely to be more stable because it will be established on its own plot. This network will include the families of Valentina, Meche, and Juan. The complete kinship diagram is shown in Figure 6.2.

Let us now discuss the exchange situation of network A, which originally included the families of Gabriela, Valentina, Teófila, and Josefa. After the two last-named families had departed from the network, a new nonkin neighbor joined. The residential situation is a U-shaped court with all the

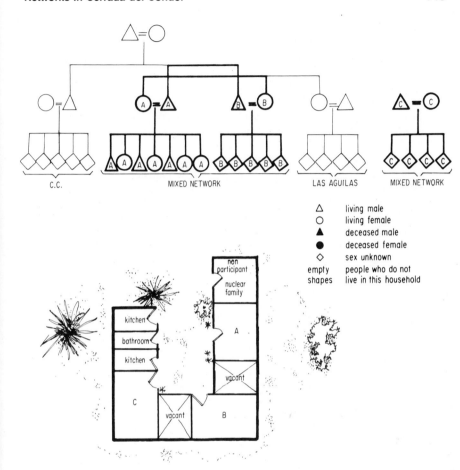

Figure 6.2.   A mixed network, containing an extended family (A, B) and a nonkin neighbor family (C). Both families are related to different macronetworks (A and B to the Guanajuato macronetwork, and C to the Villela macronetwork).

rooms in a row facing the kitchens. The inhabitants of this court share the same outhouse (Figure 6.2). There are no windows and the doors are used to let in the light as well as the air. However, since there are families in the same court who are not members of the network, curtains cover the doorways, to ensure a minimum of privacy. Of course, members of the network freely use any of the rooms pertaining to the network.

Among the other neighbors in the court there was a slightly older couple without children who became good friends with Valentina: "The lady has been very good to me, once she gave me 20 pesos so I could take my child to the doctor. I would be embarrassed to ask favors from her." The husband is a drugstore employee and enjoys a stable income; therefore this family did not join the network, as the economic basis for reciprocity was lacking in spite of the good personal relations. When the couple moved away, the vacant room was quickly snapped up by Gabriela's family.

Among the outward signs of reciprocity relations within this network, one notices that any adult will ask any of the children to bring some water, to take care of the babies, or to go on small errands. There is somewhat less familiarity when dealing with children who are not relatives, particularly when it comes to scolding a child. The women are forever borrowing money, food, pots, pans, and clothing from each other. The men as well as the women borrow and swap items of clothing. Whenever a member of the network is sick in bed, the others take care of him or her and, if necessary, take charge of the children. Again there are slight shades of difference when dealing with nonkin neighbors; thus Valentina and Gabriela address their neighbor as "comadre" or "señora," but they address each other as "sister" or simply by first names. There is a greater degree of *confianza* between sisters than there is between sisters-in-law or between nonkin neighbors.

The historical evolution of the network supports the assumption that reciprocity with nonkin neighbors is conditioned upon closeness in space. Personal friendship is not severed after a neighbor moves away, and there may be continued visiting several times a week if both families still live in the shantytown and if the women meet every day at the water faucet. However, there is no more reciprocal exchange the moment they stop being neighbors. A relation between relatives creates more *confianza* and may allow a relatively important reciprocal exchange to survive a spatial separation. In either case, though, the everyday type of reciprocal exchange as observed in networks is necessarily severed.

Thus, Meche used to visit her sisters every day; alternatively, her sisters would visit Meche, or at the very least dispatch a son or daughter as a messenger to carry news between their respective networks. The distance was about eight blocks. When Meche was working, her small boy was left in the care of the sisters. There were also frequent loans of money and food. Once Meche's husband went without a job for 2 weeks and his sisters-in-law loaned him money. Some months later, Meche's husband "was doing well." One day he noticed that Valentina was going around with a pair of torn shoes, so he gave some money to Meche with instructions to buy her sister a pair of new shoes. During Gabriela's illness,

Meche went to see her every day and took care of the children, despite the fact that there were also relatives and neighbors in Gabriela's own network who might have done the same for her. Thus the intensity of reciprocal exchange between Meche and her sisters could almost be compared to the expected intensity of exchange between members of a network. It may be predicted that the daily exchange intensity will increase once Meche is integrated into her new network with Juan and Valentina.

The intensity of exchange between members of networks A and B is quite significant. The daughters-in-law visit with their mother-in-law at least once a day, as the two networks are only half a block away from each other. The Contreras brothers go to work together every morning, they help each other out finding jobs, and they drink together. Drinking, incidentally, is a joint activity among all men of both networks including the nonkin neighbor. Brother Miguel, the occasional visitor from the village, was a constant participant in the drinking circle until the time he had a serious dispute with his brothers-in-law. Miguel then had to move to Meche's place; her husband neither works nor drinks with his brothers-in-law. This was a contributing factor in the formation of a new network around Meche. The presence of Miguel has also moderated the intensity of exchange between Meche and network A; besides, Meche already had three children and it had become more difficult for her to visit her sisters as often as she used to.

Within a given network there may be a subtle evolution of reciprocity relations according to the fluctuations in *confianza* between its members. Each of the members maintains dyadic reciprocity relations with outsiders, which may lose or gain in importance depending on changes in the internal composition of the network. Thus Juan Contreras' niece Josefa had always maintained good personal relations with the relatives of her husband, who lived in Puente Colorado. When her residential unit was ruined she was able to move in with these relatives. Teófila, Valentina's nonkin neighbor and *comadre,* had cultivated the friendship of her sister-in-law in Cerrada del Cóndor, so she moved in with her when the roof caved in on her dwelling. Valentina and Gabriela, too, have relatives in Puente Colorado and in the village who might be called upon in case of future mishaps. Their good relations with network B did come in handy in the matter of purchasing the new plot.

Compadrazgo is liberally used in order to reinforce the network structure. Not only is Valentina the godmother of Teófila's child, but their husbands are also *compadres.* There is *compadrazgo* between Josefa and Valentina, and between Gabriela and Valentina. All men in the network are tombstone polishers, neighbors, and members of the same drinking circle. Thus one may observe a mutual reinforcing interaction between kinship, neighborliness, *compadrazgo, cuatismo,* and the resulting *confianza* as generated by repeated instances of reciprocal assistance in matters of migration, transmission of useful crafts and techniques, jobs, housing, and the daily exchange of goods and services.

3. Network of nonkin neighbors. Stable networks depend essentially upon the existence of kinship among their members. If no relatives are living nearby, the settlers make do with neighbors. Such a network begins with dyadic relationships depending on the degree of *confianza* between two partners. Usually relations are initiated by the women, whose contacts in the shantytown provide more opportunities for exchange. The initial favor may be an offer of assistance in an emergency, such as taking care of the children for a neighbor who is taken to the hospital. As *confianza* takes hold, the favors gradually become more frequent, until the level of daily mutual exchange is reached: money, food, use of pots and pans and household items, joint television viewing by both families, and so on. The husbands may become friends and go out weekends drinking together, or introduce each other to new jobs. In some cases the relationship begins with a friendship among the husbands, particularly when *cuatismo* begins at work and the husband induces his *cuate* to move into a vacant room adjacent to his own. Once a friendship between two neighboring families becomes stabilized it is usually formalized through *compadrazgo,* though *compadrazgo* by itself may not guarantee a reciprocity relationship. For example, an emergency christening in case of the impending death of the child may force the mother to request the favor of godmotherhood from any handy neighbor; naturally, a *compadrazgo* relation born of such circumstances does not necessarily create enduring bonds of reciprocity.

Now, the degree of *confianza* between nonkin neighbors is invariably lower than it would be between relatives. (See Figure 6.3.) This is because certain kinds of favors are only asked from relatives: borrowing cooked and prepared foods, borrowing underwear or the use of a bathtub and the like. Señora Meche Saldivar, an active energetic woman, is a key participant in a joint kinship network belonging to the macronetwork of migrants from Villela. In addition to her membership in this network, Señora Meche maintains a close friendship with two neighbors, Paulina Gonzalez and Maria Luna, on a basis that might be described as protective female solidarity. Señora Meche knows all about the lives and problems of her two friends, and has taken over the role of an advisor especially in case of trouble with their husbands. In particular she encourages them to stand up to their husbands when they come home drunk and want to beat them.

The degree of *confianza* with each of these two friends is slightly different. With Señora Paulina she maintains an exchange of objects and facilities such as an iron or a washing tub. With Señora Luna, there is an exchange of objects and facilities, but in addition the two neighbors chat all

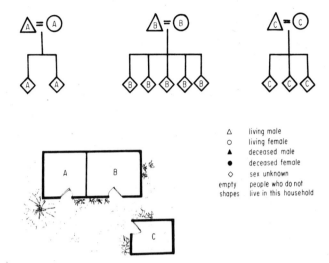

△	living male
○	living female
▲	deceased male
●	deceased female
◇	sex unknown
empty shapes	people who do not live in this household

Figure 6.3. A network of nonkin neighbors.

day long and Señora Luna's children are allowed to watch television at Señora Meche's home. The Luna family is extremely poor; Señora Luna has eight children, but is hard working and extremely nice to all her neighbors. According to her own statement, she is nice to everybody so that someone may be nice to her in case of need. She has close personal contacts with two of her neighbors: Señora Meche and Señora de la Peña.

Señora Luna is a migrant from Hidalgo who was abandoned by her first husband; she arrived in Mexico City with one of her sons and left four other sons behind. In Mexico City she worked in a tortilla bakery that belonged to the sister of some friend she had in Tula. After some years she moved in with Señor Luna, a bricklayer, who gave her two sons and also gave a home to all her earlier children, including the ones she had left behind in Hidalgo. She has no relatives in Cerrada del Cóndor; in all of the Federal District she only has one sister, who works as a maid and visits her on days off. Señor Luna never sees his relatives, if he has any. He drinks and is not working at the time. Señora Luna takes in laundry in Las Aguilas and makes about 35 pesos a day. Two of her boys are also working, one in a street market and the other as car washer. Both hand all their earnings to the mother. The daughters take care of their little brothers and work around the house. Señora de la Peña, Señora Luna's other friend, is a poor but respected woman like herself. They assist each other in many ways. Señor Luna has just one *cuate*.

In addition to these two neighbors, Señora Meche has other female friends. Thus she exchanges certain favors, such as borrowing the iron or the wash tub, with Señora Carlota Herrera, a migrant from Guanajuato. Señora Carlota and her husband migrated directly to the home of an aunt in Cerrada del Cóndor. Her husband had formerly worked for his parents, who had a small piece of land in an *ejido,* but the yield was not enough to feed them. When he got married he decided to move to Mexico City. After a while they went back to the village. Señora Carlota explains that "presumably he was missing his family." When they came back to the shantytown for good, they found that her aunt had left. However, they had made friends of their own, and the first 3 or 4 months they were able to live with one of their former neighbors, until an adjoining room became vacant. They are very poor people. They are paying rent for the plot on which they built their shack and kitchen. The husband is the only breadwinner (he is a bricklayer). They have seven children and they live as a detached nuclear family.

Another neighbor, Señora Clarita Villa, has many friends but does not seem to belong to any specific network. She has 11 children living with her in Cerrada del Cóndor, plus two married sons who live outside the shantytown. They originally came from the medium-sized town of Zamora, in Michoacan; first she came by herself and lived with a friend from her hometown, then the family followed, leaving behind a mortgaged house in Zamora. After some moving about in Mexico City they reached Cerrada del Cóndor, where they are paying one of the highest rentals (400 pesos) in one of the best houses in the shantytown. Their economic level is among the highest of the shantytown even though the husband does not work much; but Señora Clarita is very active. She operates a sewing machine and she also sells eggs from house to house within the shantytown. She buys her eggs directly from a poultry farm. Two of her sons also work to increase the family income, and one son is a student at the National Polytechnic Institute. Señora Clarita is a respected leader among her neighbors. She once organized and headed a delegation of women to petition the wife of the President of the Republic on behalf of the shantytown. Although she needs no favors and belongs to no network she is always ready to help out a neighbor and is particularly friendly with her clients and with Señora Meche's nonkin network. This might possibly be a case of emerging leadership of an energetic woman who is exchanging favors against the generalized support of a broad female clientele.

Let us now look at a different case of reciprocal exchange among neighbors. The Rivera family came from the State of Guerrero. Señora Rivera maintains very close reciprocity ties with two neighbors: Señora Juanita Ibarra and Señora Caldera. The Riveras have no relatives in Cerrada del Cóndor and rarely see their relatives in Mexico City, for various reasons. Thus Señora Rivera's sister lives in Mexico City but she is relatively well-to-do; sometimes she brings some used dresses as a present but this is done secretly as Señor Rivera considers such gifts "humiliating." Señor Rivera does not see much of his relatives in nearby Mixcoac either.

In Cerrada del Cóndor there were several families from Señor Rivera's home village who helped him gain access to a job in the brick kiln. These *paisanos* comprise two extended-family networks, totaling 10 heads of families. These heads of families are Señor Rivera's *cuate* group. Señor Rivera gives his wife 40 pesos a week for her household money, pays the rent (85 pesos a month), and spends the rest with his *cuates*. The Señora secretly takes in washing, because her husband is very jealous and does not let her go out by herself. She also earns an extra 50 pesos a month cooking for and washing the laundry of a house guest.

When Señora Rivera is in need of cash she borrows from her neighbor, Señora Juanita Ibarra. She also borrows beans, salt, or whatever else she may need. Conversely, Señora Ibarra borrows money from Señora Rivera; but she rarely borrows any foodstuffs. As is common among neighbors, they address each other formally as "señora".

There is another neighbor, Señora Caldera, who always approaches Señora Rivera whenever she needs money or some grocery item. Conversely, Señora Rivera will approach Señora Caldera for foodstuffs, but rarely for money. Whenever Señora Caldera is ill, Señora Rivera will do her laundry for free. Then there is a fourth neighbor, Señora Mancera, who borrows money or food from Señora Rivera; the latter in turn may borrow food from her, but seldom any money.

The most intense reciprocal exchange occurs between the Rivera and Ibarra families. Señora Rivera claims that she is always ready to help any neighbor in need. She helps with foodstuffs and even with cooked food, and "never turns anybody down if she has what they ask for." Señora Juanita Ibarra is her *comadre;* other fictive kin all belong to her husband's *cuate* group. Since a wife is excluded from a *cuatismo* relationship, the neighborhood network is mainly used for the needs of reciprocal assistance in domestic and family emergencies. Job assistance and other aspects of male solidarity are supplied by the husband's *cuate* network in Cerrada del Cóndor.

4. Families who do not participate in networks. The case of Señora Clarita Villa, a woman whose family is unaffiliated with any network, has been described in the preceding example. This is a case where the economic situation is sufficiently solid to make continued reciprocity relations unnecessary. However, this is only one of the possible reasons for lack of affiliation to networks.

Here is another case. Señora Alicia Mandujano's husband has recently died. They have lived in Cerrada del Cóndor for 18 years; her husband initially worked at the construction of the Tarango dam and decided to stay in the shantytown after the dam was finished. Their several sons are now married and live all over the city. Ten years ago they set up a little store in the shantytown. They live by themselves and never socialize with anybody. The widow is getting along with her store and with the assistance of an unmarried son who lives with her and helps her to carry the merchandise around. This son is a mechanic in a factory and he makes enough for a living; his friends are all from the factory and none of them live in the shantytown.

The Vivanco family (another case) lived for a year in Pericos Court in Cerrada del Cóndor. They never made any friends and were generally disliked by their neighbors. The husband was a bricklayer and they had three children, but the woman never came out of her room and never said a word to anybody. When Señora Vivanco fell ill, her mother came from somewhere in Mexico City to care for her. Eventually the family moved to Puente Colorado.

Another unattached family by the name of Romo is a young couple without children. The woman migrated to Mexico City with some girl friends, to take jobs as maids; then she met her husband, a construction worker. When they got married they moved in with the husband's parents in Barranca del Muerto (Mixcoac) but the wife did not get along with her mother-in-law so they moved to Cerrada del Cóndor. She has no relatives in the Federal District and goes to visit her mother in the village once a year. This couple lives in a court but as they have no children they feel no urgency to communicate with the neighbors.

Another case, the Aliaga family, comes from Oaxaca. Señor Aliaga worked for a builder who decided to take him along to Mexico City for a job. The family lives at the edge of Cerrada del Cóndor on a lot belonging to an engineer who works for the same building firm. Two of their eight children are working. One boy works with his father in the building firm and a daughter is working as a maid. Both contribute to the family income. Their home was built at the lot owner's expense; it includes two rooms, a kitchen, and an outhouse. The lot is fenced and is being used to raise animals. All the relatives of the family live in Oaxaca; their *compadres* have been selected from among people who live at the other end of town. They get together two or three times a year. The husband does have some friends outside the shantytown; one of them is a lawyer. His major personal contact in the city is his boss who has been providing for his needs ever since he arrived in Mexico City; thus he has no use for the solidarity of his peers. The family keeps aloof from their neighbors in the shantytown because they feel that the people are "no good"; their home was burglarized 2 months ago.

The case now to be described is in some ways opposite to the previous one. The Vazquez Gonzalez are poor and in low esteem in the shantytown. The wife had initially been a maid (together with her sister) immediately after migration to Mexico City. She got married after 4 years of courtship. The husband had lived in Cerrada del Cóndor since he was a little boy; after marriage they built a shack in Cerrada del Cóndor and have been living there for 5 years. They are paying rent for the lot. They have three children. The man used to have a trade as a roofer, but he is a heavy drinker and a loafer and works only when he feels like it. He has some brothers in Mexico City but he never sees them. She has a sister in Mexico City who is married to a "good" man, so she feels ashamed to go and visit her. The husband may often be seen in the shantytown, getting drunk with three of his *cuates* from the shantytown. He customarily mistreats his wife and has seriously hurt her before. Once she succeeded in pawning some object and running away to her mother, but he went to the village and got her back.

The standing of the family within the community is very low. Nobody talks to the wife; her children roam about the shantytown, dirty and lonely, as the mother is often forced to go out in search of some job. No one in the shantytown has asked them to be *compadres*. The children do not go to school because their mother does not have the money to send them. The man borrows from his *cuates* for drinking. Once he borrowed from a neighbor but he never returned the money so he gets no more. The wife used to have a female friend from the Saldivar network, but no one risks visiting her any more for fear of her husband, who is often found drunk on the doorstep. For the same reason, she does not dare leave the house when he is around. Gradually she has been left in total isolation and disgrace.

ANALYSIS OF A RESIDENTIAL COMPLEX: PERICOS COURT

In Cerrada del Cóndor there is a court owned by the son-in-law of Señor Obregón, who formerly owned all the land on which the shantytown is located (Figure 6.4). The court is shaped like a rectangle and contains 14 rooms facing on a central patio with two outhouses at the far end. Each room has a tiny kitchen. The rooms are of brick construction with cement floors and asbestos roofing. All rooms have electric light and a laundry bin; there is a water faucet in the center of the court. Rentals range from 250 to 280 pesos per month, depending on the size of the room.

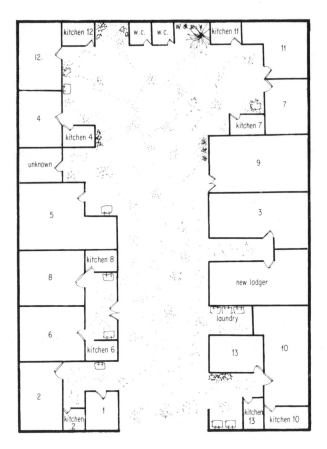

Figure 6.4. Pericos Court, a singly owned lane. Each number corresponds to a different renter (see explanation in text).

At the time of the survey there were 13 households living in Pericos Court, with the social structure shown in Figure 6.5.

1. *An extended family network in room 7, including three generations, with their members pooling all resources.* There are four breadwinners in this extended network.
2. *A mixed network consisting of a jointed household in rooms 8, 9, and 11, plus a nonkin neighbor family in room 6.* The jointed family includes one couple with their unmarried children living in room 11, one married daughter with eight children in room 8, and one married son with four children in room 9. The nonkin neighbors in room 6 represent a complete nuclear family. This mixed network contains four heads of nuclear families all of

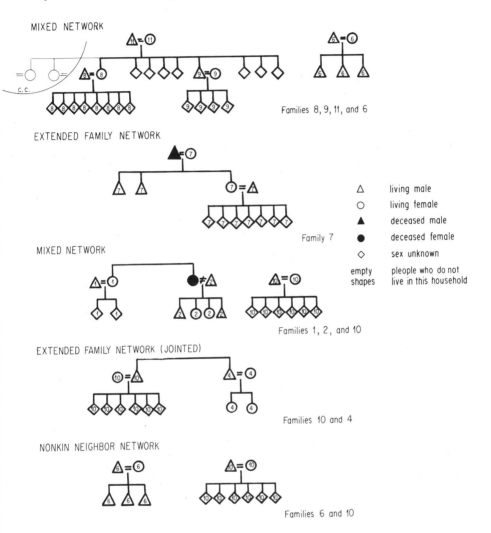

MIXED NETWORK

Families 8, 9, 11, and 6

EXTENDED FAMILY NETWORK

Family 7

△   living male
○   living female
▲   deceased male
●   deceased female
◇   sex unknown
empty   pleople who do not
shapes   live in this household

MIXED NETWORK

Families 1, 2, and 10

EXTENDED FAMILY NETWORK (JOINTED)

Families 10 and 4

NONKIN NEIGHBOR NETWORK

Families 6 and 10

Figure 6.5. Some different types of networks found among the residents of Pericos Court. The numbers refer to the residential distribution shown in Figure 6.4. Note that some networks overlap, and that some families (3, 5, 12, and 13) do not participate in networks.

whom are immediate neighbors and have jobs. They are also *compadres* to each other and have a *tanda* among themselves.

3. *A mixed network including a jointed family (rooms 1 and 2) and a nonkin neighbor family (room 10).* Each household contains one provider; there is *compadrazgo* among the three families.

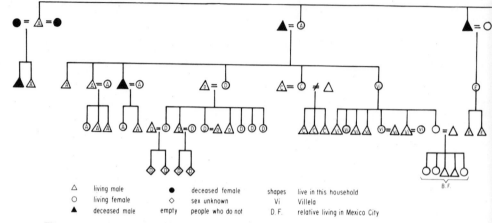

Figure 6.6. The Villela macronetwork. Vi, still living in Villela; A, jointed household network; B, single-roof network, expense sharing; C, jointed household network; D, single-plot network, no expense sharing; E, single-roof network, expense sharing. D.F., Federal District.

4. *A jointed family in rooms 4 and 10.* This family overlaps with the preceding network, since the nonkin neighbor in room 10 is also the brother of the head of household in room 4. They are not immediate neighbors though they live in the court.

5. *A network of nonkin neighbors in rooms 6 and 10, overlapping the two preceding networks.* Rooms 6 and 10 face each other across the court; their respective families maintain intense reciprocal exchange as well as *compadrazgo* ties.

6. *Families 3, 5, 12, and 13 participate in no reciprocity networks within the shantytown.* The head of household in room 3 is an employee of the Federal District administration who has a stable job and only one child. His wife is a friend to the woman in room 1 but they have no steady reciprocal exchange. Room 5 contains a childless couple without relatives in the shantytown; they do not socialize with anyone. The family in room 12 never tried to make friends with anyone in the court; they left the shantytown within a few months. Finally, in room 3 both husband and wife are working; they have a 12-year-old boy. They are *compadres* with the neighbors in room 2, but it is a case of an emergency *compadrazgo* and no reciprocity relation has developed, perhaps for lack of time and opportunity.

Thus the social structure in the court may be analyzed in terms of reciprocal networks based on shadings of *confianza*. The highest level of *confianza* is found in the extended family network, which is fully autonomous and maintains no relations with other people in the court. Networks based on jointed families are

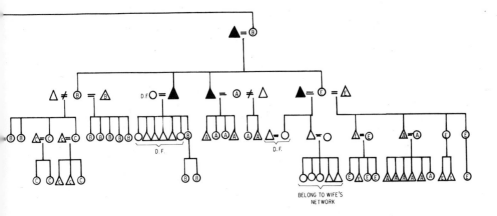

less exclusive and do admit the incorporation of nonkin neighbors. The larger networks are more functional and more stable; they are based on kinship. In addition there are dyadic relations that may produce multiple affiliation of a nuclear family to more than one network. Thus, in the case of the family in room 10, the wife participates in a relationship of *compadrazgo* and reciprocal exchange with the three women in rooms 1, 2, and 6, and her husband maintains a similar relationship with his own brother who lives in room 4.

NETWORKS AND KINDREDS:
THE VILLELA MACRONETWORK

In Chapter 3 I described the process that gave rise to the migration of a kindred of 25 nuclear families from Villela, in the State of San Luis Potosí. Genealogically speaking, we may distinguish two major branches in this kindred, descendants of two sisters and matriarchs (Figure 6.6). For reasons of topography and land tenure in the shantytown, the various Villela families have become clustered in five different networks according to the availability of dwellings. Solidarity with the macronetwork of Villela has survived this partitioning of the kindred into separate reciprocity networks. There is still a great deal of interpersonal contact as well as reciprocal exchange among relatives who live in different networks.

Figure 6.6 describes the composition of each of the networks. In general these networks are not homogeneous, since they include members of both major branches of the kindred. Naturally enough, close relations continue to exist between members of the same branch who live in different networks. Incidentally, the physical distance between the five networks is not very great; the average distance between two networks is about half a block.

I have already described the typical features of the exchange between Villela migrants. The men are carpet layers who drink together and who have their own soccer team. Reciprocal exchange between the women is very intense and includes *compadrazgo,* mutual visiting, and exchange of goods and services.

The affine members of the macronetwork continue to relate with their orientation networks. An interesting case is the woman I have called Meche Saldivar, who has her own network of nonkin women neighbors in addition to her Villela network. Her husband is very active within the macronetwork; he is a carpet layer and the captain of the soccer team, and he drinks with his in-laws. Meche's relatives live one block away but their exchange is very intense. Her brother Isidro is a confirmation godfather to her children. Her husband's mother and sister live two blocks away, and Meche goes every day with a gift of food in spite of the fact that she expresses dislike for the members of that network. Most relevant in this case is the fact that Meche's network is relatively self-sufficient, since four people in her nuclear family (the husband, the wife, and two sons) have jobs and contribute to the household. Meche's female neighbors apparently provide adequate reciprocal exchange for her daily needs, and the Villela macronetwork supplies all needs in terms of jobs as well as ritual support. Meche's family is matrilocal, since her husband is closely integrated into his affine kinship network.

There are other macronetworks in Cerrada del Cóndor, though none as large or as powerful as the Villela macronetwork. In every case there are dyadic relations with other networks, particularly through the affine kin. These dyadic relations appear to complement the function of the macronetwork, and they may become quite important in the formation of subsidiary networks that splinter off from the original macronetworks.

NETWORKS AND KINSHIP

Kinship is the most common social foundation for reciprocity networks. There is an essential distinction, however, between networks and families, or households. Of course, all three overlap in the case of networks integrated by an extended family. Yet kinship affiliation is neither necessary nor sufficient for network formation, as one frequently finds mixed networks of extended families with jointed families or with nonkin neighbors. On the other hand, many relatives maintain no reciprocal exchange whatsoever.

There is a continuum of stability, social closeness, and intensity of exchange, and these variables may be correlated with the internal structure of the network. Kinship is a major factor of stability and intensity of exchange. At one extreme we find extended families who practice complete pooling of resources; in such networks the reciprocal exchange is exocentric, that is, each member exchanges goods and services with all other members without any centralizing person intervening in the exchange. At the opposite end we have networks of nonkin neighbors, with a type of exchange that is dominantly egocentric and dyadic. There is a similar continuum in terms of trust (*confianza*), with a pole of maximum *confianza* in extended-family networks, and minimum *confianza* in nonkin-neighbor networks. The networks with the highest degree of *confianza* are more stable and larger, from the point of view of the number of participants; at the pole of least *confianza* the networks are also more unstable and smaller.

A network may become self-sufficient when it is large and stable; its growth will tend to stabilize at that point. On the other hand, if the network is too small there is a tendency to broaden its base through the incorporation of nonkin neighbors by means of *compadrazgo*. Jointed households are more flexible than extended households in this respect, perhaps because nuclear families in a jointed household do not control each other as closely as those in an extended household. Thus they have more opportunities to establish dyadic contacts with neighbors. All such shadings in reciprocity may be translated in terms of degrees of mutual trust; in a mixed network, for example, those favors that imply higher levels of intimacy (loans of clothing or cooked meals) are largely restricted to relatives and do not apply to exchange between nonkin neighbors.

The basic element of a network is the nuclear family; affiliation is usually on a family basis rather than individually. Yet there are often certain key personalities who are felt to be essential to the internal cohesiveness of a network. In extended families with pooling of resources, this personality is frequently the mother. Kinship networks may be patrilineal as well as matrilineal; nonkin networks are often based on friendship between women, as this is where exchange begins most often in a shantytown. Husbands are incorporated later into the network.

Affiliation to a network does not exclude dyadic exchange with members of other networks. Thus there is an intense dyadic exchange between affine kin, particularly if the respective families of orientation do not live far away. In egocentric networks between nonkin female neighbors, their husbands often maintain dyadic relations with their *compadres* and *cuates*. However, such external dyadic relations tend to wane as *confianza* increases within a network. In all exocentric networks there is a tendency for male members to work and drink together.

The genesis of an extended or jointed network, in cases where the network is established on a single plot, may usually be traced to a paterfamilias or his wife who own or rent this plot for the purpose of housing their married offspring and collateral kin. All owners of plots in Cerrada del Cóndor, with the single exception of a lone widow, have formed networks in this fashion.

The importance of *confianza* as a variable of social relations and exchange will be discussed more fully in Chapter 9. Shadings of *confianza* are also revealed through the external forms of address. Thus, close consanguineal kin not only borrow each other's articles of personal use but also behave toward each other with more familiarity. Among nonkin neighbors, the common forms of address are "señor," "señora," "compadre," "comadre," and so on. A child of a nonkin neighbor is not to be scolded or to be sent on errands. Requests to nonkin neighbors are always couched in terms of respectful language and formal behavior, and it is important that no hint of services previously rendered be made when requesting a favor. Reciprocity must be implicit, never explicit. If a request is turned down there is no insisting and no recrimination; one merely puts a stop to any further attempts at exchanging goods and services. If a person wishes to comply but is in no physical or economic position to do so, that is another matter. In such cases one may often verbally accede to the request and make excuses afterward. The main point is the show of good will in implementing a reciprocity relationship, even when there may be no means of performing the service as requested.

Borrowed objects are to be returned within a reasonable amount of time; if necessary the owner may request them if he needs them. Borrowed money is returned as soon as possible, and it is not customary to borrow any cash from people one still owes money to. Such loans would require a specific explanation or a clear emergency situation. Any person who fails to return a borrowed object is considered a thief, particularly if he denies possessing the borrowed object. Usually one hears it said that favors are to be performed and objects loaned only to people whose character and good disposition are personally known to one. This implies *confianza* as well as an economic level relatively similar to one's own. Otherwise one might find oneself in the awkward situation of having to turn down a request for reciprocity, and "having to say no is very unpleasant."

There are few families without a network or lacking any dyadic exchange between neighbors: fewer than 10 cases in Cerrada del Cóndor. These cases belong to one of four specific situations: (1) transients or new arrivals who have not yet made any personal contact in the shantytown; (2) old people who are supported by their children; (3) very poor families who are not respected, often because the husband is a drunk or a *marihuano;* and (4) families of higher than average economic income who do not stand to benefit from reciprocal exchange, either because the husband has a steady job or because there are several breadwinners in the family. The exceptional character of these cases tends to confirm the central importance of reciprocal exchange as a mechanism of economic safety and as the main reason for generating and maintaining reciprocity networks.

7

Compadrazgo

Porque matar a un compadre es ofender al Eterno.
[Killing one's *compadre* is an offense against the Almighty.]
—Mexican popular ballad

In this chapter I shall analyze the traditional institution of fictive kinship (*compadrazgo*) as it is found in an urban shantytown. This analysis may help evaluate the changes that have occurred in this important social institution under the impact of the new conditions of marginality. The role of *compadrazgo* is a mechanism for strengthening social solidarity in the networks of reciprocal exchange. If a reciprocity network is a social field based on exchange relationships, this social field may reinforce and strengthen its solidarity texture by means of certain traditional institutions that are recombined in such a way as to meet new and unfavorable ecological challenges, such as urban marginality.

Family and kinship in the shantytown have been shown to adapt certain new features, new modes of interaction within the extended family, new spatial arrangements, and a redistribution of domestic functions. These changes produced a new type of household called *jointed,* which represents an adaptation of the extended household to specific shantytown conditions. A similar analysis may be attempted in order to describe the changes in the *compadrazgo* institution as a result of the new type of reciprocity networks developed under urban marginal conditions.

Mintz and Wolf (1950:341–367) have pointed out the flexibility and adaptability of the *compadrazgo* institution to a wide range of social situations and structures in Europe and Latin America. A very complete study of different types of fictive kinship in Mexico, including the related rituals, rights, and obligations as well as the differences between real and ideal behavior, has been made by Forbes (1971). Some relevant conclusions as related to the present study were the following: *Compadrazgo* strengthens social ties between equals, furthers social mobility and economic advancement, and affords a magic symbolic protection against latent interpersonal aggression. Forbes agrees with Foster (1965:10–11) and Kemper (1971:165) in describing *compadrazgo* as a relationship essentially between *compadres* rather than between godparents and godchild.

My Cerrada del Cóndor informants described the ideal model of *compadrazgo* behavior in terms that agreed neither with my observations nor with the perception of the real situation by the informants themselves. I therefore distinguish three different levels of the model and aim the analysis at the discrepancies between these three levels. The ideal model of *compadrazgo* in Cerrada del Cóndor is very much like the rural ideal model. The real model as perceived by the informants, on the other hand, resembles the description made by Roberts of *compadrazgo* in Guatemala: ''The category of *compadre* was hardly ever cited as a possible recourse in times of emergency or in need of financial help. . . . In choosing godparents, families said that they tried to choose people whom they respected and who were not such close friends as to make them too familiar [1973:173].'' On the strength of such information, Roberts reached the following conclusion: ''I found little evidence that *compadrazgo* relationships served as a basis for continuing interaction of any kind within the urban milieu. People might interact with their children's godparents, but this was seen as part of the normal relationship between friends [1973:173].''

Finally, direct observation in Cerrada del Cóndor revealed that people continue to seek out *compadres* and to widen and broaden the number and variety of *compadrazgo* ties, including and going beyond the traditional ritual occasions such as baptism or confirmation. One finds a whole range of secular or voluntary circumstances, such as give rise to *compadrazgo de santos, compadrazgo de hábitos, compadrazgo* on graduating from primary school, *compadrazgo* on the occasion of a child's first haircut, and so on. This insistence on maintaining and broadening the scope of application of the *compadrazgo* institution, which after all involves expenses to both parties, would be difficult to explain if it were true that *compadrazgo* is losing importance as a mechanism of human and social interaction. A similar conclusion may be derived from the continued use of special forms and address (''mi compadre,'' ''mi comadrita'') as well as the change from the familiar to the respectful form of address ("usted" instead of "tú") which is invariably observed between friends on becoming *compadres*.

On the basis of participant observation as well as on the strength of my survey data from Cerrada del Cóndor, I have provided an interpretation of the differences between the two levels of the ideal model and the true situation in respect to *compadrazgo*. The discrepancies become intelligible once we understand the connection between *compadrazgo* and reciprocity networks. Networks are indispensable for survival of the individual in the shantytown. Since the networks are conditioned on physical neighborhood and social proximity or *confianza*, we may expect *compadrazgo* to develop particularly among neighbors and relatives. This is indeed the situation. In other words, the outstanding flexibility of the *compadrazgo* institution as a mechanism for reinforcing social solidarity has been mobilized to increase the cohesion within the reciprocal exchange networks.

But how can we understand the discrepancy between the real and the professed behaviors of informants as related to *compadrazgo?* This discrepancy might seem to reveal some degree of ambivalence of the informants toward the values of the *compadrazgo* institution itself. However, this is not the only possible explanation. A *compadrazgo* relationship involves simultaneously two opposite attitudes: embracing someone, and keeping him at arm's length. Suppose that two men become friends to the degree of using the familiar form of address; then they become *compadres* and at once they revert to the respectful form of address. The form of address between *compadres* paradoxically would seem to indicate an *increase* in the social distance, even though we know that the opposite is true; an extremely close social relationship has just been ritualized. In other words, *compadrazgo*, because of its very flexibility and diversity of functions, is in itself ambiguous. It may be used either to formalize an existing close human relation, or to formalize a social distance perceived as potentially conducive to interpersonal aggression. In either case the content of the relationship is given by the preexisting relationship and not by the institution of *compadrazgo* as such.

The ideal model of *compadrazgo* as described by informants corresponds to the traditional teachings of Mexican culture, both rural and urban. It includes a compendium of rights and duties as prescribed between *compadres,* and between godparents and godchild, which may be found in the literature (see also Berruecos 1972). The ideal quality that is expected to characterize the *compadrazgo* relationship more than any other is *respeto,* a combination of personal affection, mutual admiration, and social distance.

Thus, I find that among close relatives *compadrazgo* is preferably used to confer a distinction, to particularize: "Among all my relatives *these* are the ones who count, and *who can be counted upon.*" The great number of *compadrazgos* among relatives in Cerrada del Cóndor is significant, precisely because it contradicts the ideal model. On the other hand, *compadrazgo* between unrelated persons implies a wish to confer or to receive a distinction, and simultaneously to allay the chances of mutual conflict. In the marginal urban situation there are frequently utilitarian motivations as well. *Compadres* are often people who may be approached for assistance in an emergency. They are an indispensable social resource in the large city.

The frequently heard claim: "I don't see my *compadres* and I don't need them" may refer more to the ideal model as described by Forbes (1971), used to prevent interpersonal aggression, than to the real situation. In Cerrada del Cóndor, the preponderance of *compadrazgo* relations between relatives and neighbors flagrantly contradicts this ideal model by implying that the *compadrazgo* institution is being used in the shantytown to make preexisting reciprocity relations more solid and permanent. This kind of use of *compadrazgo* particularly interests us in this book.

A Latin American uses and relies on two types of social resources: horizontal relations (e.g., *compadres*) and vertical relations (e.g., godparent–godchild). This basic model may be extended to any kind of relations, even though they are not necessarily ritualized through *compadrazgo* (Foster 1961:1173–1192, 1963:128–129; Lomnitz 1971). Thus, if we think of the relative situation between patron and client, or between different social classes or groups, in terms of their use of the two types of relationships, we may hypothesize as follows: Marginals as a group rely very little on godfatherly "protectors," on account of their lack of upward social mobility. Neither do they have any "godchildren" since they already occupy the lowest echelon on the social scale. Hence their lack of meaningful vertical social relations causes them to rely largely on horizontal relationships. This may explain the increased importance of *compadrazgo* (a formalization of equalitarian social ties) in the marginal situation. I agree with Safa (1974:61–64) in that cooperation between equals is a result of necessity born of the social structure. If one lacks a powerful godfather one must make do with *compadres*.

COMPADRAZGO IN CERRADA DEL CÓNDOR

In 1971 I carried out a *compadrazgo* survey in Cerrada del Cóndor among female heads of households. Each of these residents was asked about the *compadres* who had been requested by herself or her husband, about the number of times she herself had been required as a *comadre*, the number of *compadrazgos* contracted before and after migration, and the types of *compadrazgos* in each case. The survey was incomplete because of the emphasis on female *compadrazgo*. (See Table 7.1.)

TABLE 7.1

Compadrazgos Reported by 142 Female Heads of Residential Units

Type of *compadrazgo*	Requested by family	Requested by *compadre*
Baptism	521	196
Confirmation	295	83
First communion	68	18
Matrimony	29	9
Evangelios	17	3
Muerte, corona y cruz	5	10
Fifteenth birthday	4	4
Santos	7	3
Niño Dios	2	2
Graduation from primary school	1	2
Hábito	0	2
Others[a]	9	1
Total	958	333

[a] Includes *coronación, cuadro de la Virgen, alumbración, consagración, vestido de San Martín,* home, and a barbershop inauguration.

Each informant reported having made an average of 6.7 requests of *compadrazgo* (either by herself or through her husband or both) and having received an average of 2.4 requests of *compadrazgos*. The difference between these two figures may be attributed to (1) the fact that the survey does not include cases where only the husband has been requested to be a *compadre,* and (2) the fact that the age of the godparents often exceeds the age of the parents of the godchild. Thus, the age span of procreation is normally between 18 and 45, whereas

TABLE 7.2

Who Selects the *Compadres?*

	Number	Percentage
The husband	387	29.9
The wife	229	17.7
Both	305	23.5
Unknown	370	28.9
Total	1291	100.0

TABLE 7.3

Compadrazgos Contracted in the City or in the Country Reported by 142
Female Heads of Residential Units

Type of *compadrazgo*	Contracted in the countryside	Contracted in the city
Baptism	142	575
Confirmation	87	291
First communion	7	79
Matrimony	7	31
Alumbración	3	0
Muerte, corona y cruz	4	11
Others[a]	3	51
Total	253	1038

[a]The following types of *compadrazgo* have not been recorded or re-
called by informants prior to migration: *muerte y corona, santos, niño
Dios*, fifteenth birthday, *evangelios, hábito*, grade school graduation,
escapulario, consagración, vestido de San Martín, and inauguration.

the age of being a godfather or godmother has no such limitations. Therefore,
any sample containing a high percentage of young heads of households should be
expected to feature a higher number of *compadrazgos* contracted by the head of
the household than of cases where he or she was the requested party. The
difference corresponds largely to elderly persons attached to households whose
heads are younger men or women.

According to informants, the *compadres* were often selected by their husbands
rather than by themselves. This is shown in Table 7.2.

The survey also revealed that the reported number of *compadrazgo* cases should
be taken as a lower limit rather than as a true figure. An informant reports: "I
must have around 50 *compadres* but most of them I don't see and I don't
remember well." The tabulated figures refer to those *compadres* who maintained
a significant social relationship with the informant at the time of the survey. An
important proportion of such cases of *compadrazgo* was contracted prior to
migration, as Table 7.3 shows.

Godparenthood (*Compadrazgo de Bautismo*)

Godparenthood or fictive parenthood is numerically and socially the most
important form of *compadrazgo*. Every child must have a godfather and a godmother. A *compadre* at baptism is the *compadre* par excellence; all other kinds of
compadrazgo imply lesser duties and responsibilities on both sides.

The ideal duties involved in baptism *compadrazgo* may be gathered from the following explanations, which were collated from a number of informants: (1) The *compadres* must always talk to each other respectfully and must greet each other wherever they meet; (2) the godparents must buy certain items of clothing for the godchild, particularly the shawl, diapers, and dress the baby will wear for the ceremony; (3) the godfather pays the church and makes the offering; (4) if the godchild dies, the godfather buys the wreath; (5) in case of death or inability of the parents, the godfather must take over the economic maintenance of the godchild; (6) the godparents take the godchild to the fount and "take the horn away" (the devil's horn); this implies the right and the duty of the godparents to advise, educate, and if necessary reprimand the godchild, and to be a model and spiritual guide.

Now, concerning the model that most informants consider to be real, it is usually accepted that the effective duties of a godparent terminate as soon as the ceremony is over. The single persisting obligation concerns a respectful relationship between the *compadres* and a moral obligation to take care of the child if the parents die. Informants claim that *compadres* do not help each other, and that requesting the assistance of a *compadre* is not a good idea if one wishes good relations to be maintained. Quite often it is said that a neighbor is better than a *compadre* for mutual assistance. Nevertheless, Table 7.4 shows that *compadres* are recuited precisely among neighbors. Such declarations seem to indicate that the image of the *compadrazgo* relationship is somewhat defensive, since the need to prevent a deterioration of the relationship is stressed above the need for cooperation. This ideal model differs from urban reality, where we find neighbors in a situation of reciprocal exchange to be preferred as *compadres,* and to continue to cooperate and help each other without impairing good relationships in the least.

TABLE 7.4

Relation between *Compadres* at 575 Baptisms in the Federal District

Relationship	Number	Percentage
Relatives living close by	146	25.5
Relatives in the metropolitan area	65	11.0
Relatives in the countryside	27	4.7
Neighbors (nonkin)	200	34.8
Friends at work	53	9.2
Others	84	14.6
Total	575	99.8

Table 7.4 shows that 346 out of 575 godparents were neighbors (whether relatives or not). The 27 cases of parents who returned to the countryside to have their children baptized are all families with deep roots in the village or those who intended to return to the village eventually. On the other hand, the 65 informants who selected a godparent from within the Federal District but outside the shantytown are from families who had no relatives in Cerrada del Cóndor and preferred to choose relatives as godparents, for some of the reasons to be described later. These data tend to modify both models proposed by the informants. Godparenthood in Cerrada del Cóndor is definitely a social relationship that plays a role in the reciprocal networks, as shown by the preference for neighbors, whether they are relatives or not. More than 60% of the instances of godparenthood were contracted between neighbors. The hypothesis of a relationship between godparenthood and networks was tested and confirmed through personal observation and unstructured interviews. In all cases it was found that the godparenthood relationship was being utilized as a reinforcement of reciprocal exchange relationships within networks. Without exception, every single network contained internal *compadrazgo* relations. Explaining the personal criteria for selection of godparent, most of the informants stressed the condition of equality of economic wants as one of the positive qualities a godparent should be expected to fulfill.

Let me reproduce here some representative opinions on the matter of criteria for the selection of *compadres:* ''We always invite people who are just as poor as we are,'' ''One must select a poor *compadre* so that people won't say that you are acting in self-interest,'' ''When looking for a godfather you have to remember to look for a decent man, a good friend, and if it is a couple, see that they are properly married,'' ''I wanted him because I trusted him, because we come from the same part of the country and we have known each other for many years,'' ''I asked him because we had been playmates since we were kids,'' ''Because of mutual liking and friendship,'' ''Because he was respectful and kind,'' ''Because he was already a godfather to several of my children,'' ''Because he got a job for my husband,'' ''Because he was just as poor as we are and he is not ashamed of it, and he likes children,'' ''Because they were helping us a lot and we were unable to get even with them in any other way,'' ''Because we are neighbors.'' The preceding explanations refer only to godparenthood between nonrelatives.

Defensive reasons do exist in a small number of cases: ''We wanted him because we have had some trouble, and we have no more fights now.'' Somewhat more frequently one finds the case of selection under stress of emergency, or for lack of a better choice: ''We knew nobody in the Federal District so we asked the neighbors,'' ''The child was dying and so I asked him as an emergency,'' ''We couldn't find anybody.'' Quite often the initiative is of the future godfather or godmother, rather than the parents of the child. In either case the net effect is one of establishing or reinforcing neighborhood relations.

A large number of godparents (41.2%) are relatives. Among relatives, those who live in the same household or in a reciprocity network are preferred (25.5%). This pattern disagrees with the ideal model of *compadrazgo,* according to which godparents are selected among friends and acquaintances, not among relatives. The striking preference for relatives may be rationalized as follows: "I selected nearby relatives because they are handy," "Because they are relatives," "Because they are trustworthy," "Because he already is godfather to one of my kids, so he might as well take two or three," "Because we are neighbors and in-laws and we live on the same lot," "Because I wanted my sister to be my *comadre,*" "Because if he were just a friend we would hardly ever see him," "Because one has got to reciprocate and since they are members of the household it was easy to see that they wanted the child," "Because I didn't have any money and couldn't afford to have a godfather who was not a relative," "Because I had no money for a party after baptism and my relatives live with me and know I can't afford it," "To have them nearby so that the children can know them."

Once again I point out the discrepancy between such reasoning and the model that prescribes that nothing is to be asked or expected from a *compadre.* The economic stress of marginal life has produced an actual modification of the *compadrazgo* institution, thereby serving the needs of social solidarity as required for survival. This is a new confirmation of the vitality of the *compadrazgo* institution. *Compadrazgo* has become a mechanism for conferring official status to a situation of social closeness, for expressing and consolidating preexisting trust, and for preventing potential conflict within reciprocity networks.

Brothers and sisters have become favorite *compadres* in the shantytown. Also, it has become quite usual for a young couple to ask their parents or parents-in-law to become godparents. In general, *compadres* are selected among relatives who are close enough to be trusted or neighbors in good standing, i.e., those who have an ongoing exchange relationship with the couple.

Tomasa and Valentina, for example, were neighbors. Their husbands were also friends and worked together; for this reason Valentina's husband had suggested to his friend to take up a residence next to his own. Since that time, the two families have gotten along quite well; the men are buddies at work and at play, and help each other out. Tomasa's family became integrated in the reciprocity network formed by Valentina's kin (see Chapter 6). Tomasa has now requested Valentina to be her *comadre,* "because she is very good and we help each other a great deal." In this fashion fictive kinship was used to formalize a neighborly relationship within a network formerly constituted by kin only.

Now, Tomasa happens to have another neighbor, a woman who is married to a drugstore clerk and who enjoys a certain amount of economic independence; the ensuing inequality of wants has prevented her from joining the network. However, this neighbor "is very good" and has bestowed various presents and kindnesses upon Tomasa. In order to reciprocate and honor her, Tomasa decided to offer one of her daughters to be her neighbor's goddaughter.

Compadrazgo is also used as a means of neutralizing potential conflict within a kinship relation. Several years ago, Mercedes was Salvador's girl friend. Today both are married (but not to each other), and have become neighbors within the same reciprocity network because Salvador's brother happened to marry Mercedes' sister. Unfortunately the internal peace of the network was being threatened by Salvador's wife, who was jealous of Mercedes on account of their former courtship. In order to prevent any further friction within the network, Mercedes decided to offer her son to Salvador's wife. Thus the relation between Mercedes and Salvador was raised above suspicion, since on becoming *compadres* they had to treat each other with a formal respect that excluded any idea of flirting.

Who Selects the Godparents? In Table 7.2, we saw that husbands decided more often than wives about the selection of a godparent, or at least that the choice is made by both parents. However, it happens quite often that the husband selects the godfather and the wife selects the godmother. When the godfather is a friend of the husband's at work, the question of who makes the selection is hardly in doubt. On the other hand, if those involved are neighbors the decision is usually reached jointly. In some families it is always the husband who selects the *compadres;* in others, if the child is a boy the *compadre* is selected by the husband, and if the child is a girl, by the wife. Sometimes the spouses take turns in selecting the *compadres.* In conclusion, there seems to be no definite rule regarding the initiative in the matter of selecting a *compadre.* Godfather and godmother are not necessarily a couple though this is indeed very common. In some parts of the country three children are offered to the same godparent or couple, and such local customs tend to be preserved in the shantytown.

Certain families have never been called upon for *compadrazgo.* They are either very young people or they belong to the lowest status in the shantytown, on account of extreme poverty or because they are drunks or "indecent people." Evidently *compadrazgo* entails recognition of a status of respectability, since its most outstanding outward attribute is indeed respect.

Compadrazgo de Confirmación

The relationship of *compadrazgo* entered upon religious confirmation of a child is similar to that of baptism in many ways. Table 7.5 indicates that the proportion of neighbors and relatives among such *compadres* is quite high.

TABLE 7.5

Relationship between *Compadres* at 291 Confirmations in
the Federal District

Relationship	Number	Percentage
Relatives living close by	64	22.0
Relatives in the metropolitan area	39	13.5
Relatives in the countryside	20	6.9
Neighbors (nonkin)	77	26.4
Friends at work	32	11.0
Others	59	20.0
Total	291	99.8

The alleged reasons for selecting a given *compadre* on the occasion of confirmation are quite similar to those described in connection with godparenthood. The purpose is to give recognition and solidity to a social relationship by conferring a distinction to the recipient, thus ensuring permanence and trustworthiness to reciprocity relations.

The duties of a *compadre de confirmación* are less important, particularly in respect to the godchild. Even the ideal model entails rather vague obligations for the confirmation godparent: "None that I know of," say some informants, whereas others suggest: "To buy the child a pair of pants and shoes for use in the ceremony," "To buy the breakfast," "To pay the church," "To give some money," as well as some economic and moral assistance to the godchild. In general such obligations tend to be more or less voluntary, depending on the relationship between the *compadres,* which is the essential factor.

This kind of *compadrazgo* is often used in order to confirm a preexisting friendship: "We were friends," "I found it easy to make the request," "We had a liking for each other," "They asked for it themselves," "We are neighbors," "We are *compadres,*" "I wanted my sister to be my *comadre,*" "He works with my husband," "They were people to be trusted," "They already were godparents to one of ours," "Our husbands used to drink together and in a drinking session my husband offered him our boy," "I liked him as a *compadre,*" "We used to get along."

Other Types of *Compadrazgo*

Fictive kinship connected with holy communion (*compadrazgo de primera comunión*) is predominantly an affair between godmothers. Here the mother is usually the one who selects the *comadre.* On the other hand, this is also a

TABLE 7.6

Relationships between *Compadres* at 79 First Communions in
the Metropolitan Area

Relationship	Number	Percentage
Relatives living close by	20	25.3
Relatives in the metropolitan area	10	12.7
Relatives in the countryside	2	2.5
Neighbors (nonkin)	30	38.0
Friends at work	1	1.2
Others	16	20.0
Total	79	99.7

compadrazgo between neighbors and relatives. The *compadres* may occasionally present their godchild with a gift of clothing, a candle, or a luncheon, but often nothing is given. There are also collective holy communions where the priest is the godfather of all the children. Table 7.6 shows the distribution of social relations among *compadres* in this particular case.

Because of the predominantly female character of this *compadrazgo* one finds hardly any work companions among such *compadres*. Also, it is not customary to go back to the countryside or to the village to celebrate holy communion.

Wedding *compadrazgo* (*compadrazgo de matrimonio*) entails certain obligations, such as leading the couple to the church, sometimes sharing the expenses of the wedding party, and eventually giving advice to the people "if they take up bad living." The wedding *compadres* are selected for a number of reasons: "Because they were neighbors and good friends," "Because they were good to us," "Because we didn't have the money for the party," "My mother-in-law picked them for us," "My brother asked one of his friends to be *padrino*," and so on. Neighbors and relatives outside the shantytown are preferred for this type of *compadrazgo,* as one may see in Table 7.7.

Compadrazgo de santos is found practically only among women who are friends and neighbors. This consists in going to church together and blessing an image. The *comadres'* only duty consists in going to pray to the image once a year. When the *compadrazgo* is between men the relationship is the same. All residential units in Cerrada del Cóndor have images of saints, and the ceremony of blessing these images has become one more opportunity for reinforcing the ties between friends and neighbors, as the request for such a *compadrazgo* is a testimony of respect. Of 13 reported cases in the shantytown, 9 were between *comadres* who were otherwise unrelated.

The *compadrazgo* "*corona y cruz*" (or *coronación y muerte*) is apparently found only among neighbors who are relatives. When a child dies the *padrino de*

TABLE 7.7

Relationship between *Compadres* at Matrimony

Relationship	Number	Percentage
Relatives living close by	5	16.0
Relatives in the metropolitan area	9	29.0
Relatives in the countryside	1	3.1
Neighbors (nonkin)	10	32.1
Friends at work	3	9.9
Others	3	9.9
Total	31	100.0

corona places the wreath and buys the coffin. Eight days later, he must be present for the blessing of the cross. Usually relatives who are requested for this duty are very close both residentially and socially. Among extended households the expenses of a funeral are frequently shared and the *padrino de corona* is a member of the household.

On the other hand, nonkin neighbors are preferred for the so-called *compadrazgo de evangelios* (or *escapulario*). When a child becomes seriously ill, the *padrino de evangelios* takes him to church, gives him a scapular, and prays for his health.

There are other *compadrazgos* of religious origin such as the *compadrazgo de hábito* and the *compadrazgo de arrullo del Niño*. The first occurs when somebody makes a vow to wear the habit of some order (such as that of the Carmelite nuns) during a certain period of time. In such cases it is customary to look for a *madrina* whose duties consist of presenting the habit and offering a dinner after the penitence has been fulfilled. All three cases detected in Cerrada del Cóndor were among women, two between relatives and neighbors and the remaining case between nonkin neighbors.

The *compadrazgo de arrullo del Niño* is also called *compadrazgo de Niño Dios*. It consists in taking an image of the child Jesus to church on December 24 and dressing the image on the same date for 3 consecutive years. The *comadre* or *compadre* gives the church donation, makes a present of sweets, and may continue to perform these duties beyond the 3 mandatory years. The *compadrazgo* relationship persists however, in theory at least, after the religious duties have been fulfilled.

Some *compadrazgos* are nonreligious in origin but have acquired a religious form, including *compadrazgos* customary upon certain celebrations: the fifteenth birthday, graduation from grade school, and various types of inaugurations (including in one case the opening of a barbershop). The fifteenth birthday is celebrated only for girls. Four of the 10 detected cases were among neighbors.

Upon graduation from grade school the *padrino* may occasionally pay for a graduation mass or a dinner party.

SOME CONCLUSIONS ON *COMPADRAZGO* IN CERRADA DEL CÓNDOR

The data obtained from my survey indicate that *compadrazgo* in Cerrada del Cóndor is an institution of frequent use, so much so that informants tended to recall only those cases in which *compadrazgo* represented a milestone in a durable social relationship. Godparenthood at baptism is most important and features a definite preference for *compadres* selected among very close neighbors. Many such neighbors are also relatives.

There is some evidence that a preference for relatives as godparents existed prior to migration, as shown in Table 7.8.

There is a significant preference for relatives as godparents in the countryside. On the other hand, at confirmation the preference in the countryside appears to favor neighbors or friends as *compadres*. The urban tendency is toward a greater proportion of working companions and other nonneighbors for this type of *compadrazgo*. Otherwise there are no significant differences between the kinship preferences in the city and in the countryside.

There are very few cases in Cerrada del Cóndor of vertical *compadrazgo*— i.e., *compadrazgo* between persons of different social status (Berruecos 1972). This differs from the situation as reported by anthropologists who have de-

TABLE 7.8

Relationship between *Compadres* in the Countryside and in the City According to 142 Female Heads of Residential Units

Relationship	In the countryside		In the city	
	Number	Percentage	Number	Percentage
Compadrazgo at baptism				
Relatives	83	58.4	242	42.0
Neighbors or friends	55	38.7	253	44.0
Others	4	2.8	80	14.0
Total	142	99.9	575	100.0
Compadrazgo at confirmation				
Relatives	37	42.5	123	42.3
Neighbors or friends	46	52.9	109	37.5
Others	4	4.5	59	20.0
Total	87	99.9	291	99.8

scribed *compadrazgo* in rural Mesoamerican societies (Mintz and Wolf 1950:341–367). On the contrary, there is a great stress on an equalitarian ideology based on the sharing of similar wants. *Compadres* are people who are typically neighbors and poor. Mutual assistance among neighbors, in the form of a regular daily exchange of goods and services, is the criterion I have been using to define exchange networks; the frequent occurrence of *compadrazgo* among members of such networks suggests a close connection with reciprocal exchange.

I do not believe that *compadrazgo* is deliberately sought as a means of obtaining economic assistance, though such a motivation cannot always be ruled out. However, in the vast majority of cases the intent of both partners is to grant formal sanction to a social relationship, whether already existing or merely incipient, which is recognized as potentially useful in the future. The ideal model sees the *compadre* as a person who inspires respect and should not be bothered with petty requests, except in emergencies directly relating to the godchild. But in the real world of Cerrada del Cóndor *compadrazgo* is a legitimation of certain mechanisms of mutual assistance among neighbors and relatives that span a wide range of motivations: mending the torn web of kinship ties after a traumatic migration experience; distinguishing members of a kindred who have earned a high measure of trust; conferring a special honor upon relatives, neighbors, or friends; consecrating an interpersonal truce in cases of potential conflict; and generally conferring a status of permanence and honor to the small coin of daily life solidarity so essential to survival in the shantytown.

Many conventional obligations of *compadrazgo* that may still have been important in the village lose all relevance in the urban context. The quality of a *compadre* is not judged by the generosity of his ceremonial gifts but by the intensity and trustworthiness of the reciprocal exchange that develops afterward. Thus the flexibility of the *compadrazgo* institution fits the situation of reciprocity networks and may be used to strengthen the exchange relations or to prevent internal conflicts within networks. All reciprocity networks in Cerrada del Cóndor contained *compadrazgo* relations among at least some of their members.

Compadrazgo is a durable contract that lasts for the lifetime of the partners. Actually, however, many *compadres* are swallowed up by the great city and are never heard of again. This happens when a reciprocity network disbands and its members disperse. Rarely, *compadrazgo* may also be terminated by aggression or disrespectful behavior between *compadres*. Mutual respect is considered essential to *compadrazgo* even when other ritual, social, or economic duties are not met.

In conclusion, I submit that *compadrazgo* as practiced in Cerrada del Cóndor is an example of a ritual institution harnessed to the needs of a new social situation. The surviving formal duties of a *compadre* are mostly of a ritual nature; they are definitely shrinking in importance beside the informal duties as contained in the prevailing ideology of mutual assistance. In the end, the performance of these informal duties is the content of the *compadrazgo* relationship. *Compadrazgo* is emptied of all significance and actually disappears as an effective social relationship when the *compadres* move away and stop seeing each other regularly; much the same is true of kinship relations. On the other hand, *compadrazgo* becomes most meaningful and active in the context of reciprocity networks.

Obviously such a postulated relationship between *compadrazgo* and networks is difficult to verify quantitatively, since there is no objective difference between the exchange practiced between *compadres* and those not *compadres* within a given network. It should be kept in mind, however, that the statistics on *compadrazgo* as given in this chapter refer predominantly to intranetwork relations. The use of the *compadrazgo* institution among men and women alike represents a further indirect confirmation that networks are constituted by nuclear families and are not merely centered around women. Of course there are quite a few cases of *compadrazgo* that project outside the networks involving, among others, relatives and work companions who live elsewhere within or beyond the shantytown. It seems, however, that such *compadrazgo* relationships are often conducive to the *compadres* moving in closer together. Hence *compadrazgo* may also be used to provide certain elements of mobility indispensable to the dynamic growth of reciprocity networks.

Formal and Informal Associations

CUATISMO

Cuatismo (from the Nahuatl *cuatl,* "twin brother") is a native category describing a complex of norms, values, and social relationships built up around male friendship in Mexican culture. My interest in *cuatismo* is here necessarily limited to one specific question, namely its relationship to the internal structure of reciprocity networks in Cerrada del Cóndor.

When I made my first observations on these networks I was led to formulate the hypothesis that they were based on daily interaction among women, i.e., among housewives who were also neighbors. Later I discovered that *all* members of a nuclear family participate in reciprocal exchange. In particular, men help one another in the search for housing and work, borrow money from one another, and share other forms of self-help. There was still a possibility, however, that the network phenomenon might be centered on the aid and solidarity as practiced by housewives, rather than on some similar relationship between the husbands.

The analysis of real and fictive kinship in Cerrada del Cóndor supplied data on the importance of the male element in network formation, as shown by predominant forms of patrilineal and patrilocal kinship, or by the fact that *compadres* are selected more often by the husband than by the wife. Hence it may be inferred that reciprocity networks do involve a significant social relationship among husbands as well. Further confirmation of this inference was found in the structure of male friendship groups in the shantytown. Seen as a whole, the data amount to a conclusive chain of evidence against the initial assumption of a dominantly matrilocal structure of the exchange networks.

Field research on *cuatismo* is difficult, especially for a woman anthropologist, because of the exclusive character of this social relationship. According to a male informant, a man grades his male friends according to categories such as "friends," "good friends," and *"cuates."* These shadings of friendship imply the existence of a scale of behavior among friends, with particular bearing on the behavior patterns as related to the mechanism of requesting and granting favors.

The observations I am about to describe have been obtained in two different ways: (1) from a selected group of trusted male informants; and (2) from a survey of 142 female heads of residential units in Cerrada del Cóndor, who supplied information on their husband's *cuates.* I shall begin by describing the dyadic relationship between friends; then I shall discuss the *cuate* group and its relationship with reciprocity networks.

Cuatismo as a Dyadic Relationship

To a settler of Cerrada del Cóndor, a plain friend is an acquaintance on cordial terms with him. This relationship lacks any particular emotional content and does not necessarily imply a degree of familiarity such as would be required in order to request a favor. All it implies is a possibility of locating the person in the social field.

If two plain friends meet with some regularity and if such meetings are conducive to a more direct personal contact, they may become closer friends. This intermediate stage may entail sufficient familiarity for the mutual exchange of small favors. Yet the social forms between such friends still imply some social distance. With *cuates,* on the other hand, there is a special relationship, which is often emotional to the point where it may represent the most intense interpersonal relationship in a man's life. Of course, there is a range of intensity and function in the *cuatismo* institution. In Cerrada del Cóndor, a *cuate* is first of all a companion for leisure activities, particularly drinking. There are also other kinds of *cuates:* the sportsman *cuate,* the *cuate* for heart-to-heart talks, the *cuate* among relatives, and so on. The act of getting drunk together creates a bond that implies both interpersonal trust and a release from formal manners: "Getting drunk is a liberation, people get rid of their inhibitions. When you are sober you cannot say the kind of things that you can say when drunk; these are your truths." Verbal or physical violence among *cuates* is a release of pent-up undifferentiated aggression repressed in the course of normal social life even among close relatives. As an example, an uncle and his nephew always maintain a formal respectful approach toward each other even if they are members of the same household. Should there be a difference of opinion between them, such as might arise when watching a soccer match, the nephew cannot talk back to his uncle openly. If uncle and nephew are also *cuates,* on the other hand, it would be perfectly acceptable for the nephew to tell his uncle the next time they are drinking together: "Listen uncle, I respect you a lot, but don't say such-and-such again to me." Such disrespectful talk would not be tolerated at home; but in the tavern anything goes among *cuates.* If things get rough it is always possible to make excuses the day after and "put the blame on the drinking."

One of his informants told Roberts (1973:29) that male friendship in Guatemala meant "trusting someone, getting drunk with him and being quite open in one's confidences." In Santiago, I heard Mapuche migrants comment that if you want to have friends you have to drink (Lomnitz 1969:47–71). An informant from Cerrada del Cóndor told me: "I do not drink so I don't have any friends." In all three cases the term *friend* refers to a very special kind of male friendship. Drinking relations are important on a social plane and may eventually extend into other directions. Thus, a *compadrazgo* proposition will often originate during a drinking session. Psychologically speaking, two or more men who drink together implicitly agree to leave aside all mental reservations, to have no secrets before their *cuates.* Getting drunk together represents a high degree of trust (Lomnitz 1969:69).

Mutual obligations among *cuates* include sincerity, helpfulness with advice, siding with one another in a fight, and lending assistance to each other. The ideal attitude among *cuates* is one of unrestricted generosity, as symbolized by the custom of buying drinks in public places.

The following passage describes well the nature of *cuatismo:*

> Emotional friendship involves a relation between ego and an alter in which each satisfies some emotional need in his opposite number. We should expect to find emotional friendships primarily in social situations where the individual is strongly embedded in solidary groupings and where the set of social structure inhibits social and geographical mobility. In such situations, ego's access to resources is largely provided by solidary unions; and friendship can at best provide emotional release and catharsis from the strains and pressures of role playing [Wolf 1969:10–11].

The Group of *Cuates*

A set of dyadic relationships centered around some common interest (sports, games, partying) may become suffused by intense personal emotional attachment and a relationship of mutual assistance. Thus a group friendship among three or more *cuates* is born. Joint activities among groups of *cuates* may be varied: drinking, talking, playing cards, playing soccer, watching television, playing *rayuela* (a pitching game), going to the movies or bullfights, going for a walk, or simply going out to have fun together. Women are absolutely excluded from membership in such friendship circles.

In Cerrada del Cóndor, the *cuate* groups usually include 4 or 5 men, though certain groups may have up to 10 members. The shantytown soccer teams are associations based on *cuatismo*. Three of these teams are based on a single macronetwork among kinship-related migrants from a village in San Luis Potosí; the fourth team (called Club Mexico) is based on neighbors who are not necessarily interrelated. The membership of the latter team tends to be more urbanized and open to the fluidity of social relationships in the city, as opposed to conservative migrants who tend to stay encapsuled in their familistic network relationships. Butterworth (1972:29–50) made a similar distinction between two groups of *cuates* in Mexico City, one of which included relatives only whereas the other was constituted by friends who had met at work.

The existence of a *cuate* group is made official through its joint drinking activities. Within the drinking circle, any *cuate* in possession of cash feels obligated to buy drinks for his companions; one might say that *cuatismo* involves an economic leveling mechanism through drink, by ensuring that no member of the *cuate* group can ever gain economic prominence above the common denominator of his friend's resources. Thus *cuatismo* discourages individual savings that might introduce power differentials within the group. In addition to drinking together, *cuate* groups are also fighting associations for mutual defense, and self-help groups for mutual assistance in housing and many other chores. In a word, the *cuate* group is the effective community of a male in the great city. This pattern is reminiscent of that which I observed among Mapuche migrants in Santiago, who "transfer the functions and values of their former indigenous community to a group of friends. Drinking among such groups is a necessary condition for acceptance and membership [Lomnitz 1969:51]."

Cuatismo and Reciprocity Networks

Table 8.1 shows the results of a *cuatismo* survey carried out among female heads of residential units in Cerrada del Cóndor who were asked to inform about their husband's *cuates*. The figures in this table correspond to heads of residential units. The number of *cuate* groups should actually be smaller, because each *cuate* group may contain more than one head of residential unit. Again, heads of residential units are less frequent among *cuate* groups made up of kinsmen than among *cuate* groups that include unrelated neighbors. Such neighbors are often heads of their own residential units; this explains the high incidence of nonrelatives in the table. If a *cuate* group contains only relatives, many of them would share the same household with the head of the residential unit and therefore would not be included in the table.

TABLE 8.1

Composition of *Cuate* Groups According to 142 Female Heads of Households

All are neighbors and	
Relatives	21
Both kin and nonkin	20
Nonkin	45
All live outside of Cerrada del Cóndor and are	
Relatives	1
Both kin and nonkin	1
Nonkin	9
All live in village of origin	2
Some live in Cerrada del Cóndor	9
Residential units lacking a male head of household	34
Total	142

One important conclusion is that about 80% of the *cuate* groups of heads of residential units are recruited among men who are immediate neighbors. A large proportion of these are also all-relative groups. Only 1 out of 10 heads of residential units has his *cuate* group outside the shantytown, mostly because they are recruited at work. This would correspond to the "urban" *cuatismo* pattern, according to Butterworth (1972:50). A further tenth of the groups recruit their *cuates* partly among neighbors and partly among relatives or friends met at work.

In order to interpret the social significance of these figures, one can hardly overlook that most *cuate* groups are composed of neighbors and relatives. Field observations, as described in previous chapters, confirm the fact that *cuate* groups frequently overlap with the male sector of networks of reciprocal exchange. Networks making use of the *cuatismo* institution also appear to benefit from a closer social relationship and a more generalized and more intensive exchange of goods and services.

I have given at least one example of separate networks based on *cuatismo* for the male sector of a household, and kinship for the female sector of the same household. In one of these cases the household was residentially located halfway between both networks. In another case there was a matrifocal network of reciprocal exchange among neighborhood housewives, and each husband had a *cuate* group of his own. The reciprocal exchange relationships in such networks were relatively less generalized and intense, with a tendency toward dyadic relationships.

In general, those networks featuring an exocentric relationship, which is both stable and self-sufficient, are precisely those utilizing all available social institutions (including kinship, *compadrazgo*, and *cuatismo*) to reinforce and legitimize the network relationships. Such networks may be described as highly integrated, all the social resources of their members having been mobilized on behalf of the network.

Quite a few networks show the influence of patrilineality in the tendency of the male element toward decision making, particularly concerning the more important economic and social issues. *Cuatismo* lends emotional content to the solidarity between males within a network; it provides an outlet to pent-up aggressive tendencies, thus forestalling serious conflict and maintaining equality through the dispersal of any cash surpluses through drinking. These are important elements favoring a continuing reciprocal exchange in the network context. When a network is centered on the extended family, *cuatismo* may also help explain the continuity of the network structure beyond the lifetime of the head of the household. Domestic functions may continue to be supervised by the widow; yet such an apparent matriarchy could hardly function without an underlying structure of male friendship within the network.

Observations on *compadrazgo* as a mechanism in the dynamic growth of networks may thus be extended to *cuatismo*. A drinking circle is a sufficiently flexible structure to include *cuates* belonging to other networks, and these friendships develop into valuable dyadic reciprocity relations. Such *cuatismo*-based relations are eventually utilized when a network begins to branch out, or when a member wishes to change to another network. In conclusion, the prevalence of *cuatismo* among male members of reciprocal networks, in particular the more integrated networks, supports the view that both men and women are active participants in the network relationship. Women are formally excluded from the *cuatismo* relationship, but the relation of economic exchange includes all members of the nuclear family.

LOCAL AND NATIONAL ASSOCIATIONS

The network of reciprocal exchange is the effective community of the individual in a situation of marginality. This is perhaps the central idea put forward in this book. If correct, such a fact should be reflected in other than merely economic aspects, for example in the political and social situation of the shantytown. Thus one would expect a low participation of shantytown settlers in all kinds of local or national associations unrelated to networks.

Such a low level of participation would also be expected from the work of Adams (1974), who defined marginality in terms of the underparticipation of a social group in the process of decision making within the society at large. The effective influence of a given group in local or national affairs is obviously very small when such a group lacks representation at the decision-making level. In order to deal with these important questions I shall present the results of a special survey conducted in Cerrada del Cóndor, on the participation of the settlers in political, religious, educational, social security, labor, sports, and other associations.

The actual figures on lack of participation in local or nationwide institutions, impressive as they are, fall short of giving an idea of the true extent of marginalization. A more complete description of the situation, amounting to a nearly complete lack of influence and control over urban and national institutions, would have to include a description of the passivity among those few individuals who do belong to associations beyond reciprocity networks. Most of the affiliations observed are passive, including membership in the social security system by virtue of legal requirements, not to be compared to membership in local groups created for the improvement of the political, social, or economic situation of their participants. The latter type of association has not been observed in Cerrada del Cóndor.

Lack of membership in labor unions or trade associations can have serious consequences in the Mexican political system, which tends to channel political participation through pressure groups rather than political parties. Specifically, in Cerrada del Cóndor those few settlers who are union members generally abstain from active participation in union activities. Settlers who are covered by social security may make use of a few economic facilities within the social security system but abstain from all activities that might bring them into contact with other members of the social security system.

These general observations lead one to the fact that there is no local authority in Cerrada del Cóndor, elected or otherwise. There are only informal organizations based on exchange networks, outwardly invisible but effective and absorbing for the individual. These autonomous social organisms have a dynamic of their own; they may not control the shantytown as such but they are not subjected to external control either. The lack of articulation of the marginals with local or national formal associations also means that as a group they are beyond the control of the urban industrial system. In fact they largely escape the political control of the nation as well. In its attempts to grapple with the "problem" of marginality, the urban industrial system has been utterly unable to regulate or control this growing population sector in any significant way. I am reminded of Adams' analogy between marginalization and waste in an industrial society (1974). Industrialization may be described as a process of differentiation of human and material resources; after processing there is always a remainder that is not further processible. Ultimately the accumulation of waste materials and waste populations forces society to undertake expensive programs for recycling these populations and materials in order to reincorporate them to production and social control.

Participation in National Associations

Households in Cerrada del Cóndor participate in national culture through public education and the mass media. This participation may be thought of as

TABLE 8.2

Participation in National Associations[a]

Participants per residential unit	Residential units	
	Number	Percentage
None	97	68.3
One or more	43	30.2
Unknown	2	1.4
Total	142	99.9

[a] Based on a survey of 142 residential units.

passive; nevertheless it is large in comparison with the low levels of participation that still prevail in the countryside. I estimate that at least 80% of shantytown children below the age of 12 go to school; 81% of the residential units in the shantytown have a radio, and 39% of them have a television set. There is considerable consumption of popular literature (comics, photo-romances, sports sheets). All these media are carriers of the values, norms, and aspirations of urban national culture.

All settlers are also members of the Catholic religion, which they observe to a greater or lesser extent. At the very least they all observe the ceremonies connected with the life cycle (baptism, confirmation, wedding, burial). Each residential unit has an altar with images, most commonly the Virgin of Guadalupe, Saint Martin of Porras, and the Sacred Heart of Jesus. Even settlers who do not regularly participate in religious observances live their common faith as a set of norms and values perceived as part of the national identity.

With these exceptions in mind, the survey reveals a low degree of participation in specific national associations. Table 8.2 shows that fewer than one-third of the residential units are implicated in any way with associations at the national level.

TABLE 8.3

Membership in Associations Outside of Cerrada del Cóndor

Association	Number of affiliated
Social security	29
Unions	13
Religious organizations	13
Parent-Teacher Associations	6
Sport clubs at place of work	5
Political parties	4
Total	70

Table 8.3 presents a detailed rundown of the types of affiliations found in the shantytown.

The law requires that all industrial workers, employees, and civil service workers must belong to social security. Under the provisions of this affiliation they have a right to medical services covering their nuclear families. The coverage extends only to the worker unless he is legally married. This provides an incentive for making sexual unions legally valid.

Membership in labor unions should theoretically overlap the membership in social security, as both should be automatic for jobholders in industry or government. In practice, however, most construction workers hold temporary jobs, which they change frequently, and few employers take the trouble to affiliate their workers in the social security systems, not to mention labor unions. At any rate, membership in a labor union is rarely a matter of the worker's free choice.

The following religious organizations are represented in the shantytown: Sacred Heart Congregation, Brotherhood of the Sanctuary of Atotonilco, Catholic Action, Legion of St. Mary, Congregation of the Virgin of Carmen, and Congregation of Saint John. There are no members of Protestant or other denominational non-Catholic associations. A few families are affiliated to more than one Catholic fraternity or congregation.

Six families said that they participated at least once a year in meetings of the Parent–Teacher Association.

Table 8.3 also includes five members of soccer teams outside the shantytown; such membership is significant since soccer clubs are typically urban associations. The fact that there are soccer teams available inside the shantytown may lead us to see membership in teams outside the shantytown as an indication of a higher degree of urbanization.

Membership in political parties was distributed as follows: two members, both of economic level A, were registered with Partido Revolucionario Institucional (PRI), and two informants were said to belong to Partido Acción Nacional (PAN). Membership appeared to be purely formal, with the possible exception of one informant who occasionally distributes political handbills.

In conclusion, whatever little participation in outside associations was detected in the shantytown appears to be sporadic and largely nominal. The most significant and continuous participation is found in sports and religious associations. Thus, national associations appear to have no significant direct influence on the shantytown, judging by the low level of participation found among the settlers.[1]

---

[1]Cornelius substantially agrees with our point of view in the sense that lack of membership in national organizations is significantly correlated with political marginality: "Numerous studies have demonstrated that people who are members of voluntary organizations tend to participate in politics more than those who are not, irrespective of their social status characteristics and attitudinal orientations. My findings are quite consistent with this generalization [1975:199]."

Participation in Local Associations

All major local associations observed in Cerrada del Cóndor are directly related to reciprocity networks. This is notably true for the soccer teams, which
may be regarded as the most active local associations in the shantytown.

A further type of local association closely connected with networks is the
informal rotating credit group called *tanda*, which has been more fully described
in Chapter 4. *Tandas* and soccer teams both derive their membership directly
from neighborhood networks and may be seen as subsidiary activities of such
networks rather than local associations in their own right.

Because of the absence of local government in the shantytown, the need to
solve certain acute local problems may give rise to sporadic action groups. Such
ad hoc associations arise over issues and tend to disappear after the crisis has
subsided. There are very few examples of sporadic associations in the history of
the shantytown. The two best known examples follow:

1. Several neighboring family groups met a few times for the purpose of
   petitioning the authorities concerning the installation of a public water
   faucet.
2. Another time, four women decided to get together in order to request an
   audience with the First Lady, for the purpose of lodging a complaint
   against a refinery that was causing brushfires in the ravine and endangering
   the shantytown.

The exceptional nature of such emergency associations and the low level of
participation of the settlers in these temporary groups represent further indications of the lack of community organization at the shantytown level. Cerrada del
Cóndor cannot be said to constitute a community in any formal or informal sense.
Roberts (1973) has observed that formal organizations in shantytowns normally
arise as a result of external pressure and not as a consequence of the natural needs
of the settlers.

The medical center of Cerrada del Cóndor is an example of an organization
created by an external agency. The credit for the creation of this medical center
belongs primarily to a group of middle-class women who live in the adjacent
neighborhood of Las Aguilas. The uncomfortable and potentially threatening
proximity of the shantytown induced these women to take the initiative in establishing a small neighborhood health center with the assistance of the local parish.
The Children's Hospital of Mexico (which belongs to the Department of Health
and Welfare) took an interest in this center and appointed a medical student as a
resident, particularly for serving the children of the shantytown. A group of
doctors also became interested in the possibility of carrying out a study on

nutrition and mental health among the children. The women's group of Las Aguilas also contributed some money to cover the salary of a social worker.

These modest facilities were all that was needed to turn the health center into an important institution in the daily life of the shantytown. In addition to its use as a clinic and a center for preventive medicine, it became a meeting place for children, mothers, and particularly for adolescent girls, because of the presence of the understanding social worker. At various times courses in carpentry, electricity, and similar trades were conducted for men and boys; there were also special classes for children who had failed to fulfill the entrance requirements for primary school. Among the more successful free courses offered was a "health-promoter's course" led by a doctor of the Children's Hospital. The young girls who took this course learned some elements of first aid and nursing. All such experiments were unfortunately sporadic since they lacked the backing of a settler's organization on the local level. The continuity of the efforts rested solely on the support of the middle-class women's group. The Children's Hospital withdrew from Cerrada del Cóndor in 1970. For over a year the women's group continued on its own, but finally it too withdrew from the shantytown.

At this point the doctor in charge of the health center decided to go directly to the settlers; he succeeded in setting up a neighborhood association for the provisional support of the center. This association included five settlers, who organized some shantytown benefits and announced a monthly assessment to be collected from Cerrada del Cóndor settlers, for the maintenance of the health center. After this, the doctor also withdrew, but the health center survived; a private university has taken it over as a center of social work. In the afternoons there is medical service (for a small fee), provided by a medical student and a dentistry student. The fees pay for the light bill and for the services of a woman caretaker who is a shantytown resident. Three or four settlers have continued to take an interest in the center and have volunteered to take part in its maintenance and administration. These settlers live on the edge of the shantytown and actually belong to the middle class.

The apparent lack of ability of shantytown settlers to organize at the local level has been attributed to the heterogeneity of origins among the settlers as well as to their residential and occupational mobility within the city. These factors are assumed to interfere with the development of the sufficiently broad basis of confidence and cooperation needed for the existence of a community of local interests (Roberts 1973). This explanation fails to take into account the presence of the networks of reciprocal exchange, which have developed a high degree of confidence and cooperation. Rather, the mistake of all "organizers" from the outside is the assumption that the shantytown represents a community, when it is actually an agglomeration of networks, each of which represents a separate community to its members. This is not the same as an excessive "integration" of the marginals to the urban environment, as Roberts proposes, but on the contrary an effect of their lack of integration in the urban industrial socioeconomic system. In Mexico City there are mature shantytowns with semiurban facilities and fully legalized ownership of marginal property, where local government is just as lacking as it is in Cerrada del Cóndor, though sporadic action groups come up under a leader's direction to petition the government for the solution of specific problems (Cornelius 1975). The lack of formal organizations at the shantytown level persists even when the settlers are homeowners and their residential mobility has become lower than it would be among most middle-class families. I infer that the social and organizational structure of shantytowns is not a result of rootlessness among the settlers.

The medical center could never have been created by the shantytown settlers themselves, for a very obvious reason: lack of information on the functioning of the bureaucratic system, and lack of personal contacts. The involvement of the Children's Hospital of Mexico was due primarily to a personal contact of a member of the women's group in Las Aguilas. Marginal people are entirely lacking in such contacts or in the elementary knowledge of the state apparatus these contacts presuppose. Assuming that the right contacts had been available to them, they would not have been eligible for free medical assistance because of their lack of incorporation in the national social security system. In other words, the health center could only have arisen through outside initiative, as a charity coupled to the interest of the hospital in using the health center as a research facility.

Normally the health center would have suspended operations the moment that the hospital and the women's group withdrew from the shantytown. It was saved through the personal intervention of a middle-class doctor, who had to step in to organize the shantytown settlers, precisely because such organization is not a normal feature of marginality. A shantytown-wide service such as a health center cannot easily arise or be maintained, since it has no obvious connection with the indigenous social organization of the shantytown. On the other hand, organizations that arise directly from the network structure, such as the local soccer teams, are stable and enjoy a broad participation on the part of the settlers.

It may be worth recalling that many of the larger shantytowns develop a type of local leader called a *cacique,* who may be seen as a broker between the marginal settlers and urban modern society. The characteristic fragmentation of land tenure in Cerrada del Cóndor has so far prevented the rise to power of important *caciques;* but this is not typical of Mexico City squatter settlements. More often the shantytown features at least one *cacique* "who stands guard over the crucial juncture or synapsis of relationships which connect the local system to the larger whole [Cornelius 1975:158]." A *cacique* is a political broker who controls vital resources (land, water, work protection) and therefore enjoys a broad local following as well as personal relations with politicians and officials.

He is in a position to perform useful services for the population of the shantytown in exchange for a profitable personal control. Thus a certain amount of political control over marginal populations is achieved by the system through utilization of traditional preindustrial mechanisms. Although not directly observed in Cerrada del Cóndor, *cacicazgo* is a widespread form of traditional leadership in Mexican peasant communities. Some of the mechanisms that give rise to *cacique* leadership have been described in Chapter 6.

Reciprocity and Confianza

In this chapter I shall discuss some theoretical implications of the networks observed in Cerrada del Cóndor. A systematic analysis of these observations involves, first, a discussion of reciprocity as an *economic system;* second, an analysis of the social conditions that give rise to reciprocity; and third, the relationship between reciprocal exchange and market exchange. Then I shall attempt to define the intensity scale of reciprocal exchange within the framework of a network typology derived from shantytown observations, and I shall describe the *confianza* parameter that determines the type and intensity of reciprocal exchange. The chapter concludes with some general observations on exchange in relation to scarcity or abundance of resources in a social group.

WHAT IS RECIPROCITY?

Following Polanyi (1957:234–269) and Dalton (1968:143–187), I define reciprocity as a form of exchange of goods and services having the following characteristic features: (1) It develops as part of a social relation; (2) the reciprocal flow of goods and services persists beyond a single transaction; (3) it is not governed by the law of supply and demand. "Reciprocity may be attained through a sharing of the burden of labor according to definite rules of distribution as when taking things 'in turn.' Similarly reciprocity is sometimes attained through exchange at set equivalencies for the benefit of the partner who happens to be short of some kind of necessities [Polanyi 1957:253]."

This specific use of the term *reciprocity* should be carefully distinguished from the more general usage as employed by Blau (1964), Gouldner (1960), Homans (1958:597–606), Levi-Strauss (1967:189), and Mauss (1954) when they speak of the *principle of reciprocity* as the basis of all social life. In this book I use the term *reciprocity* to designate a specific mode of exchange to be distinguished, for example, from market exchange. Polanyi holds that this type of exchange is based on the principle of generosity, in contrast to market exchange, which is supposedly based on a purely individualistic and rational maximization of profit. Most studies on reciprocal exchange were made in "primitive societies," and were connected with the problem of social solidarity (see Sahlins 1968:139–236). Members of the "formalist" school of economic anthropology, such as Burling (1962:704), Firth and Dyamour (1970), and Cook (1968:188–208), have reacted against this approach; they claim that any economic exchange is necessarily based on the maximization principle. The "substantivist" model proposed by Polanyi and his followers was decried as romantic and as influenced by the "antimarket mentality" of anthropologists. Cook (1968:210) dismissed it as "a theory which was specifically designed for the analysis of certain types of moribund economies."

In Cerrada del Cóndor reciprocal exchange is an integral part of an economic system that does not follow the law of supply and demand. It is connected with the existence of social networks, i.e., social fields defined simultaneously by social and economic exchange relations. It is possible to argue that these social networks are structures that maximize an important commodity, namely security. Indeed, reciprocity always implies a flow of goods and services in both directions. The basis of generosity, if this is the proper term, is not altogether unselfish. Whatever interpretation one may prefer to use, the fact remains that networks of reciprocal exchange do exist in the shantytown and are by no means limited to "primitive" cultures in the process of extinction.

Perhaps the concept of generosity as applied to reciprocal exchange should not be understood as a moral category but rather as an effect of economic necessity: "for it is scarcity and not sufficiency that makes people generous [Evans-Pritchard 1940:90–91]." Here is an essential difference from market economy, which I propose to dwell on. "Maximization" of resources presupposes a supply of goods in sufficient amounts to raise the question of several plausible alternate strategies: to sell or not to sell, to select a job offer among various available possibilities, and so on. Reciprocity, on the other hand, arises in situations of lack of resources. Whenever the physical or social survival of a group is threatened, people mobilize their social resources for whatever economic value they may afford. The Spanish saying "*hoy por ti, mañana por mí*" ("your turn today, my turn tomorrow'') summarizes the principle of reciprocal exchange in a situation of balanced scarcity assumed to persist indefinitely for both partners.

The condition of equality of wants has implicitly been noted by several authors. Thus, Sahlins points out that ''a difference in affluence—or in capacity to replicate wealth—would lower the sociability content of balanced dealing [1968:166].'' On the other hand, Blau has shown that every act of exchange implies a power transaction, and that imbalanced exchange generates power differentials. Whenever one of the partners of the exchange needs it more than the other, he finds himself in the situation of the ''poor nephew,'' who has to endure the meddling of his rich uncle in his personal affairs. ''Indeed, a major impetus for the eagerness of individuals to discharge their obligations and reciprocate for services they receive by providing services in return is the threat of becoming otherwise subject to the power of the supplier of services [Blau 1964:28].''

Polanyi gives no specific definition of a dyadic reciprocal exchange. Instead, he speaks of reciprocity as a form of exchange between symmetrical social *groups* within a given society. In this he largely uses field observations by Malinowsky. Sahlins, on the other hand, sees reciprocal exchange as ''a momentary episode in a continuous social relation. The social relation exerts governance: the flow of goods is constrained by, if part of, a status etiquette [1968:139].''

In my analysis of the so-called *compadrazgo* exchange in the middle class of Chile (Lomnitz 1971), I proposed that social relations may be convertible into economic resources through a reciprocity mechanism. As in the Chilean middle class, there is no dominance of the social aspects or vice versa in Cerrada del Cóndor. Both are inseparable aspects of one and the same relationship.

SCALES OF RECIPROCITY IN CERRADA DEL CÓNDOR

The networks of reciprocal exchange in Cerrada del Cóndor feature different kinds and degrees of reciprocity. In general these variations depend on the internal structure of the network, and on the physical and social closeness among its members.

The term *intensity of exchange* is used to designate a measure of the frequency of exchange as well as of the range of goods and services traded. Reciprocity between close relatives may often be very intense; favors and objects of every kind are frequently exchanged, physical distance permitting. Of course, a daughter does not normally spend 2 hours and 5 pesos on bus rides merely to ask her mother for a cup of cooking oil. A neighbor is handier for such daily emergencies of marginal life. On the other hand, physical closeness by itself is not sufficient to guarantee an intense reciprocal exchange relation; social closeness is also a requirement. More subtle shades and differences in exchange intensity may depend on the complex factor of *confianza*.

The internal structure of the network depends primarily on the type of household, as analyzed in Chapter 5:

Extended networks with expense sharing
Extended networks without expense sharing
Jointed networks
Mixed networks (relatives and nonrelatives)
Neighbor networks (nonrelatives only)

The intensity of exchange in these various types of networks appears to describe a continuous scale from high to low intensity, as follows:

Pole of high intensity				*Pole of low intensity*
Extended with expense sharing	Extended without expense sharing	Jointed	Mixed	Nonkin

The exchange intensity within a given network may also be translated in terms of certain features, which one might generally relate to the "efficiency" of the network. These features are listed in Table 9.1.

The most efficient network is the extended family that lives under the same roof or on the same plot and practices expense sharing. The least efficient network would be a network of neighbors unrelated through kinship. The terms *generalized reciprocity* and *balanced reciprocity* have been borrowed from the reciprocity spectrum proposed by Sahlins (1968). In generalized reciprocity the goods and services may flow in one direction over long periods of time, as happens for example between parents and children; the absence of equivalent return does not necessarily interrupt the relationship. In balanced reciprocity, on

TABLE 9.1

A Continuum of Intensity of Exchange

Pole of high intensity	Pole of low intensity
Generalized reciprocity (pooling)	Balanced reciprocity
High stability	Low stability
High autonomy (closed network)	Low autonomy (open network)
Large number of participant families	Small number of participant families
Exocentric exchange	Dyadic exchange
Low formality (familiarity)	High formality (etiquette)
Centralizing personality (emotional leader)	Noncentralized neighborhood network

the other hand, the value of the things exchanged is closely equivalent and the exchange occurs by turns at relatively short and regular intervals.

By *stability* I mean the permanence of a network as a functioning economic and social structure. In Cerrada del Cóndor the extended family networks have a high degree of stability; networks formed by nonkin neighbors are not nearly as durable, since frequent residential changes tend to scatter neighbors whenever a kinship relation is lacking. The older networks develop a great deal of *autonomy* because of the number and stability of their membership. In other words, the numerical size and stability of a network determine its economic viability. Networks between nonkin neighbors, on the other hand, normally include two or at most three nuclear families, which is seldom sufficient for satisfying all the economic needs that arise within the network. Members of such networks therefore tend to complement their economic security requirements through dyadic exchange relations with outsiders to the network (usually relatives or *cuates*). These dyadic relations exert a definite centrifugal attraction, which reduces the stability of the network.

The relative absence of formality in a reciprocal relationship may be used to gauge the intensity of the exchange. As an example, I have observed that members of extended networks with expense sharing often borrow objects from each other without asking permission. In fact, quite a few belongings are shared by the group and have no individual owner. Mutual assistance among members tends to be unconditional and quite informal. On the other hand, exchange between nonrelatives invariably follows a protocol, which includes a set of prescribed courtesies (forms of address such as "señora," "vecina," or "comadre"); this protocol extends to the formalities for requesting and returning favors.

As a final observation, I have noticed that networks where the regime of reciprocal exchange is very intense are often organized around a central figure who commands the loyalty and affection of all network members, thus helping to consolidate a familistic network over long periods of time. Usually it is a mother or an elder sister. Female emotional leaders may be very important in the structure of a network, since they embody and sustain the ideology of mutual assistance within the social group. Such strong personalities are rarely found among networks based on nonkin neighbors, since the corresponding familistic structures are lacking. In this case, mutual help must rely on the ebb and flow of economic circumstances and above all on the degree of *confianza* between members of the network.

CONFIANZA: A VARIABLE OF RECIPROCAL EXCHANGE

Confianza is a psychosocial dynamic variable that measures the ability and desire of two partners to engage in reciprocal exchange of favors, goods and services, and information.

An exchange is a dyadic event. The generalized exchange observed in reciprocity networks has been termed *exocentric,* because each of the participants tends to exchange goods and services with every other member of the network. This exocentric exchange evidently results from a sequence of dyadic reciprocal exchanges that keep occurring among all members of the social group.

Consider the ideal model of intensity of reciprocal exchange. This model appears to be governed by a continuum of social distance (see, for example, Lomnitz 1971:103). The ideal scale of favors in terms of social distance may be gathered from an open survey of 142 women in Cerrada del Cóndor. Table 9.2 totals the number of possible replies given during the survey. Its statistical significance is more qualitative than quantitative, since each informant may have given more than one affirmative reply. The questions used in the survey referred to a hypothetical ideal situation and not to an actual occurrence.

Ideally, relatives may be approached for any kind of favors; the help of a *compadre,* on the other hand, should more properly be reserved for emergency situations. Fully 86% of all positive replies concerning "all kind of favors" corresponded to relatives and neighbors. This ideal model of reciprocal exchange is dominated by favors of social and physical closeness. Figure 9.1 attempts to convey the ideal of an intensity field of exchange governed by these two variables. Here the different types of networks are represented as points on the social distance axis, in an attempt to symbolize the ideal model of reciprocity as found in Cerrada del Cóndor. Actually, of course, there are shadings and differences within each category of social distance. Within any family some brothers may be closer than others; some cousins may be preferred over others. Even friendship terms (whether among kin or nonkin) include distinctions such as "just friends," "good friends," and "*cuates.*" There are acquaintances by sight, acquaintances on greeting terms, buddies (work companions), friends of a friend, and so on, in endless nuances. Furthermore, the actual dyadic relationship does not always reflect the formal social distance: A *cuate* who is a neighbor and a drinking companion may enjoy a more intense relationship of reciprocal exchange than a

TABLE 9.2

Kinds of Favors Requested

Social distance	Any favor	Loans of money	Emergencies	No favor
Relatives	50	58	6	16
Neighbors	10	48	7	45
Compadres	6	35	12	63
Friends	3	30	7	72
Acquaintances	0	4	6	92

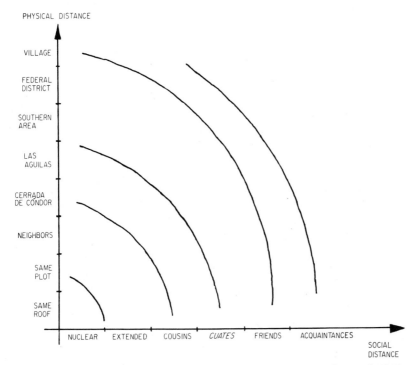

Figure 9.1. An ideal model of intensity of reciprocal exchange, according to physical and social distance between partners. The intensity of the flow of exchange increases toward the origin of the graph. In this model, each particular exchange relationship may be represented by a point on the graph.

brother who lives somewhere else in the Federal District. Hence the definition of *confianza* as the real or effective psychosocial distance between individuals, as opposed to the formal or ideal social distance between categories. The latter is represented by degrees of kinship or by dyadic forms of a more or less ceremonial character (such as *compadrazgo* or the privilege of the familiar form of address). *Confianza,* on the other hand, represents the subjective and personal evaluation made by a participant concerning his momentary status within a given reciprocity relation.

A further factor that determines *confianza* is physical proximity. An effective implementation of prescribed or expected norms of behavior depends on actual opportunities of performance. The opportunity of mutual assistance is greatly diminished by intervening physical distance; here *confianza* dies on the vine. On the other hand, any successful act of reciprocal exchange increases the *confianza* for future exchange. In a shantytown the limitation interposed by physical distance on every kind of social contact is particularly severe. This factor can be objectively measured (in minutes needed to walk somewhere or in pesos of busfare). It may be quantified and plotted as proposed in Figure 9.2. Physical closeness is a vital component of *confianza* and may actually dominate a reciprocity relationship over and above the expected social behavior.

A third factor influencing *confianza* is socioeconomic equality. Even among relatives, greater *confianza* exists among those who share the same economic position; conversely, socioeconomic differences can estrange even brothers. This observation is explained by the fact that *confianza* lies at the base of reciprocity, and reciprocity is possible only in a situation of equality of wants. Economic and status differentials impede reciprocal exchange just as effectively as social or physical distance.

Finally, *confianza* presupposes a minimum degree of mutual knowledge among partners, including particularly the cultural and personal aspects. This should be self-evident in the case of members of a nuclear family who share the same household and who were brought up with the same set of norms and values. In the case of neighbors who are not relatives, mutual knowledge is still an essential factor in establishing a *confianza* relationship. Thus, among neighbors there is a definite preference for *paisanos,* neighbors who come from the same part of the country and are therefore expected to share a similar subculture or set of regional values. *Cuatismo* is a friendship institution that increases the level of *confianza* between participants through the mutual exchange of personal confidences. The importance of drinking in *cuatismo* may largely be traced to the relaxing effect of alcohol on social inhibitions, thus accelerating the soul-baring process between members of the drinking circle (Lomnitz 1969).

In a different cultural context one may find other kinds of mechanisms for accelerating the process of mutual acquaintance among potential participants of a reciprocity relation. For example, in the Chilean middle class one finds a peculiar ideology of friendship, which specifies a high degree of intimacy between friends even without the use of alcohol. This ideology is encouraged from childhood onward: "A good friend is generous in the broadest meaning of the word, he shares the good and bad moments of his life, his experiences and feelings, and he is always well disposed towards his friends [Lomnitz 1971:100]." This is the basis of the institution of *compadrazgo,* a system of reciprocal exchange of favors that has a well-defined survival value in the Chilean middle class.

What Is *Confianza?*

If the preceding observations are at all significant in terms of the economic behavior of man in society, it follows that *confianza* represents a cultural trait that should be ethnographically described in every given situation, and that may be expected to evolve with time. A person feels *confianza* in another when he trusts the other to have the ability, the desire, and the good disposition to initiate a personal relationship of reciprocity exchange, or when his own familiarity with the other would encourage him to make the first approach himself. Such an initial move usually consists of requesting a favor or in offering to perform a favor, without risking a misinterpretation of this gesture. Another form of expressing *confianza* is the act of volunteering an item of personal information of an intimate character, thus implying faith in the discretion and friendly disposition of the other person. *Confianza* must necessarily be described ethnographically, since each culture features different obstacles or inhibitions about establishing reciprocal exchange relations; also, each type of exchange is valued in a different way. Not only will a given reciprocal transaction imply more or less *confianza* in one culture than in another, but the external demonstrations or marks of *confianza* may vary from one culture to another.

Simmel (1964) has described *confidence* as "one of the most important synthetic forces in our society." He defines confidence in the following terms:

1. It is a cognitive category: "Confidence is intermediate between knowledge and ignorance with respect to a man [p. 318]."
2. It is found in groups of intermediate social distance: "A person who knows totally does not need confidence—a person who knows nothing cannot afford confidence [p. 319]."
3. It evolves dynamically: "Our relations develop on the basis of reciprocal knowledge and this knowledge is based on the relations themselves; both are intrinsically interrelated [p. 309]."
4. It requires personal knowledge of individuals: "In order to produce the necessary confidence in spite of a lack of knowledge of the objective circumstances, a much higher degree of knowledge of personal circumstances is required [p. 317]."
5. This personal knowledge has a social survival value: "All purely general knowledge extending only to the objective elements of a person, which do not touch on his secret, personal or individual aspects must be precisely supplemented with the knowledge of these aspects, whenever a mutual association is to acquire an essential significance in terms of the total existence of its members [p. 319]."

On a more elementary level this might be paraphrased by saying that no society can function without a minimum degree of confidence among its members. In modern complex societies, for example, an individual must trust any stranger he may meet on the street not to inflict any damage on him. Goffman (1959, 1966) has described the signals and symbols used in the urban culture to express this kind of elementary confidence: styles of dress, haircut, body motions, eye movements, and so on. An individual may thus learn to classify strangers in terms of their potential danger or trustworthiness.

In small societies an individual may characteristically "relate repeatedly with the same person in practically all social situations [Benedict 1966:23].'' Members of small societies tend to move within culturally prescribed roles, and these roles include the specification of mutual assistance. Everyone knows who is to be helped and who is to be approached for help; *confianza* is implicit in the social relation. As a society grows and becomes more complex, the social, economic, and occupational mobility of its members increases and the total roles found in small societies become fragmented. The family tends to break up and the force of the prescribed duties as implied in kinship roles begins to weaken. In this situation the individual is led increasingly to depend on institutions, such as banks, credit unions, hospitals, social security, employment agencies, unemployment insurance, and retirement funds. *Confianza* relationships are relegated to certain less critical areas—at least from a standpoint of physical survival—for example, the emotional aspects of social life.

However, many complex societies have failed to develop an institutional apparatus to the point where the survival needs of all members of society are adequately ensured. In most Latin American urban societies, for example, the available social security protection is not adequate to guarantee a minimum economic level of subsistence for a majority of the population. Simultaneously, a large sector of the population has abandoned the relative shelter of their small communities, with their prescribed roles and their stable and direct interpersonal relations. In such a society it becomes vital for an individual to enjoy the support of a social group for which he feels sufficient *confianza,* to rely on it for major emergencies as well as for the satisfaction of his most immediate daily needs in many cases.

Depending on the degree of *confianza,* a given relative or friend may be approached in different reciprocity contexts; one friend is good for a loan, another might be approached in a major emergency, still another might be trusted with confidential information. Thus *confianza* tends to be distributed across a set of individuals, beginning with close relatives and spreading out as far as possible depending on one's social resources.

In conclusion, urban industrial societies institutionalize mutual assistance; small peasant societies, on the other hand, tend to prescribe it through social roles. In either case social solidarity is channeled through mechanisms that depend relatively little on personal initiative, as long as the individual conforms to the norms and values of his culture. But there are also many halfway industrialized societies that contain large urban groups lacking adequate and effective coverage by social security institutions; such groups face a serious problem of survival. The individual may then gather his social resources and build them up into a reciprocity network. *Confianza* is the cement used to produce cohesion in these networks, thus making them operational for purposes of reciprocal exchange in the interest of survival.

In Cerrada del Cóndor the network of reciprocal exchange has become the effective community of the individual. Such informal economic groups of mutual assistance must be seen as indispensable to the individual and collective survival of the shantytown settlers. As the objective conditions in the shantytown are extremely severe, the solidarity found in the networks is proportionately strong. This implies a high level of *confianza* among network members. In each case *confianza* evolves as does the relationship; it grows with the intensity of reciprocal exchange and eventually it becomes identical with the exchange relationship itself. The traditional role patterns from the village are no longer adequate. The shantytown settler no longer asks, "Who are my relatives?" Rather, he asks, "Who are the people I can trust?"

CONFIANZA AND EXCHANGE IN CERRADA DEL CÓNDOR

In 1970 the shantytown of Cerrada del Cóndor contained 45 social networks as defined by an underlying criterion of mutual reciprocal exchange of goods and services. I have attempted to study these networks by means of an operational field method, using the economic function as a common standard for the definition of each network. The intensity of the exchange decreases as a function of the physical or social or economic distance between partners; this is reflected in a decrease in the trust or *confianza* between partners of an exchange. Thus *confianza* emerges as a decisive factor in network formation, since it involves the entire complex of cognitive and affective signals indicating to the partners that their offers or requests of reciprocal exchange will not be turned down.

Confianza as a psychosocial indicator of reciprocity is extremely sensitive to economic differences. Here there emerge a number of important distinctions between *confianza* and concepts such as represented by the terms *confidence* and *trust* in English or the German *Vertrauen*. A feeling of trust may be based on written information or on other factors, including kinship, which do not necessarily involve direct personal acquaintance. *Confianza,* on the contrary, refers specifically to the conditions for reciprocal exchange; this necessarily includes some prior personal contact as well as other social and cultural preconditions. In general (at least under conditions of marginality), *confianza* implies an equality of wants as prior condition in establishing a reciprocal exchange. This is not only true among marginals but also among other strata of urban Latin American societies such as the middle class (Lomnitz 1971) and even some privileged sets of the upper class (Lomnitz and Pérez 1974).

The case histories described in this book show, among other things, that a woman who is poor because of marriage to a worthless husband may lack the necessary *confianza* for approaching her own sister if the sister is economically

better off. A man may have more *confianza* with his in-laws than with his own
blood relatives, without upsetting his excellent relations with his consanguineal
kin in the least. An individual may decide to rely economically on his boss and
thereby derive a stable income, to the extent that no relations of *confianza* with
his neighbors can develop. An equality of wants is not enough for *confianza* to be
established. The partners must also share some social and cultural categories,
such as kinship, a common geographical origin, or an interpersonal affinity
(*simpatía*).

Mutual relations generate forms of reciprocal exchange that may be classified
along a continuum from generalized and exocentric pooling (as in extended-
family networks) to formal and egocentric dyadic exchange (as in nonkin
neighbor networks). The so-called mixed networks of kin and nonkin neighbors
may be considered as intermediate cases. One example of a mixed network
between extended, jointed, and nonkin households, is shown in Figure 9.2. The
structure of this network is self-explanatory and its analysis is left to the reader.

The goods and services exchanged within a reciprocity network may be
classified as follows:

1. *Information.* A wide range of information items are exchanged, including
   instructions for migration, tips on residential opportunities and jobs, general and specific orientations for urban living, and personal gossip.
2. *Job assistance.* When joining a network the economically active members
   are introduced to the trade or craft that is the mainstay of the whole
   network. New arrivals are taken along as unpaid apprentices and the host
   shares his salary with them as long as they cannot earn their way.
3. *Loans.* Such loans may include money, food, tools, clothing, and all kinds
   of articles for home and personal use.
4. *Services.* Among the services most commonly exchanged are the following:
   accommodation of new migrants from the countryside and temporary
   visitors; feeding and providing the primary needs of families during the
   initial period or urban adaptation; assistance to relatives in need (particularly widows, orphans, and the ill); mutual assistance in building and
   maintaining homes; and a host of minor services such as shopping, taking
   care of children, and carrying water.
5. *Moral support.* Networks are mechanisms that generate solidarity. This
   solidarity is extended to all events in the life cycle. It has implications of
   friendship and may often be formalized through *compadrazgo* and through
   cuatismo, as well as through joint participation in ritual occasions.

Dyadic relations of reciprocity beyond the network boundaries often prove
useful in terms of social mobility, as they determine the changes in affiliation
from one network to another. A reciprocity network is a dynamic structure,
which changes according to the life cycle and the economic circumstances of its

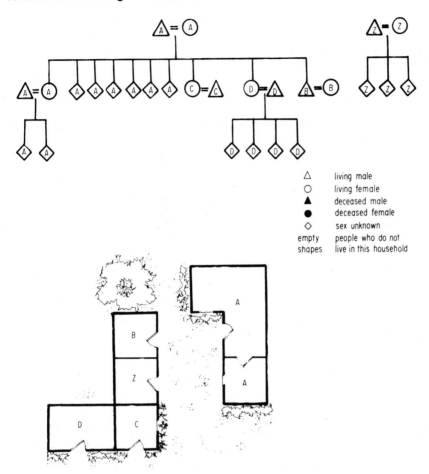

Figure 9.2. A mixed network, containing an extended family (A, B, C, D) and a nonkin neighbor family (Z), living closely together in a jointed-type arrangement. Household A is of the single-roof, expense-sharing type.

membership. Network splitting is due to the fact that, because of restrictions of the shantytown property situation, the physical dimension of a network cannot extend beyond a certain maximum size. This process may lead to the formation of macronetworks, or networks of networks, within the shantytown. Exchange relationships represent a prime factor that determines the reorganization of a network in the process of splitting or dispersing. The outward formalities of exchange in the shantytown may be described in terms of degrees and shadings of *confianza*. The act of requesting a favor represents in itself a demonstration of *confianza*, and is appreciated as such. Any such request carries an implicit commitment to grant an equivalent future favor to the person whose assistance is requested. The time and manner in which the reciprocal favor will eventually be requested remains open. For maximum *confianza* to exist between partners, the exchanges should occur at random in both directions without keeping account of the balance in either direction.

However, even at the low end of the *confianza* scale there is never any explicit reckoning; that would be tantamount to debasing a social relationship to the level of a business transaction. *Confianza* is translated in terms of forms of address and social amenities, and may often be reinforced through fictive kinship and through *cuatismo*.

PATRON–CLIENT RELATIONS: THE *CACIQUE*

A patron–client relationship is characteristically nonsymmetrical:

> The parties involved are unequal in terms of access to the goods and services that are the basis of the exchange. The key word is *access*. The commodities in question are assumed to be scarce, and invariably their source is some organized unit of the society. The potential patron does not necessarily own the goods or services in question. Through his intermediary, however, they can be made available to selected outsiders . . .[and] provide the client with access [to an outside organization] at a price [Greenfield 1966:3].

Incipient patron–client relationships are found in the shantytown of Cerrada del Cóndor. For instance, a bricklayer foreman tends to become a broker between the shantytown settlers and the builders or engineers, as he is usually entrusted with recruiting the members of his bricklayers' crew. Eventually he may gain access to other scarce resources, such as land, water, and political protection; then he will be termed a *cacique*. *Cacicazgo* is a well-known brokerage system that has been described in the Mexican countryside. It has not been observed in Cerrada del Cóndor, perhaps because the shantytown is too small or because the property situation is relatively stable. It is also clear, however, in Cerrada del Cóndor as elsewhere, that settlers who gain power or ascendancy over others do not leave the shantytown, as might be expected, but tend to become brokers or intermediaries between the settlers and the outside world.

A shantytown patron expects loyalty from his clients in exchange for the access to scarce goods and services he provides. Thus a bricklayer foreman expects the cooperation of his gang or crew and may negotiate new jobs without consulting them. The tacit social contract between the foreman and his workers becomes an important economic resource for both parties. Reciprocity networks are the initial groups out of which such crews may develop, particularly since the male membership of a network tends to ply the same trade. Thus, asymmetric patron–client relationships may grow out of symmetric reciprocal exchange networks. Full fledged *caciques* are found in the larger shantytowns of Mexico City

(Cornelius 1973). Their power tends to grow in proportion to their economic and social ascendancy over the settler. Subjectively speaking, an existing relationship of *confianza* is converted into loyalty. At a higher level, political power over marginal population groups may be exchanged against patronage, which filters down to the individual settler in the form of jobs, land, water, and other scarce commodities. Reciprocity turns into redistribution, in which case the *cacique* or broker often retains the lion's share for himself. Such mechanisms of patron–client relations often account for the effective articulation between reciprocity networks at the shantytown level and the urban industrial society at large.

In conclusion, we may distinguish between three different patterns that tend to characterize different levels of social organization:

1. *The rural pattern.* This consists in the leveling (usually through alcohol consumption) of economic inequalities within the network. This pattern, as observed in the Villela macronetwork, for instance, is very closely related to the *cuatismo* ideology.
2. *Cacicazgo.* The emergence of a patron or broker, who succeeds in converting his social resources into personal power, has often been described in Mexico. Shantytown *caciques* are intermediaries between the settlers and the urban industrial society, and indirectly between the city and the countryside.
3. *The urban pattern.* Finally, where differentials in power translate into noticeable economic differences or changes in the life-style (home, furniture, electrical appliances, or moderation in the drinking pattern), the dependence on reciprocity may decrease abruptly. This eventually entails a decrease in *confianza* and a tendency toward social isolation of the individual family. Families with rising incomes break away from the networks and eventually move out of the shantytown into urban, working-class, or lower middle-class type neighborhoods.

These three patterns tend to confirm the specific function of reciprocity networks as a response to economic insecurity. Once a family enjoys some degree of economic security its membership in such a network becomes dysfunctional, since more affluent members would have to divest themselves of their excess means without gaining any appreciable advantage in return. Consequently, the ideology of mutual assistance that prevails within the networks stresses the economic equality among its members.

A FINAL NOTE ON FORMS OF EXCHANGE

Polanyi originally distinguished between three forms of exchange: reciprocity, redistribution, and market exchange. According to his critics (e.g., Cook 1968), this model involves an implicit value judgment, because of an alleged preference for reciprocity (based on generosity and social solidarity) over market exchange. In Cerrada del Cóndor, however, the use of reciprocity is a result of need rather than social idealism. In general, it may be stated that reciprocal exchange in complex modern societies is not some lingering remnant held over from romantic or obsolete ceremonies of the past. Rather, it represents an economic way of life to a large and growing population sector.

First, whenever a human group encounters a situation of extreme scarcity, as happens periodically in the case of certain tribes in Uganda (Laughlin 1973:2; Turnbull 1967:63–71), social solidarity may be totally lost. Children will snatch food away from their parents, and vice versa. Here individual survival overrules the need for continuity of the most elementary social relations, as society itself is threatened with extinction. Laughlin has observed that in this case some rudiments of market exchange may still persist, as individuals will sell their last remaining resources to members of other tribes.

Second, at a slightly higher economic level, one finds human groups living continuously close to the edge of starvation. There is an economic basis of subsistence but this basis is uncertain, scarce, or irregular. Most important, there is a *structural insecurity* of the satisfaction of the material needs of members of the group. This insecurity may be due to physical causes (periodic disasters, cyclic droughts), ecological processes such as exhaustion of the soil, or socioeconomic processes (marginality). Social solidarity is then mobilized as a resource for survival. The group tends to practice reciprocal exchange; depending on social distance among members of the group, reciprocity may become generalized to the extent of pooling of resources. If one recalls that human survival has always been precarious for a majority of the world's population, one may infer that reciprocity has probably played an important role since the earliest days of humanity.

The survival problem may be stated in different terms among different social groups. Thus, among middle-class Chileans the question is not so much one of biological survival but of social survival of a group that characteristically lives *above its means*. A member of such a social group perceives the possibility of being forced to earn a living through manual labor as extremely threatening, and therefore the maintenance of certain externally identifiable symbols of fictitious prosperity becomes almost as important as physical survival itself. Here the economic function of mutual assistance is as clearly an adaptation to a situation of scarcity as it is in the case of Cerrada del Cóndor, though the ideological content and the social forms of reciprocity are quite different.

Finally, if the resources of the group exceed the average minimum required for biological and social survival of the individual, interpersonal solidarity tends to lose much of its economic justification and may even be seen as an obstacle in the path of economic progress of the more ambitious individuals. In this case we find a dominance of market exchange; the group tends to replace such values and social forms as were characteristic of reciprocity with the values and forms of free enterprise. Competition is prized above solidarity, the "rules of the game" prevail over the rules of courtesy, and the ambition of getting ahead is idealized over and beyond the amenities of social life and the values of mutual assistance. The conflict between these two different ideologies has been analyzed at some length in the case of the middle class of Chile (Lomnitz 1971:99–101).

These comments are intended to clarify the theoretical relation between different forms of exchange. In certain complex societies the practice of reciprocal exchange may coexist with a dominant market economy, at least among certain important sectors or social groups. A problem arises as to how to define the mode of exchange in terms of its articulation or insertion in the dominant economic system: complementarity or conflict?

Perhaps it should be pointed out that different forms of exchange are not necessarily mutually exclusive in practice. The settlers of Cerrada del Cóndor practice market exchange whenever possible or economically convenient. Their basic means of subsistence originate in the market economy of the industrial city in which they live. But the economic sustenance derived by the marginals from the sale of their labor force is inadequate as well as unreliable. Their income derived from the market economy is unpredictable and severely limited. The practice of reciprocal exchange may therefore be seen as a regulatory device that provides a minimum income level through the mobilization of their social resources in the mutual-assistance networks. There is a basic complementarity in the alternate use of market exchange and reciprocity, since each of them taken by itself cannot guarantee survival.

Last but not least, it is necessary to point out that networks of reciprocal exchange can and do exist in any social strata. They are not restricted to Cerrada del Cóndor or to the middle class of Chile. The principle of reciprocal exchange may be put to a great variety of uses, from survival among the marginals to clan formation for economic and political purposes among the high bourgeoisie. An example of the latter use of reciprocity networks has been found in the analysis of a kindred group of the Mexican upper class (Lomnitz and Pérez 1974), where the exchange of presents, visits, invitations, gossip, and commercial or political information preserves and enhances the solidarity of the familistic group. This enables the kindred to act like a corporation or conglomerate in their dealings with banks, government, and competing enterprises, even though the actual feelings or behavior among members of the various branches of the family are not friendly or helpful. Thus even groups that most fervently subscribe to an ideology of market exchange and free enterprise may stoop to antimarket strategies if this is likely to increase their political power and their economic advantage over competitors. The tendency toward intermarriage between such familistic money clans may be seen as another indication of the use of reciprocity networks in the world of big business and finance. Here, as in the shantytown, reciprocity occurs between economic equals.

One might think that the rich would have no use for reciprocity networks when the advantages of the market economy are at their fingertips; such a view, however, does not take into account the real nature of reciprocity. The business of the preservation of privilege at the top may be pursued with the same intensity and the same kind of urgency as the struggle for bare existence at the bottom. Goods and services that pass from hand to hand in a reciprocity network may range from a few beans to a hot tip on the stock exchange. The basic principle is the same. Only the structural features of the network change according to the social and economic level.

Conclusions

SOME BASIC CONCEPTS

Some of the major concepts in this book have evolved over a period of time, as undercurrents of thought rather than as isolated factual findings. In this section I shall make an attempt to summarize the basic concepts used in describing the reality of Cerrada del Cóndor. None of them were present in my mind at the time of the fieldwork; therefore, they may truthfully be said to represent central research findings of this investigation.

A cleavage is developing in the Latin American working class. A new social stratum, the urban industrial proletariat, is rising to prominence. This emerging labor elite is becoming increasingly differentiated from the peasantry, on the one hand, and from the migrants of rural origin on the other. To the extent that they have not become integrated into a modern industrial system, the traditional masses have remained largely segregated from the urban economy. Marginality was once regarded as a transient phase of the industrialization process in Latin America; however, in shantytowns such as Cerrada del Cóndor it appears that the second generation of shantytown-born settlers has, on the whole, even less opportunity of access to industrial jobs than their parents had.

Yet the rural migrants keep streaming into the cities from the countryside. By their own standards, migration to the shantytowns is a successful process. How do they survive? In order to do justice to this question it becomes necessary to view the marginal reality in all its complexity. I have attempted to develop a global ecological framework that integrates the closely interwoven problems of marginality, shantytowns, migration, and urban poverty. Cerrada del Cóndor is not treated as a "community" in the traditional anthropological sense, but rather as a part of the national ecosystem. The field data are interpreted in terms of nationwide statistics. I have tried not to lose sight of the causal thread running through the history of urbanization and industrialization in Latin America, leading up to the modern plight of the settlers of Cerrada del Cóndor.

What is marginality? Physical segregation in shantytowns is one part of the story. As one examines marginality as a way of life, one finds that the major economical barrier is the *security* question. The industrial proletariat is protected by legal safeguards (unions, social security), but the marginals have access only to jobs that are temporary, intermittent, menial, devalued, and generally unprotected. Underemployment is the rule.

The marginal dilemma, then, is not so much a problem of how to live on an inadequate income as of how to survive during the recurrent periods of zero income. There is one way out of this dilemma: using the social resources of the individual. Kinship, *compadrazgo, cuatismo,* and friendship are the resources used by the marginal for this purpose. This is also true for the relatively more skilled segment of the marginal population (artisans, skilled foremen) who work on a contract basis and therefore lack the job security of an industrial worker.

Most chapters of this book have dealt with the details of how the social resources of the marginals are converted into economic security. The process is not a new one. Kinship and other forms of social solidarity have provided the mechanisms of survival during much of the history of mankind. The settlers of Cerrada del Cóndor may be compared to the primitive hunters and gatherers of preagricultural societies. They go out every day to hunt for jobs and gather the uncertain elements for survival. The city is their jungle; it is just as alien and challenging. But their livelihood is based on leftovers: leftover jobs, leftover trades, leftover living space, homes built of leftovers. Even their poultry and livestock are raised on leftovers. To borrow an example from ecology, the marginals live like crabs; they inhabit the interstices of the urban industrial system and feed on its waste.

From the point of view of the urban industrial economy, although marginality may be said to represent a "surplus population" (Quijano 1970 and Nun 1969) in some respects, in other respects it performs important though perhaps as yet unrecognized social functions. In particular, the rise of an urban middle-class in Latin America is greatly indebted to cheap labor and services provided by marginals: domestic servants, gardeners, delivery boys, drivers, and a host of menial helpers of every description. If there is a symbiotic relationship between urban society and marginality, its major beneficiary is undoubtedly the middle class.

NETWORKS

Since marginals are barred from full membership in the urban industrial economy they have had to build their own economic system. The basic social economic structure of the shantytown is the reciprocity network. This is not a social group or institution; rather, it is a social field defined by an intense flow of reciprocal exchange between neighbors. The main purpose of a reciprocity network is to provide a minimum level of economic security to its members.

The principal findings about shantytown networks may be summarized as follows:

1. Reciprocity networks are groups of neighbors who cooperate in the daily task of mutual economic survival.
2. Membership in networks is based on family units, not individuals.
3. The networks are constituted and disbanded according to a dynamic process ruled by economic and social factors, such as the historical evolution and property structure in the shantytown, the geographical origins and family structure of the settlers, the major incidents in the life cycle, and the daily ups and downs of shantytown life.
4. The size, stability, and intensity of exchange in a reciprocity network depend on the social closeness between member families. All-kin networks tend to be more stable, more self-sufficient, and larger in size than networks of nonkin neighbors.
5. Association in networks is based on a fundamental equality of wants among member families.

The reciprocal exchange of goods and services among shantytown settlers was found to be a central fact of their economic existence, so much so that many other features of the social and economic life of the marginals were organized around or in terms of networks of reciprocal exchange. Family structures, residential patterns, occupational structures, household organization, leisure time activities, alcohol consumption, and the use of traditional institutions such as *compadrazgo* and *cuatismo* were all modified and directed toward protecting and furthering reciprocity relations among kin and neighbors. Some examples of adaptive changes in traditional structures and institutions found in Cerrada del Cóndor are the extensive use of *compadrazgo* among members of reciprocity networks, whether kin or nonkin; the widespread use of the jointed household as a means of preserving the extended-family structure in the fragmented property and land ownership conditions of the shantytown; the prevalent recruitment of *cuate* groups and drinking circles among the male segments of reciprocity networks, and the egalitarian ideology that stresses and idealizes reciprocal assistance and solidarity under conditions of mutual equality of wants.

It is hardly possible to overlook the large extent to which prevalent rural patterns of individualism and mistrust have become superseded by powerful tendencies toward integration, mutual assistance, and cooperation. Rural migrants are housed, sheltered, and fed by their city relatives in the shantytowns; the men are taught a trade and oriented toward available urban jobs, in direct competition with their city kin. The reason for such "altruistic" behavior must be sought in the fact that migrants become integrated in local kinship reciprocity networks, which represent an overriding survival value to all their members. Contacts between the migrants and their communities of origin in the countryside become oriented in terms of the new reciprocity structures in the shantytown. Kinship is the major factor promoting migration. The extended family in the shantytown has become a unit of production and of consumption. Important economic collaboration is provided by women, old people, and children. The result is a complex economic system largely based on the sale of unskilled manual labor by the men, service occupations by old men and women, and the active gathering of surplus and waste materials by all members of the household. A new typology of households for Latin American marginality is a result of this study.

LIVING IN CERRADA DEL CÓNDOR

Nearly 70% of the heads of families and their spouses in Cerrada del Cóndor are migrants of rural origin. These migrants belonged to the poorest economic strata of the peasantry: disowned or landless farm workers, working seasonally on *ejidos,* for small wages. Fewer than 20% were from towns of more than 25,000 inhabitants. Most migrants came from depressed areas in the neighboring states of México and Guanajuato, and from rural areas within the Federal District. Many of the latter were "passive migrants"—peasants who lived in small rural communities surrounding the metropolitan area, and who were displaced by explosive urban growth. These people did not have to move from their villages to the city; rather, the city moved and engulfed their villages.

Up to 90% of the migrants were assisted during and after migration by relatives already living in the city. Most migrants moved directly from their villages to Mexico City, without intermediate stops. Subsequent moves within the metropolitan area were likewise conditioned by the presence of relatives in other shantytowns or marginal settlements. Most migrants tended to move within a given sector of the city (the southern area, in the case of Cerrada del Cóndor). A pattern of moving first to downtown slums and later on to the peripheral shantytowns, as reported from other Latin American countries, was not observed.

The population of the shantytown is comparatively young. Nearly 60% of the heads of families and their wives are under 40. Illiteracy is high. Among the same group (heads of families and their wives), nearly 30% are illiterate, and slightly over 2% have schooling beyond the sixth grade. Nuclear families tend to be complete and relatively stable. In cases of marital desertion, most women seem to be able to find another man within a reasonably short time. Children of previous unions born out of wedlock are commonly accepted by the husbands on an equal footing with their own. In general, most heads of households are married both legally and through the Catholic religion; less than 18% live in consensual unions. The average fertility is high. In spite of the predominance of young couples in the shantytown, a majority of nuclear families have more than four live children. A high proportion of settlers lives in extended households comprising up to four generations. Depending on available vacancies and other peculiarities of the property system in the shantytown, these households may either live under a single roof, in separate dwellings within a single plot, or in independent adjoining housing units.

The basic economic facts of shantytown life revolve around the question of economic insecurity. Four economic levels may be distinguished, according to material possessions. Levels A and B may be described in a general way as *urban;* they include 16% of the residential units in Cerrada del Cóndor. The remaining residential units feature rustic-type furniture and construction; thus, 60% of all residential units belong to level D, which corresponds to the lowest rung in terms of material possessions. In terms of income, the average monthly earnings per residential unit in all four levels is less than $100. However, in terms of job security and occupational structure, the number of unskilled laborers and others subjected to chronic underemployment is significantly higher in level D than in level A. Also, the rate of incidence of alcoholism and illiteracy is significantly higher in level D. Most of the settlers in level A are owners of their housing units. More than half of the residential units lack any bathroom facilities. On the average there were about three residents per bed, but many settlers, especially children, slept on the floor.

The occupational structure of wage earners in the shantytown (both men and women) is largely based on unskilled labor. The most frequent occupation among men is that of *peon,* i.e., manual laborer who may work at various trades according to demand. The highest demand for such labor is in the building trade, for bricklayers and construction workers in general. Among women the most frequent paid occupation is that of domestic servant. Industrial jobs account for about 10% of the employment among male breadwinners; however, they represent jobs of the lowest category, namely janitors, doormen, watchmen, and the like. The common denominator of practically all shantytown jobs, including commerical and service occupations, is the lack of a steady income or social and job security.

Life in Cerrada del Cóndor is organized around neighborhood networks. Because of rigidly defined sex roles, the emotional content of marital relations is generally low. A man's life revolves around his male friends (the *cuate* group) and a woman's affections are largely centered on her children and other kin. Men are supposed to be somewhat unreliable and irresponsible (this is an accepted trait of masculinity); women tend to develop a resilient, strong, and resourceful character. When women are allowed to work, their earning power is as high as that of their mates. In addition to their economic contribution, women play an important role in cementing the network of reciprocal exchange, because of their constant daily use of it through the borrowing of small quantities of money and food, and the exchange of kindnesses, services, and emergency assistance. The larger kinship networks are often held together by the authority of an elder matriarch.

Compadrazgo in the shantytown has blossomed forth into a variety of hitherto unknown forms. Typically urban occasions, such as the opening of the barbershop, are consecrated through the use of *compadrazgo*. The frequent occurrence of *compadrazgo* among members of reciprocity networks suggests that this traditional institution is being used as a means of consolidating interpersonal relationships within these networks. Another traditional institution, *cuatismo* (the Mexican form of male friendship), is similarly utilized. The *tanda,* a typically urban form of rotating informal credit, was also found to exist predominantly among members of reciprocity networks.

THE FUTURE OF RECIPROCITY

The secret of the survival of huge marginal populations in Latin American cities lies in the efficient use of their social resources. Some social scientists have claimed that reciprocity is an archaic form of economic exchange, well on its way to extinction. Perhaps so, though I have found it alive and well in Cerrada del Cóndor. The generalized use of reciprocal exchange occurs in human populations that exist under conditions of chronic economic insecurity. Under such conditions, cooperation has greater survival value than competition as found in market exchange. Reciprocal exchange in Cerrada del Cóndor is governed by a set of factors, including social and physical distance, equality of economic wants, plus a psychosocial variable I call *confianza*. As found in Latin American societies, *confianza* measures the readiness of two individuals to engage in reciprocal exchange of goods and services. *Confianza* between neighbors and members of a reciprocal exchange network fluctuates according to the flow of goods and services exchanged. It may be officially acknowledged by reducing the social distance between the partners through kinship, *compadrazgo, cuatismo,* and other forms existing in the culture.

Latin American marginality represents a successful evolutionary response of traditional populations to the stresses of rapid urbanization and industrialization.

The marginals have carved out an ecological niche within the urban milieu, one that provides for their basic survival needs. How will they evolve? Will the shantytowns gradually become absorbed by an increased demand for industrial labor, or will they continue to grow, feeding on the surplus population of the depressed countryside? Will they play an important role in the sociopolitical evolution of Latin America? If so, will their impact be on the side of tradition or on the side of revolution?

The challenge met by the settlers of Cerrada del Cóndor is the universal human predicament of survival. Their example may teach us a valuable lesson. Human societies have always been threatened; moreover, the experience of Cerrada del Cóndor is particularly relevant to the threats we are facing today. The economy of the marginals has proved to be efficient in two respects: (1) the utilization of social resources for economic ends, and (2) the recycling of surplus and waste materials toward their maximum utilization. There is an obvious contrast between the successful adaptation of the marginals to a situation of scarcity of resources, generating mechanisms of social solidarity and methods of intense utilization of waste, and the crisis of Western industrial societies attributed precisely to a lack of social solidarity and a wasteful utilization of dwindling resources. The reciprocity networks I have attempted to describe in the shantytown of Cerrada del Cóndor may well prove to be a prototype for the social structures needed for the survival of mankind. Market exchange may still be the most efficient economic system as long as the resources of a society are abundant in terms of the population it supports. But as long as there are segments of humanity confronting a dwindling pool of natural resources or threatened by physical extinction, reciprocity as a system of socioeconomic exchange will have a future.

References

Acevedo, Marta
  1973   La mujer de clase media en México. Paper presented at the AAAS Symposium on The
         Mexican Woman.
Adams, Richard
  1974   Harnessing technological development. In *Rethinking modernization. Anthropological
         perspectives,* edited by John J. Poggie, Jr., and Robert N. Lynch. Westport, Connecticut:
         Greenwood Press.
Alejo, Javier
  1973   Crecimiento demográfico y empleo en la economia mexicana. Conference at the Population
         Symposium. Congress of AAAS: La ciencia y el hombre.
Alemán, Eloisa
  1966   *Investigacion socioeconómica directa de los ejidos de San Luis Potosi.* Instituto Mexicano
         de Investigaciones Económicas.
Antochiew, Michel
  1974   Asentamientos habitacionales planificados y no planificados. *Cuadernos Técnicos AURIS*
         No. 9 (Gobierno del Estado de Mexico).
Arriaga, Eduardo
  1970   *Mortality decline and its demographic effects in Latin America.* Population Monograph
         Series No. 6. Berkeley: Univ. of California Press.
Ashton, S.
  1972   The differential adaptation of two slum subcultures to a Colombian housing project. *Urban
         Anthropology* 1(2).
Balán, Jorge, Harley L. Browning, and Elizabeth Jelin
  1973   *Men in a developing society.* Austin: Univ. of Texas Press.

Barnes, J. A.
  1954   Class committee in a Norwegian island parish. *Human Relations* 7:39–58.
Bataillon, Claude, and Hélène Rivière d'Arc
  1973   *La Ciudad de México*. Mexico City: Sep/Setentas (Secretaría de Educación Pública).
Bazdresh, Carlos
  1973   La política económica (de México). *Plural* 22 (July): 18–20.
Bender, D.
  1967   A refinement of the concept of household: Family coresidence and domestic functions.
           American Anthropologist 69:493–504.
Benedict, B.
  1966   Sociological characteristics of small territories and their implications for economic de-
           velopment. In *The social anthropology of complex society,* edited by M. Banton. ASA
           Monograph No. 4. London: Tavistock.
Berruecos, Luis
  1972   Comparative analysis of Latin American *compadrazgo.* Thesis submitted to Dept. of An-
           thropology, Michigan State University.
Blau, Peter
  1964   *Exchange and social power*. New York: Wiley.
Bonilla, Frank
  1970   Rio's *favelas:* The rural slums within the city. In *Peasants in cities,* edited by William
           Mangin. Boston: Houghton Mifflin.
Brandes, Stanley H.
  1975   *Migration, kinship and community*. New York: Academic Press.
Brown, Jane Cowan
  1972   *Patterns of intraurban settlement in Mexico City*. Latin American Studies Program Disser-
           tation Series No. 40, Cornell University.
Browning, H.
  1965   Recent trends in Latin American urbanization. In *Contemporary Latin American culture,*
           edited by George M. Foster. Berkeley: Univ. of California Press.
Browning, H., and W. Feindt
  1971   The social and economic context of migration to Monterrey, Mexico. In *Latin American
           urban research,* Volume 1, edited by F. Rabinovitz and F. Trueblood. Beverly Hills,
           California: Sage Publications.
Bryce-Laporte, R. S.
  1970   Urban relocation and family adaptation in Puerto Rico: A case study in urban ethnography.
           In *Peasants in cities,* edited by William Mangin. Boston: Houghton Mifflin.
Burling, Robbins
  1962   Maximization theories and the study of economic anthropology. *American Anthropologist*
           64:802–821.
Butterworth, D.
  1962   A study of the urbanization process among Mixtec migrants from Tilaltongo in Mexico
           City. *América Indígena* 22(3):257–274.
  1971   Migración rural–urbana en América Latina: El estado de nuestro conocimiento. *América
           Indígena* 31(1):85–106.
  1972   Two small groups: A comparison of migrants and non-migrants in Mexico City. *Urban
           Anthropology* 1(1):29–50.
Cardona, R., and A. Simmons
  1976   Toward a model of migration in Latin America. In *Migration and urbanization,* edited by
           B. Du Toit and H. Safa. The Hague: Mouton.

Castells, Manuel
   1971   *Problemas de investigación en sociología urbana*. Madrid: Ed. Siglo Veintiuno.
   1974   *La cuestion urbana*. Mexico: Ed. Siglo Veintiuno.
Cohen, J. (Editor)
   1968   *Man in adaptation*, Volumes 1 and 2. Chicago: Aldine.
Cook, Scott
   1968   The obsolete "anti-market" mentality: A critique of the substantive approach to economic anthropology. In *Economic anthropology*, edited by E. E. Le Clair, Jr., and L. Schneider. New York: Holt, Rinehart and Winston.
Cornelius, Wayne
   1971   The political sociology of cityward migration in Latin America: Toward an empirical theory. In *Latin American urban research*, Volume 1, edited by F. Rabinovitz and F. Trueblood. Beverly Hills, California: Sage Publications.
   1973   A structural analysis of urban *caciquismo* in Mexico. *Urban Anthropology* 1(2):234–261.
   1975   *Politics and the migrant poor in Mexico City*. Stanford, California: Stanford Univ. Press.
Cornelius, W., and L. Lomnitz
   1975   The role of citizens in squatter settlements. Mimeographed.
Dalton, George
   1968   The economy as instituted process. In *Economic anthropology*, edited by E. E. Le Clair, Jr., and L. Schneider. New York: Holt, Rinehart and Winston.
Dirks, Robert
   1972   Networks, groups and adaptation in Afro-Caribbean community. *Man* 7(4):565–585.
Du Toit, B.
   1976a Migration and population mobility. In *Migration and urbanization*, edited by B. Du Toit and H. Safa. The Hague: Mouton.
Du Toit, B.
   1976b A decision-making model for the study of migration. In *Migration and urbanization*, edited by B. Du Toit and H. Safa. The Hague: Mouton.
Du Toit, B. and H. Safa (Eds.)
   1976   *Migration and urbanization*. Mouton: The Hague.
Evans-Pritchard, E.
   1940   *The Nuer*. Boston: Oxford Univ. Press.
Firth, R., and J. Dyamour
   1970   Family and kinship in Western society. In *Modern sociology*, edited by Peter Worsley. London: Penguin.
Forbes, J.
   1971   *El sistema de compadrazgo en Santa María Belén Atzitzimitlán, Tlaxcala*. Tesis para obtener el título de maestría en Antropología Social. México: Universidad Iberoamericana.
Foster, George
   1961   The dyadic contract: A model for the social structure of a Mexican peasant village. *American Anthropologist* 63:1173–1192.
   1963   The dyadic contract in Tzintzuntzan II: Patron–client. *Review American Anthropologist* 65:128–129.
   1965   The dyadic contract. In *Readings in contemporary Latin American culture*, edited by G. Foster. Berkeley: Univ. of California Press.
Ganz, Herbert
   1965   *The Urban villagers*. New York: Free Press.

Garigue, Philippe
  1970   French-Canadian kinship and urban life. In *Modern sociology,* edited by Peter Worsley. London: Penguin.
Geertz, Clifford
  1962   The rotating credit association: A "middle range" in development. *Economic Development and Culture Change* 10(3):241–263.
Goffman, Irving
  1959   *The presentation of self in everyday life.* New York: Doubleday.
  1966   *Behavior in public places.* New York: Free Press.
Gouldner, Alvin
  1960   The norm of reciprocity: A preliminary statement. *American Sociological Review* 25(2).
Greenfield, S.
  1966   Patronage networks, factions, political parties and national integration in contemporary Brazilian society. Mimeographed.
Hole, Frank
  1968   Investigating the origins of Mesopotamian civilization. In *Man in adaptation,* Volume 1, edited by J. Cohen. Chicago: Aldine.
Homans, George
  1958   Social behavior as exchange. *American Journal of Sociology* 62:597–606.
International Labor Organization ILO, PREALC
  1974a La política de empleo en América Latina: Lecciones de la experiencia de PREALC. Santiago, Chile.
  1974b La subutilización de la mano de obra urbana en paises subdesarrollados. Documento de trabajo. Santiago, Chile.
Kemper, Robert V.
  1971a El estudio antropológico de la migración a las ciudades en América Latina. *América Indígena* 30(3):609–634.
  1971b Migration and adaptation of Tzintzuntzan peasants in Mexico City. Doctoral dissertation, Dept. of Anthropology, Univ. of California, Berkeley.
  1974   Social factors in migration: The case of Tzintzuntzeños in Mexico City. *América Indígena* 1:1095–1118.
  1976   *Campesinos en la ciudad.* Mexico: Sep Setentas.
Leeds, Anthony
  1969   The significant variables determining the character of squatter settlements. *América Latina* 12 (3):44–86.
Levi-Strauss, Claude
  1967   *Structural anthropology.* New York: Anchor.
Lewis, Oscar
  1952   Urbanization without breakdown. *Scientific Monthly* 75:31–41.
  1959a The culture of the *vecindad* in Mexico City: Two case studies. Actas del XXXIII Congreso Internacional de Americanistas 1, San José, Costa Rica.
  1959b *Five families.* New York: Wiley.
  1964   *Los hijos de Sánchez.* México: Fondo de Cultura Económica.
  1966   The culture of poverty. *Scientific American* 215:4.
  1969a *La antropología de la pobreza.* México: Fondo de Cultura Económica.
  1969b The possessions of the poor. *Scientific American* 221:4.
Lomnitz, Larissa
  1969   Patrones de ingestión de alcohol en migrantes Mapuches en Santiago. *América Indígena* 29(1):43–72.

1971 Reciprocity of favors in the urban middle class of Chile. In *Studies in economic anthropology*, edited by George Dalton. Anthropological Studies No. 7. Washington: American Anthropological Association.

1976a The role of women in an informal economy. Mimeographed.

1976b Networks and migration. *Current perspectives in Latin American urban research*, edited by A. Portes and H. Browning. Austin, Texas: Institute of Latin American Studies, University of Austin Press.

Lomnitz, L., and M. Pérez

1974 Historia de una familia de la Ciudad de México. Paper present at the Annual Meetings of the American Anthropological Association, Mexico City.

Mangalam, J., and H. Schwarzweller

1968 General theory in the study of migration: Current needs and difficulties. *International Migration Review* 3(1):3–18.

Mangin, William

1967 Latin American squatter settlements: A problem and a solution. *Latin American Research Review* 2(3):65–98.

1970 *Peasants in cities*. Boston: Houghton Mifflin.

Matos Mar, José

1962 "Migración y urbanización" las barriadas limeñas: Un caso de integración a la vida urbana. In *La Urbanización en América Latina*, edited by P. N. Hauser. Paris: UNESCO.

Mauss, Marcel

1954 *The gift*. London: Cohen, West.

Mayer, Adrian

1968 The significance of quasi-groups in the study of complex societies. In *The social anthropology of complex societies*, edited by M. Banton. ASA Monograph No. 4. London: Tavistock.

Mayer, Philip

1961 Tribesmen or townsmen: Conservation and the process of urbanization in a South African city. Cape Town: Oxford Univ. Press.

Mintz, S., and E. Wolf

1950 An analysis of ritual co-parenthood (*compadrazgo*). *Southwestern Journal of Anthropology* 6:341–367.

Mitchel, J. Clyde

1969 *Social networks in urban situations*. Manchester, England: Univ. Press.

Morse, Richard

1965 Recent research on Latin American urbanization. *Latin American Research Review* 1(1):35–74.

Munizaga, Carlos

1961 *Estructuras transicionales en la migración de los araucanos de hoy a la ciudad de Santiago, Chile*. Notas del Centro de Estudios Antropológicos 6. Santiago: Universidad de Chile.

Muñoz, H., O. Oliveira, P. Singer, and C. Stern

1972 *Migración y desarrollo*. Buenos Aires: CLACSO.

Muñoz H., and O. Oliveira

1972 Migraciones internas en América Latina: Exposición crítica de algunos análisis. In *Migración y desarrollo*, edited by H. Muñoz, O. Oliveira, P. Singer, and C. Stern. Buenos Aires: CLACSO.

Muñoz H., O. Oliveira, and C. Stern

1972 Migración y marginalidad ocupacioal en la Ciudad de México. In *El perfil de México en 1980*. Mexico City: Siglo Veintiuno.

Nelson, Joan
    1969   Migrants, urban poverty and instability in developing nations. Cambridge, Massachusetts:
           Center for International Affairs, Harvard University.
Nun, José
    1969   Sobrepoblación relativa, ejército industrial de reserva, y masa marginal. *Rev. Latinoamer.
           Sociol.* 5(2):178–236.
Nutini, H.
    1968   *San Bernardino Contla.* Pittsburg, Pennsylvania: Univ. of Pittsburg Press.
Palerm, Angel
    1969   *Productividad agrícola: Un estudio sobre México.* México: Centro Nacional de Pro-
           ductividad.
Parra, Rodrigo
    1972   Marginalidad y subdesarrollo. In *Migraciones internas,* edited by R. Cardona. Bogotá,
           Colombia: Andes.
Peattie, Lisa R.
    1974   The concept of "marginality" as applied to squatter settlements. In *Latin American urban
           research,* Volume 4, edited by W. Cornelius and F. Trueblood. Beverly Hills, California:
           Sage Publications.
Polanyi, K.
    1957   The economy as an instituted process. In *Trade and market in the early empires,* edited by
           K. Polanyi, C. M. Arensberg, and H. W. Pearson. New York: Free Press.
Portes, Alejandro, and John Walton
    1976   *Urban Latin America.* Austin: Univ. of Texas Press.
Pozas, I. R. *et al.*
    1969   La ciudad. *Acta Sociologica de la Facultad de Cienclas Politicas y Sociales.* UNAM.
Prebisch, Raul
    1970   Transformación y Desarrollo en América Latina. Informe presentado al Banco Interameri-
           cano de Desarrollo (BID). Washington, D.C.
Quijano, Aníbal
    1970   Redefinición de la dependencia y proceso de marginalizacion en América Latina. Santiago:
           CEPAL (Comisión Económica para América Latina). Mimeographed.
Radcliffe-Brown, Alfred R.
    1968   *Structure and function in primitive societies.* New York: Free Press.
Roberts, Bryan
    1973   *Organizing strangers.* Austin: Univ. of Texas Press.
Safa, Helen
    1974   *The urban poor of Puerto Rico.* New York: Holt, Rinehart and Winston.
    1976   Introduction. In *Migration and development,* edited by H. Safa and B. Du Toit. The Hague:
           Mouton.
Sahlins, Marshall
    1968   On the sociology of primitive exchange. In *The relevance of models for social anthropol-
           ogy,* edited by M. Banton. Monographs No. 1. London: Tavistock.
Sayers, Robert, and Thomas Weaver
    1976   Explanations and theories of migration. In *Mexican migrations,* edited by T. Weaver, and
           T. Downing. Tucson: Bureau of Ethnic Research, Dept. of Anthropology, Univ. of
           Arizona.
Secretaría del Trabajo y Previsión Social
    1975   Dirección general del servicio público de empleo. Cuadernos de Empleo No. 1.
Simić, Andrei
    1970   *The peasant urbanites: A study of urban mobility in Serbia.* Doctoral dissertation, Univer-
           sity of California, Berkeley.

Simmel, George
1964   *The sociology of George Simmel,* edited by K. H. Wolff. New York: Free Press.
Singer, Paul
1975   *Economía política de la urbanización.* Mexico City: Siglo Veintiuno.
Sotelo, Ignacio
1972   *Sociología de América Latina.* Madrid: Tecnos.
Souza, Paolo, and Victor Tockman
1975   El sector informal urbano. Grupo de Trabajo sobre Ocupación y Desocupación. Santiago, Chile: CLACSO.
Stepick, Alex
1973   Predicting behavior from values. Social Sciences Working Paper 46b. School of Social Sciences, Univ. of California, Irvine.
Stepick, Alex, and Gary Hendrix
n.d.   Predicting behavior from values. Mimeographed.
Stepick, Alex, and Carol Stepick
1975   Migration theories. Paper presented to the Symposium on New Approaches to the Study of Migration, American Anthropological Association Annual Meeting, San Francisco.
Sunkel, Osvaldo
1971   El desarrollo latinoamericano y la teoría del desarrollo. Mexico City: Siglo Veintiuno.
Turnbull, Colin M.
1967   The Ik: Alias the Teuso. *Uganda Journal* 31(1).
Turner, John
1970   Barriers and channels for housing development in modernizing countries. In *Peasants in cities,* edited by William Mangin. Boston: Houghton Mifflin.
1971   *Low-income housing in Mexico City.* Internal report. Toluca, México: AURIS.
Turner, J., and W. Mangin
1968   The barriada movement. *Progressive Architecture* (May 1968):154–162.
Unikel, Luis
1971   The process of urbanization in Mexico: Distribution and growth in urbal populations. In *Latin American Urban research,* vol. 1, edited by F. Rabinowitz and F. Trueblood. Beverly Hills, California: Sage.
1976   *El desarrollo urbano de México.* Mexico City: El Colegio de México.
Urquidi, Victor L.
1969   La ciudad subdesarrollada. *Demografía y Economía* 3(2):137–155.
Uzzell, Douglas
1975   Ethnography of migration: Breaking out the bi-polar myth. In *New approaches to the study of migration,* edited by D. Guillet and D. Uzzell. Houston: Rice Univ. Press.
Veckemans, Roger, and Ismael, Silva F.
1969   El concepto de marginalidad en *DESAL, Marginalidad en America Latina.* Barcelona.
Ward, Peter
1975   Una Comparación entre colonias paracaidistas y ciudades perdidas de la ciudad de México. Hacia una nueva politica. Mimeographed.
1976   The squatter settlement or slum or housing solution: Evidence from Mexico City. *Land Economics* 52(3):330–345.
Weaver, T., and T. Downing
1976   *Mexican migration.* Tucson: Bureau of Ethnic Research, Dept. of Anthropology, Univ. of Arizona.
Whiteford, Michael
1975   Reaching for a good life, a comparative analysis of urban adaptation. Mimeographed.
1976   Adaptations to an urban environment. In *New approaches to the study of migration,* edited by D. Guillet and D. Uzzell. Houston: Rice Univ. Press.

Whiteford, Scott
  1976   Migration in context: A systemic historical approach to the study of breakdown before
         urbanization. In *New approaches to the study of migration,* edited by D. Guillet and D.
         Uzzell. Houston: Rice Univ. Press.
Wolf, Eric
  1969   Kinship, friendship and patron–client relations in complex societies. In *The social an-
         thropology of complex societies,* edited by M. Banton. London: Tavistock.
Wolfe, Alvin W.
  1970   On structural comparisons of network situation and social network in cities. *Canadian
         Review of Sociology and Anthropology* 7(4).
Wright, Connie
  1976   Internal Mexican migration. In *Mexican migration,* edited by T. Weaver and T. Downing.
         Tucson: Bureau of Ethnic Research, Dept. of Anthropology, Univ. of Arizona.
Young, M., and P. Wilmott
  1957   *Family and kinship in East London.* London: Penguin.

Index

A

Acquaintances, favors and, 194
Adults, number working, economic level and, 85, 86
Age
  at migration, 49
  shantytown population, 45, 210
  at starting work, 68
  at time of survey, 60
Agriculture, decline of, 16
Aguascalientes, migrants from, 45
Alcohol
  consumption, economic level and, 85
  problem solving and, 123
Arrimados, families and, 97
Asentamientos informales, 19
Associations
  local, 180–181
    participation in, 184–187
  national, 180–181
    participation in, 181–183
Asunción, underemployment in, 14
Atzcapotzalco, informal settlements in, 24
Aurora, relatives in, 128

B

Barranca, relatives in, 129
Barriada movement, squatters and, 8
Beds
  number of persons using, 82–83
  per residential unit, 84

Birthplace, parents of migrants, 50–51
Brick factory, shantytown and, 25
Brokers, marginality and, 13

C

Cacique
  patron–client relations and, 202–203
  shantytowns and, 186–187
Cali, slums, household types in, 117
Calzada de Puebla, relatives in, 128
Capitalism, Latin American, 4–5
Capulín, relatives in, 128
Case histories
  economic levels, 72–76
  household types
    extended jointed, 114–117
    extended single-plot with expense sharing, 108–112
    extended single-plot without expense sharing, 112–114
    extended single-roof with expense sharing; 104–106
    extended single-roof without expense sharing, 106–108
    nuclear, 103–104
  marital roles, 94–96
  reciprocity networks
    jointed family, 136–139
    mixed kinsmen and neighbors, 139–146
    nonkin neighbors, 146–149
    nonparticipating families, 149–151
Catholicism, settlers and, 182

Cerrada del Cóndor
  compadrazgo, 162–164
    conclusions on, 172–174
  confianza and exchange in, 199–202
  cuate groups in, 178
  ecological model of migration
    and imbalance, 46–48
    and stabilization, 53–55
    and transfer, 48–53
  economy
    case histories, 72–76
    economic level and lifestyle, 84–88
    housing and property ownership, 78–81
    income and economic level, 76–78
    informal rotating credit institution, 88–89
    material belongings, 81–84
    occupational structure, 64–67
    occupation and economic level, 76
    schooling and economic level, 88
    summary and conclusions, 89–91
    unpaid family labor, 67–72
  kinship system in, 123
  living in, 210–212
  location and size, 19–21
  maps of, 22, 23
  marital roles in, 93–97
  medical center and, 184–186
  migration into
    case histories, 58–61
    ecological model, 46–55
    general characteristics of settlers, 44–46
    intraurban, 55–61
  migration out of, 26–27
  networks in, 135–136
    case histories, 136–151
  nuclear families in, 97–99
  reasons for moving to, 26
  reciprocity scales in, 191–193
  relatives in the country, 129–130
  residential pattern, 118–123
Chihuahua, migrants from, 45
Children, *see also* Offspring
  broken marriages and, 96
  female, roles of, 94
  number per nuclear family, 98–99
  unpaid labor of, 67–69
Children's Hospital of Mexico, medical center
    and, 184, 186
Cities
  Latin American, 4–5

population growth, 7
  rural islands in, 37–38
City contacts, migrants, 54
Ciudades perdidas, population of, 19
Coahuila, migrants from, 45
Colonialism,
  Latin American, 4, 5
Colonias de paracaidistas, 19
Colonia(s) Popular(es), 19
  nuclear families in, 117
Commercial occupations, *see also* Jobs, Occupations
  Cerrada del Cóndor, 64, 65, 66
Compadrazgo
  ambiguity of, 161
  in Cerrada del Cóndor, 162–164, 212
    conclusions on, 172–174
  first communion and, 169–170
  ideal model, 160, 161, 162
  marginality and, 208
  migrants and, 46, 48
  other types, 169–172
  reciprocity networks and, 134, 138, 140,
    145–146, 155, 156, 157, 173–174, 209
  role, social solidarity and, 159–160, 161
  survival and, 3
  ties, varieties of, 160–161, 163, 164
  weddings and, 170, 171
Compadrazgo "corona y cruz," 170–171
Compadrazgo de Confirmación, 168–169
Compadrazgo de Niño, 171
Compadrazgo de santos, 170
Compadres
  favors and, 194
  relation between, 165
  selection, 163, 164
    reasons for, 166–167
Confianza
  definition of, 4
  and exchange in Cerrada del Cóndor, 199–
    202
  forms of address and, 158
  meaning of, 134
  nature of, 196–199
  networks and, 144, 145, 146, 154, 157, 158,
    161
  reciprocity and, 193–196
  tandas and, 89
Confidence, definition of, 197
Conflict, *compadrazgo* and, 168

Construction types, shantytown, 80
Contreras, relatives in, 128
Copilco, relatives in, 128
Countryside, Latin American, 4
Credit, marginals and, 83
Cuates, group of, 177–178
Cuatismo
  confianza and, 196
  as dyadic relationship, 176–177
  marginality and, 208
  marital role and, 94
  networks and, 146, 149, 175–176, 178–180, 209
  problem solving and, 123
  survival and, 3

D

Daily life, shantytown, 31–33
Del Valle, relatives in, 128
Dress, in shantytowns, 27, 30
Drinking, *cuates* and, 176–177, 178, 180

E

Earnings, shantytown, 70
Ecology, human, 39
Economic distance, reciprocity networks and, 134
Economic level
  income and, 76–78
  life styles and, 84–88
  material belongings and, 81–84, 211
  occupation and, 75, 76
  property status and, 79
  ratings of variables used, 71
  stratification of, 73
Economic status
  confianza and, 199–200
  relatives and, 128–129
Economies, Latin American, 5
Economy
  agricultural, 6
  growth of, 15–16
  shantytown, general, 63
Ejido-hacienda Villela, migrants from, 46
Elderly, earning by, 69
Electrical appliances

ownership of, 83–84
  rating of, 70, 71, 72
Electricity, shantytowns and, 24, 29
Emergencies, associations and, 184
Employee, definition of, 65
Employment, *see also* Jobs, Occupations
  industrial, 7
Entropy, social, 10–11
Eventuales, definition of, 65
Exchange, forms of, 203–206

F

Families, *see also* Household(s)
  extended, 100, 102
    jointed, 114–117
    single-plot with expense sharing, 108–112
    single-plot without expense sharing, 112–114
    single-roof with expense sharing, 104–106
    single-roof without expense sharing, 106–108
  jointed, networks and, 136–139
  networks, neighbors and, 139–146
  not participating in networks, 149–151
  nuclear, 97–99, 100, 102, 103–104
    exocentric networks and, 135–136
  without networks, 158
  without relatives, 127
Family life, migrants, 53–54
Favelado, daily life of, 8
Favors
  kinds and of whom requested, 194
  return of, 158
Federal District
  migrants from, 45, 50
  relatives in, 128
Feedback, migration and, 40
Fertility
  Cerrada del Cóndor, 99
  shantytown families, 211
Folk society, migration and, 37
Formal social distance, networks and, 133
Fraccionamientos ilegales, 19
French Canadians, kinship system, 126
Friends, favors and, 194
Friendship, marginality and, 208
Furniture, rating of, 70, 71, 72

G

Generosity, reciprocity and, 190
Geographical origin, migrants, 45
Godparents
    compadrazgo and, 163–168
    duties of, 165
    selection, reasons for, 166–167
Guanajuato, migrants from, 45, 210
Guayaquil, underemployment in, 14
Guerrero, migrants from, 45

H

Hacienda system, duration of, 43
Hidalgo, migrants from, 45
Holidays, shantytown, 32–33
Homes, shantytown and, 24–25, 27, 29, 30
Household(s), see also Families
    comparisons of, 117–118
    definition of, 99–100
    extended, evolution of, 121
    jointed, reasons for, 122
    types of, 100–103
        case histories, 103–117
Housing
    economy and, 78–81
    government-sponsored, 19
    low-income, 18–19
    rating of, 70, 71, 72
Husband(s), conceptions of wives, 94

I

Imbalance
    migration and, 39, 56, 61
        Cerrada del Cóndor, 46–48
Income, economic level and, 76–78, 84
Industrialization, marginality and, 11–12
Industries
    concentration, effects of, 5–6
    Latin American, 5
    workers, Cerrada del Cóndor, 64, 65, 66
Informal rotating credit institution, see Tanda
Information, confianza and, 200
Interaction, migration and, 40
Iquitos, underemployment in, 14

J

Jalisco, migrants from, 45

Jobs, see also Employment, Occupations
    assistance, confianza and, 200
    marginal populations and, 24

K

Kinship
    households and, 100
    marginality and, 208, 210
    migration and, 2, 38, 48–49, 53–54, 55
    reciprocity networks and, 133, 135, 156–158
    shantytowns and, 21, 25–26
    survival and, 3
Kinship system, Cerrada del Cóndor, 123–129
Kitchen, location of, 80–81

L

Laborers, unskilled, Cerrada del Cóndor, 64, 66, 67
Labor reserve force, marginality and, 12
Las Aguilas
    Cerrada del Cóndor and, 21, 56
    facilities in, 21, 24
    medical center and, 184, 185, 186
    relatives in, 128, 129
Latin America
    cities, domination by, 4–5
    migration processes in, 41–42
    social structure, 9–10
    working class, cleavage in, 207
Life style, economic level and, 84–88
Lima, shantytowns in, 56
Literacy, migrants, 51, 52, 210–211
Livestock, raising of, 69
Loans, confianza and, 200
Lomas de Plateros, Cerrada del Cóndor and, 21, 24
London, migrants, residential pattern, 118
Los Alpes, relatives in, 128

M

Maestro, definition of, 65
Managua, underemployment in, 14
Marginality
    cheap labor and, 208
    compadrazgo and, 167

core group, definition of, 13
rural and urban, 90 •
security and, 208
transience of, 207
Marginalization, theory of, 9-14
Market exchange, economic group and, 205
Marriage(s)
broken, 96
types of union and, 97-98
Marriage status, at time of migration, 54
Material belongings, economic level and, 81-84
Medical center, Cerrada del Cóndor, 184-186
Men, female view of, 94
Merced Gómez
Cerrada del Cóndor and, 21, 24
relatives in, 128, 129
Mexican Institute for Childhood Protection,
shantytowns and, 24
Mexico
economy of, 11
migration in, historical, 43-44
population growth in, 6
underemployment in, 16-17
urbanization and growth of, 15-16
México, migrants from State of, 45, 210
Mexico City
labor force, per capita net product, 17
low-income housing in, 18-19
marginal employment in, 63
migration into, 17-18, 43-44
population, growth of, 17
slums, household types in, 117-118
unemployment and underemployment in, 18
Michoacán
migrants from, 45
population loss, 43
Migrants
characteristics of, 42
Italian, kinship system, 126
locality of origin, 45
population of, 45-46
new, residential pattern, 118, 119
passive, 45, 210
Migration
Cerrada del Cóndor
case histories, 58-61
ecological model, 46-55
general characteristics of settlers, 44-46
intraurban, 55-58
demographic studies, 35-36

ecological model, 38-40
Cerrada del Cóndor, 46-55
ecological view, 5-7
historical structuralism and, 36
intraurban
case histories, 58-59
number of moves, 59-60
in Mexico, historical, 43-44
patterns, 2
processes in Latin America, 41-42
reasons for, 46-47, 56, 58, 125
routing of, 49-50
time pattern in Cerrada del Cóndor, 51, 53
Mixcoac
moves from, 56
relatives in, 128, 129
Mobility, migrants, 60
Monterrey, migrants in, 55
Money, borrowed, 158
Moral support, *confianza* and, 200
Morelos, migrants from, 45
Mother, reciprocity networks and, 157

N

Naucalpan, informal settlements in, 24
Narvarte, relatives in, 128
Neighbors
compadrazgo and, 165-166
cuate groups and, 179
family networks and, 139-146
favors and, 194
nonkin, networks of, 146-149, 157
Networks, *see also* Reciprocity
in Cerrada del Cóndor, 135-136
case histories, 136-151
cuatismo and, 175-176, 178-180
exchange intensity and, 192
exocentric, 134-135
importance of, 209-210
kindreds and, the Villela macronetwork,
155-156
kinship and, 156-158
reciprocal exchange, 131-133
classification of, 133-135

O

Oaxaca, migrants from, 45
Occupational history, male heads of family, 66
Occupational structure, Cerrada del Cóndor,
64-67

Occupations, *see also* Employment, Jobs
  economic level and, 75, 76, 84, 211
  migrants, 47, 48, 51
Offspring, *see also* Children
  reciprocity networks and, 158
Olivar del Conde, relatives in, 128
Olivar de los Padres, moves from, 56

P

Paisanos, confianza and, 196
Parent–teacher associations, participation in,
  182
Peon, definition of, 64
Pepenadores, salvage and, 91
Pericos Court, analysis of, 151–155
Physical distance, reciprocity networks and,
  133–134, 195–196
Piloto, relatives in, 128
Political parties, participation in, 182, 183
Population
  density per room, 81
    rating of, 70, 72
  growth, 6, 15
  in Mexico, 43
  of locality of origin, 45–46
Poverty, migration and, 41
Power, reciprocity and, 191
Property owners, Cerrada del Cóndor, 65
Property ownership, economy and, 78–81, 84
Psychosocial distance, reciprocity networks and,
  134
Puebla, migrants from, 45
Puente Colorado
  Cerrada del Cóndor and, 21, 26
  relatives in, 128, 129
Puerto Rico
  shantytown, household types in, 117

Q

Querétaro, migrants from, 45

R

Radios, ownership of, 83–84, 182
Rain, shantytowns and, 27, 30
Ravines, shantytowns and, 27
Reciprocity, *see also* Networks
  confianza and, 193–196

future of, 212–213
nature of, 189–191
scales in Cerrada del Cóndor, 191–193
survival and, 3–4
Relatives
  compadrazgo and, 162
  effective community of, 128
  favors and, 194
  godparents and, 167
  priority of preferences in decision to live with,
    127
  rural, contacts with, 129–130
  visits to, 124–125, 126
Religious objects, economic level and, 83
Religious organizations, membership in, 182,
  183
Rents, variations in, 80
Residence
  household type and, 100
  most recent, of migrants, 50
Residential complex, analysis of, 151–155
Residential pattern, Cerrada del Cóndor, 118–
  123
Roles, marital, 93–97
Rooms, number in residential unit, 81

S

San Angel, relatives in, 128
Sandpits, Cerrada del Cóndor and, 21, 25, 48
Sanitary facilities, per residential unit, 82
San Jerónimo, relatives in, 128
San Luis Potosí, migrants from, 45, 46
San Salvador, underemployment in, 14
Santo Domingo, underemployment in, 14
Santo Domingo de los Reyes, nuclear families
  in, 117
Santa Maria del Rio, population of, 48
Scarcity, social solidarity and, 204
School, percent attending, 182
Schooling
  economic level and, 87, 88
  migrants, 51, 52
  shantytowns and, 24, 32
Security
  marginality and, 208
  reciprocity and, 190
  wife's kin network and, 94
Service occupations, Cerrada del Cóndor, 64,
  65, 66

Services, *confianza* and, 200
Settlement, migration and, 40
Settlers
Cerrada del Cóndor, general characteristics, 44–45
Shantytown(s)
anthropologist's view of, 8
contributions of, 9
definition, 8
economy, general, 63
life, impressions of, 27–33
origin of, 25–27
population proportions, 9
urban growth and, 7–9
water and, 24
Shops, shantytown and, 24
Slums
development of, 8
Soccer teams
cuatismo and, 178
membership in, 183, 186
Social distance, reciprocity and, 195, 196
Social organization
patterns
cacicazgo, 203
rural, 203
urban, 203
Social security
confianza and, 198
settlers and, 181, 182, 183
Social structure, survival and, 3
Society
urban, marginals and, 208
Solares, Cerrada del Cóndor and, 21
Spanish, as colonists, 4
Sport clubs, participation in, 182
Squatter settlement, *see* Shantytown
Stability, networks and, 193
Stabilization
Cerrada del Cóndor, 53–55
migration and, 40, 42, 61
Stove, rating of, 70, 71, 72
Strangers, confidence and, 197
Street vendors, shantytowns and, 32
Survival
design for, 3–4
social group and, 204
Sympatía, confianza and, 200

T

Tacuba, relatives in, 128
Tacubaya, relatives in, 128
Tamaulipas, migrants from, 45
Tanda, organization of, 88–89
Tarango, Cerrada del Cóndor and, 21
Television sets
ownership of, 83–84, 182
shantytowns and, 30, 32
Third World, development of, 11
Tizapán
moves from, 56
relatives in, 128
Tlacopac
moves from, 56
relatives in, 128
Tlalpan, relatives in, 128
Tlaxcala, migrants from, 45
Trades, marginals and, 12–13, 14
Transfer
migration and, 39–40, 61
Cerrada del Cóndor, 48–53
Transportation, migrants, 51, 53
Tzintzuntzan, migrants, household types, 117

U

Uncles, maternal, 94, 96
Underemployment
rural, 18
types of, 13–14
Unions
marginality and, 12
settlers and, 181, 182, 183
Unpaid family labor, Cerrada del Cóndor, 67–72
Urban growth, shantytowns and, 7–9, 60–61
Urban society, migration and, 37

V

Vecindades
Cerrada del Cóndor and, 21, 23
households and, 100
population of, 19
Veracruz, migrants from, 45, 50
Villela
inhabitants, 47, 48, 51
land conditions, 47
macronetwork of, 155–156

W

Wage earners, number per residential unit, 69
Washing, in shantytowns, 27, 28, 31
Waste, marginality and, 91, 213
Water, shantytowns and, 24, 28, 31
Wives, affective life of, 94
Women
  brothers and, 94
  earning by, 69, 95
  friction between, 122–123
  literacy of, 88
  marital roles, 94, 96–97
  occupations of, 65

Z

Zacatecas
  kindred from, 123–126
  migrants from, 45
Zaragoza, informal settlements in, 24